How to Cure Yourself of
Narcissism

How to Cure Yourself of Narcissism

Copyright ©2020 Seth McDonough

All rights reserved. No part of this book may be reproduced or transmitted in any form or by any means without permission in writing from the author.

The author has made every effort to ensure the accuracy of the information within this book was correct at time of publication. The author does not assume and hereby disclaims any liability to any party for any loss, damage, or disruption caused by errors or omissions, whether such errors or omissions result from accident, negligence, or any other cause.

ISBN-13: 978-1-7770925-0-4 *(Paperback Edition)*

ISBN-13: 978-1-7770925-1-1 *(eBook Edition)*

Cover Design by Calum McDonough

Interior Typesetting and Layout by Melissa Williams Design

How to Cure Yourself of
Narcissism

or

Coping with

ADH-ME

How to diagnose and manage your Attention-Deserving Hyperactive and Mistreated Ego

SETH MCDONOUGH

You are looking at everyone's favourite person!

(Place your photo in this box.)

For YOU—you have made writing this book a pleasure. Thank you!

And for all my friends and family who have inspired it. ;)

Table of ADH-Contents

Prologue: You're Great! So What's the Problem? — 1

Chapter 1: Finding ADH-You — 4
   Oblivious You — 6
   Cheap-You — 9
   Mute-You — 12
   Snob-You — 14
   Attention-Requiring-You — 21
   Malevolent-You — 26

Chapter 2: A General Theory of Listening For You — 29
   Listening to Descriptions — 31
   Listening to Anecdotes — 34
   Listening to Rants — 39

Chapter 3: Listening Practice For You — 44
   Listening Without Talking (In Conversation) — 45
   Listening Without Talking (In Audience) — 47
   Stream of Interruptions — 49
   You Gotta Ask Your Impending Interjection One Question — 54
   Conversational Patience — 59
   Segues in the City (Starring Carrie Bradshaw) — 61

Chapter 4: Talking You! — 63
   Conversational Hostages — 64
   On the Phone; On the Hook — 65
   Small Talking — 69
   Me-Tails: Riding vs. Hiding Your Stream of Consciousness — 70
   The Art of Ranting — 74
   Arguing You — 76
   Accidentally Mean You — 79

Chapter 5: Conversational Discretion & You — 84
   Conversations to Consider Avoiding
   (for Other People's Enjoyment) — 85
   (Depending on Context) — 88

(Because They're Not Yours to Share) — 92
(Because They're Needlessly Mean) — 93

Chapter 6: Egos & You — 96
Grace Under Ego — 97
Dogmatic You — 101
Boasting You — 104
Blunt You — 107

Chapter 7: Patronizing You — 109
"If You Think About It . . ." — 110
"No, It's X." — 112
"That's Right." — 113
"Just Do X." — 116
". . . Right?" — 117
"M'Dear" and Beyond — 120
"You're Only Saying That Because You're X Gender." — 120
Your Socratic Method — 122

Chapter 8: A Friend in You? — 124
Handshaking You — 125
Feeling for Feelings — 127
Bust Your Instincts — 128
Punctuality Now — 135

Chapter 9: Funny You — 137
Is There Really a Winner Here? — 138
"No" Humour — 140
Literal You — 141

Chapter 10: Apologetic You — 146
Empty Apology — 148
Conditional Apology — 149
"Sorry You Feel That Way" Apology — 150
Blaming Apology — 150
Story in Lieu of Apology — 151
Martyring Apology — 153
"I Said I Was Sorry" Apology — 154
"Aren't I Great for Apologizing?" Apology — 155
Apology Accepting — 156

Chapter 11: Electronically Communicating You — 159
Capital Offence — 160
Coming Up Short — 162

Ignoring is Bliss	166
Getting Forward	169
The Hostility of Sudden CC-ing	170

Chapter 12: Out In Public You — 172
The "Be Yourself" Fallacy — 173
Smoking Mad — 180
Litter by Litter — 182
Out of Bounds — 186

Chapter 13: Moving Around You — 188
Sidewalking You — 189
Umbrella Reasoning — 192
The Leash You Can Do — 192
Slow-Walking — 194
Sudden Stopping — 195
Escalator Standing — 196

Chapter 14: Commuter You — 198
Getting On Transit — 200
You're Driving — 211
Signaler Mingler — 215
Your Alarm Making — 217

Chapter 15: Commuter You vs. Commuter You — 218
Driver You vs. Pedestrians — 219
Pedestrian You vs. Drivers — 221
Cyclist You vs. Drivers — 222
Driver You vs. Cyclists — 224
Motor-Psycho You — 227

Chapter 16: Customer You — 230
Before You Rant — 231
Discriminating Manners — 236
From Red Tape to Red Face — 237
The "How Are You?" Paradox — 241

Chapter 17: Presenting You — 244
Student You — 245
Question & Answer You — 253
Presenter You — 267

Chapter 18: Work You — 274
- *Employee You* — 275
- *Co-Worker You* — 278
- *Boss You* — 285
- *Meetings & You* — 288
- *The Break Room & You* — 290

Chapter 19: Attending You — 295
- *Your ADH-Family* — 296
- *Movies* — 298
- *Parties* — 298
- *Sports* — 303

Chapter 20: Athlete You — 305
- *Recreational vs. Competitive* — 306
- *Professional* — 308

Chapter 21: Famous You — 317
- *Your Greatness* — 319
- *The Power of Humility* — 322

Chapter 22: Getting a Date with You — 325
- *Picking Up Dates* — 327
- *Online Dating* — 330
- *Speed-Dating* — 351

Chapter 23: Dating You — 356
- *Arriving at a Date* — 357
- *The Payment Debate* — 359
- *On Date* — 364
- *End Date* — 369
- *Ghostly Behaviour* — 378

Chapter 24: Wedding You — 380
- *The Wedding Script* — 381
- *Your Guest* — 384
- *You're Guest* — 387

Epilogue: Are You Free of ADH-Me? — 391

Acknowledgments — 393

PROLOGUE

You're Great! So What's the Problem?

As you know, you're a big deal.

You have an extraordinary ability to join *any* conversation already in progress and enhance it with your funny and insightful stories.

Even when you're late to a meeting, you're still able to contribute more to the discussion than anyone else.

And when you're in a good mood, the whole bus gets to tap their feet to the booming sounds of your portable dance music.

All of this you know because when you were a child, your parents, teachers, and advertisers taught you how extra special you are. Not only are you a unique snowflake like no other, you're probably the best one.

I see you nodding along, wondering why I'm stating the obvious. Well, I have some bad news. It turns out there are others like you who have also been raised as wunderkinder. Each year our society is receiving increasingly large shipments of new adults who admire themselves with the heat of a thousand suns, and unfortunately, the regular, non-special people of the world are starting to run out of adulation to bestow on all of you.

Even more troubling, some of those boring, non-special people are becoming irritable with you. Perhaps you've already noticed your least interesting co-workers trying to rush you along when you're telling a fabulously tangential story in a meeting, or maybe you've had an obnoxious stranger ask to sit in the bus seat you've reserved for your bag. You do not deserve such cruel treatment!

I hope, then, that you will take comfort in learning that your suffering is not without a name. You are the victim of an affliction called *Attention-Deserving Hyperactive Mistreated Ego* (or ADH-ME). That is, you are expertly aware of your superiority, and yet you are not always treated with the deference that your excellence deserves. In a better world, of course, your self-adulation would be recognized as right and good, but in our bizarro society, your YOU-FIRST attitude is becoming increasingly unpopular with your friends, co-workers, and pets. So the only way for you to claim the recognition and attention that you deserve will be to learn to give NON-YOUs a smidge of consideration, too.

Now, I can imagine you're thinking:

> **ADH-YOU:** This shouldn't be too hard: all I have to do is fake conscientiousness just as I fake an interest in jazz to impress people at parties, and I'll be fine.

Brilliant point, YOU! But the problem is, unlike simple trends such as skinny jeans or monogamy, reducing your ADH-TENDENCIES from your behavioural palette will require a series of minor personality modifications.

> **ADH-YOU:** That sounds annoying.

Yes, and that's why I'm here to make the ADH-REDUCTION process as painless as possible for you. I'll provide you with all the tricks of the imagination needed to help you recognize (and even consider) the experiences of those around you.

> **ADH-YOU:** Sounds complicated. What kind of tricks?

Well, let's say, for instance, that you're at the back of a lineup for a bus, and there are fewer seats available on the vehicle than there are people in the queue. What do you do?

> **ADH-YOU:** Obviously I push my way to the front of the line to make sure I get a seat.

Naturally. And certainly you deserve a seat. But what I'd like you to imagine is that the people ahead of you have prior claim on that chair, and so you should let them have first refusal of it.

> **ADH-YOU:** But how could they have a claim on a seat that I want?

Well, of course, in the grand scheme of your universal superiority, they have no right to it. But for now, if you want to get the most out of this priority-challenged world, you'll need to learn that it's considered "rude" to ignore certain social conventions, such as the unwritten hierarchy within lineups.

> **ADH-YOU:** Sorry, that's a bit too convoluted for me. How am I supposed to remember these made up "social conventions"?

That's what this book is for! If I can help you to consider the feelings and perspectives of your fellow humans, one situation at a time, then you will eventually not need to remember a strange set of rules, because they will start to seem obvious to you.

> **ADH-YOU:** I doubt it, buddy.

Yes, I know it sounds like a daunting task, but I wouldn't have asked this of you unless I knew that you could do *anything* you set your mind to. I believe in YOU!

Your fan,

Seth McDonough

Chapter 1

Finding ADH-You

ADH-YOU are blessed to be the best. You are special in a way that the rest of us are not. If the philosophers are right that the world could just be a manifestation of one person's thoughts, that person would be you.

> **ADH-YOU:** Sounds good to me. So what's your issue?

It's not you; it's the rest of us. You see, as our society collects more ADH-ME citizens, who—bafflingly!—think they're as significant as you, the best way for you to gain and retain the appreciation you crave from other people will be to put aside your (justified, but no longer tenable) insistence on preferential treatment.

> **ADH-YOU:** How I could I possibly do that?

Great question, YOU. I recommend imagining that you have the same rights *and* responsibilities as everyone else.

> **ADH-YOU:** Sounds stupid.

True, but let's begin by talking about you.

> **ADH-YOU:** You have my attention.

Okay, so it turns out that ADH-ME comes in many shapes and personalities. Let's try to figure out which role you're starring in. Here are some of the basic groupings into which you might fit. See if you can spot yourself! (And don't feel pressured to limit your self-discovery to one group: there's nothing to say that you haven't been a glorious member of multiple ADH-PERSONALITIES.)

OBLIVIOUS YOU

You Focus On You

As you know, ADH-ME is not a character flaw; in the case of the ADH-OBLIVIOUS, it is simply a lack of awareness of the world around you, and in turn, your effect on it. You rarely mean any offence when you talk loudly with the person next to you during someone else's presentation; instead, you are so focused on what is going on in your thoughts that you've innocently lost track of the volume of your voice.

> **ADH-YOU:** Exactly! So what's the big deal?

You're right; it's not a big deal, but over time a series of small deals can add up to a larger one.

> **ADH-YOU:** What's math got to do with it?

Good question, YOU! It's just that your lack of awareness of those around you can be irritating to them when, for further instance, they can't hear their own conversation over your shout talking and laughing in a restaurant. And tragically—while you would be everyone's favourite if they truly got to know you—these little episodes of obliviousness can add up to make you seem like an unpleasant person to be around. So, as you progress through this book, I'm going to ask you to contemplate the other people nearby before you unleash your full personality in every situation.

> **ADH-YOU:** Geez, buzz kill much.

Well observed, YOU!

Everyone Focuses On You

On the other side of your coin, when you *are* aware of people who aren't yourself, you reasonably assume that they have been placed there to be minor supporting characters in your life, and so you infer that they are thinking about your specific needs all the time.

> **ADH-YOU:** I do not. Prove it!

Fair enough. Tell me if this sounds familiar. When you're shopping, you are rightly annoyed when sales clerks fail to decipher your personal needs and circumstances via psychic communication. I recall that, when I worked at a bread store, ADH-YOU were mad at me one day for asking if you'd like a bag for your single loaf purchase, and then on a subsequent day, the very same ADH-YOU snapped at me for *not* offering you the same.

> **ADH-YOU:** Well, I needed it the second time for some garbage in my car.

Well said, YOU! But, unfortunately, most humans lack the ability to read your mind before you speak it.

> **ADH-YOU:** I guess that's understandable. Their brain isn't as big as mine. How could they possibly keep up with it?

Exactly! So, if you could keep our smaller minds in mind in future, that would be helpful. Consider, for further instance, when you were a customer of mine at a call centre that gave transit directions:

> **SETH:** Transit information.
> **ADH-YOU:** I need to get to Main Street and 10th.
> **SETH:** In Vancouver or in—

ADH-YOU (*annoyed*): Yup.

SETH: And where are you starting the trip from?

ADH-YOU: Home.

SETH (*hiding my amusement*): And where is home?

The above is not an exaggeration. To the question "Where are you starting out from?" I literally received answers of "Here," "Across the street from my house," "The bus stop," and my personal favourite, "You tell me: *you're* the one with the map."

On the surface, it does indeed seem perfectly obvious that you would want to begin from home—

> **ADH-YOU:** Yeah, where else am I gonna start? The barber shop?

Hee, hee, very humourous, YOU. But remember that, according to recent census data, there are many homes in the world, and so the call centre representative will need you to specify in which home you reside before they can proceed with giving you directions.

NOTE: When you have successfully reduced the symptoms of your ADH-ME, don't be alarmed if you are occasionally still guilty of this cranial stumble. Even NON-ADH-SUFFERERS make this error every once in a while because they're used to talking to their friends who are aware of their home base.

So, to determine whether you are suffering a resurgence of your ADH-ME, pay attention to your reaction to the call centre person's clarifying question, "And where's home?" If you suddenly realize your blunder and laugh at yourself, then you're fine. However, if your reaction is one of annoyance, or continued confusion about the question, then you are clearly back under the influence of ADH-ME.

CHEAP-YOU

Thriftiness is not a crime.

> **ADH-YOU:** Thank you!

Yes, it's your right not to spend more than you wish. Unfortunately, though, your thriftiness may be ruthlessly perceived as cheapness when it causes *others* to spend more. Consider the following examples.

Wallet Forgetting

You may be amongst the small percentage of people who have trouble remembering to take their wallets with them when going out.

> **ADH-YOU:** Yeah, I'm a pretty busy person, so sometimes I forget to grab it on my way out.

Yes, well explained, YOU. But, unfortunately, your wallet-forgetting tendencies will sometimes seem negligent to members of the cruel NON-ADH-WORLD who end up having to pay for you when you go for coffee with them. Polite society means no harm to one-time forgetters; however, when forgetfulness becomes so frequent that it could be construed as habit, some of your friends may start to ponder why you're not taking proactive steps to fight off your disorder.

> **ADH-YOU:** But it's not my fault that I don't have a good memory.

I see your point. But imagine that you had a tendency to forget to wear clothes when you left your dwelling: wouldn't you place a note on your door to remind yourself to put on pants?

> **ADH-YOU:** I guess.

So I suggest you do the same with your wallet.

> **ADH-YOU:** Probably won't work. I'm usually rushing, so I won't notice the note.

I'm sure you're right. But the specifics of how you solve this problem isn't really the issue.

> **ADH-YOU:** Um, then what are we talking about here?

Well teased, YOU. The moral of his particular section is that, if you have an issue that is frequently causing your companions to pay for you, then, unfortunately, it's your duty to figure out a way to restrain your problem.

Paying Back

Meanwhile, in those cases that you do cause your friends to pay for you, please remember to pay them back. That way, they won't be in the uncomfortable position of either (A) reminding you, or (B) giving up on interacting with their money again.

> **ADH-YOU:** C'mon, it's just money.

Brilliantly put, YOU! And since it is indeed just money, it shouldn't be a big deal to give it back.

> **ADH-YOU:** Well, I wouldn't expect *them* to pay *me* back.

And that's generous of you! But since you forget your wallet much more frequently than they do, they don't get the benefits of your forgiveness quite as often as you do theirs. So, to be safe, let's practise paying people back when we accidentally borrow their money.

> **HINT:** If you pay your friend back without reminder, you will have a better chance of convincing them that your forgetting-of-wallet really was an accident.

Bill Sharing

Before you and your ADH-SPOUSE go to dinner with another couple and insist on splitting the cheque (against the rival pairing's preference), remind yourself of this interaction from the delightful superhero comedy, *Mystery Men*:

> **THE BLUE RAJA:** All I'm saying is when we split the cheque three ways, the steak-eater picks the pocket of the salad man.
>
> **THE SHOVELER:** Well, you should order more.

Now, to your eye, it may look like your dining opponent is the cheap one for putting their petty financial needs ahead of the convenience of bill-splitting.

> **ADH-YOU:** Give yourself a gold star.

As always, you are right, but you might also be right if you thought of it this way: for some people, income is finite, and so they may have limited funds for their leisure activities. Thus, when going out for dinner, they may choose not to consume alcohol or steak because they want to save their money for other expenses. Consequently, when you order high-end items—and then insist on splitting the bill—you are overriding their planned financial restraint. Thus, unfortunately, when you retire from ADH-ME, we ask that you discontinue mandatory bill-splitting.

ADH-YOU: Awe, man. I liked having my steak and alcohol subsidized.

I know. And I'm sorry.

MUTE-YOU

HINT: In Chapters 14 and 18, we will talk about situations where it might be inconsiderate to impose your conversation on others (such as when a stranger is clearly enjoying their personal transit time reading a book). Here, though, I'll be referring to cases where conversation is the social expectation (such as when you're at a dinner party). If you don't see the distinction between those two cases, feel free to follow the lead of those around you.

Sometimes, during a conversation, you contribute little, leaving most of the conversational work to your counterpart(s). This is generally not a problem when you're visiting with a large group, but the smaller the set of conversationalists, the more your lack of effort can be felt by the others.

ADH-YOU: But they seem perfectly happy chattering away. Why do they need *me* to say something?

Great point, YOU! But here's the thing: conversation isn't always as easy as it looks. Sometimes, in certain social situations, the people who are talking are actually doing a lot of work to think of topics that are appropriate for that particular setting. Indeed, occasionally they can run out of material to comment on or ask about, particularly when their co-conversationalists give them only tiny responses. For instance:

TALKER: So, yeah, England was great. Have you ever been?

ADH-YOU: No.

TALKER: You should go! Do you like travelling?

ADH-YOU: I guess.

TALKER: What places have you been to?

ADH-YOU: Um, I don't know, just around North America, I guess.

TALKER: Anywhere interesting?

ADH-YOU: Not really.

TALKER: Okay, um, have you ever been tempted to go to England?

ADH-YOU: No.

TALKER: Fair enough, it's a long way away, and I guess you can always . . . um. . . . read about it?

See how the talker is starting to grasp for questions?

> **ADH-YOU:** Yeah, what a loser.

Well spotted, YOU! But, if you look even closer, you'll see that the talker is actually struggling to keep the conversation going since you're giving them so little with which to work.

> **ADH-YOU:** But I didn't have anything to say about those things.

Fair enough, that can happen. What you could do then is try asking your own question to see if your co-converser might have something to say.

> **ADH-YOU:** But if they wanted to tell me something, why didn't they just say it in the first place?

Good point, YOU. The problem is talkers are people, too, and they can lose confidence in the worthiness of their commentary if they receive no indication that you're interested in the conversation (even a non-verbal nod of interest would help).

> **ADH-YOU:** Well, sometimes I just don't feel like it.

Yes, I understand that socializing isn't always easy. But, unfortunately, when you sign up to be an adult, you take on some shared responsibilities in social interaction. This means that, even if you're tired, you are still expected to do your part.

> **ADH-YOU:** Awe, man.

I know. It's not fair. But you don't have to be a keynote participant in the conversation. Just by assisting the people who *are* by showing interest, you will meet your obligation.

> **ADH-YOU:** Fine, but I'm not going to enjoy it.

I understand.

Meanwhile, nobody is trying to outlaw technology, but if you are unable to maintain an interaction without repeatedly checking your phone, you may alienate your fellow conversers. In that case, please *do* treat yourself like a child and set a limit on your screen time.

SNOB-YOU

I admire you and your towering self-esteem.

> **ADH-YOU:** I thank you.

However, a good rule of thumb when trying to convince others to agree with your ad-YOU-lation is to ask yourself: *Does my ever-present enunciation of my greatness insult those lesser than me?* If *Yes*, then you may do well to adjust your delivery to avoid offending the fragile egos of those lesser beings.

Let's look at a few of the flavours of snobbishness that you may sometimes take on, and consider their consequences.

The Vocabulary Snob

Vocabulary is a famous tool for elevating yourself above your audience.

> **ADH-YOU:** Well, I don't know if my language is elevated, per se. Perhaps "sesquipedalian" would have been a better choice of words there, my good man.

I see your point. And I must admit I'm a fan of words, so when you use language that I don't know, I'm delighted to go to my local internet to investigate. However, there comes a point when the work of researching your impressive words exceeds the benefits. So, when you're contemplating using advanced (or jargon-scented) vocabulary, it's worth considering your audience and whether you think they'll be able to keep up with your high-flying prose. Then try to find a middle ground between (A) their occasional confusion and (B) their complete inability to understand what you're saying.

> **ADH-YOU:** But why, my fellow descendent of Australopithecine, should I dampen the effervescence of my lexicon for the assuagement of NOT-MEs?

Eloquently put, as always, YOU! My suggestion is that, whenever you're about to set your language to stun, ask yourself what the purpose of emphasizing your enhanced vocabulary is in that particular setting. If your hope is to elevate your audience's enjoyment by providing the perfect words for the ideas you're illustrating, then please proceed. If, however, your aim is to elevate your audience's opinion of you, or to hide the fact that you're not actually saying much, you may discover that people will quickly see through you.

> **ADH-YOU:** I do not recognize the semantics of your utterance. Could you please vivify?

Well, for instance: I recall a classmate in a university English class whose skills with the lost words of the dictionary were so impressive that even the professor had trouble understanding her.

> **ADH-YOU:** Sounds like someone worthy of my coterie.

Yes, I'm sure, but one day, I happened to know the meanings of the words the elitist proffered, and I discovered that her ideas were not actually that interesting.

> **ADH-YOU:** I suspect you simply did not apprehend the depth of her profundity.

Yes, I also wondered if I was missing the richness of her points, but I soon noticed that I wasn't the only one who had observed that our classmate's expensive delivery seemed to be hiding her lack of content. This is not to say that one needs to be brilliant at all times, but when you spend so much of your time trying to convince people that you're smarter than they are, they'll be less forgiving when you fail to be intelligent; in fact, they may think you're a bit of a fraud. To avoid such cruel analysis, I suggest choosing the words that best illustrate your thoughts, as opposed to those which you hope will best illustrate your impressiveness.

The Grammar Snob

When it comes to grammar, I see nothing wrong with utilizing the best you've got whenever you feel like it. (After all, unlike oversized words, grammatically correct language doesn't get in the way of comprehension.) However, you should be careful when you take it upon your talented self to correct the grammar of people who are not your children or students.

> **ADH-YOU:** But that person used a "who" where they should have placed a "whom."

Yes, I know it can be difficult to hear linguistic slip ups and not comment on them. Nevertheless, pointing them out can cause more pain than it relieves. Consider this example from the TV show *Frasier*, in which radio therapist Dr. Frasier Crane received a call from someone looking for help:

> **FRASIER:** Hello, Doug, this is Dr. Frasier Crane. I'm listening.
>
> **DOUG:** Yeah, it's about my mother. She's getting on now and she doesn't have much of a life. And, I mean she doesn't want to do anything or go anywhere and she literally hangs around the house all day. I mean it's, it's very frustrating. I think—
>
> **FRASIER:** Ah, Doug, I'm sorry, can we just go back for a second? You said that your mother literally hangs around the house. Well, I suppose it's a pet peeve of mine. But what you mean to say is that she figuratively hangs around the house. To literally hang around the house, she'd have to be a bat or a spider monkey, you see. Now back to your problem.
>
> **DOUG:** Do you mind if we stop while I tell you *my* pet peeve?
>
> **FRASIER:** Oh, not at all.
>
> **DOUG:** I hate it when intellectual pin-heads with superiority complexes nit-pick your grammar when

you come to them for help. *That's* what I got a problem with!

Line goes dead.

FRASIER: I think what he means is: that is a thing *with which* he has a problem.

Hee, hee, that's one of my favourite *Frasier* moments. Nevertheless, as brilliant as Frasier's grammatical commentary was, he was playing with emotional fire by taking it out on an individual.

ADH-YOU: Why?

Well, people take their intelligence seriously. In fact, most of us believe that we possess above-average intelligence—

ADH-YOU: That's ridiculous! How can *everyone* have above average intelligence?

Well caught, YOU! Nevertheless, most people can't help believing strongly that they have superior brains (after all, they've found themselves to possess the correct opinion on almost every issue). And, since many of those same people see grammatical criticism as a commentary on that very intelligence, they may find it rather irritating when you point out their grammatical slip-ups in open conversation.

ADH-YOU: Oh my Monteverdi. Get over themselves.

Well considered, YOU. And, to be fair, there are some people (including yours truly) who enjoy receiving helpful grammatical advice (and do not see it as a critique of our intelligence). However, I think you'll find that most people don't like your Frasierly advice, and so if you have a hankering to cure the world of grammatical flubs, I suggest targeting those who have indicated to you that they are open to your delightful grammatical assistance, and then proceed with caution.

ADH-YOU: But you're saying it's okay if I correct *your* grammar, and you won't whine about it?

Sure thing. I aint going to stop you.

ADH-YOU: You *aren't* going to stop me.

Well spotted, YOU! Thanks!

The Music Snob

One of the most popular arenas for snobbery to ply its trade is music appreciation. More than any other medium, music seems to be considered the vocabulary of the soul, and so when a NOT-YOU person chooses to dance to a tune that does not measure up in sophistication or coolness, they will be mocked by the likes of ADH-YOU for lacking a certain *Je ne sais Queen*.

ADH-YOU: But wait a minute. I have better taste in music than you do. So why shouldn't I mock you for your dumb musical choices?

That's a fair and lovely question. And I do not deny that—as a connoisseur of music—you certainly understand the nuance of your passion more than I do, so you'll be better able to categorize it into "high" and "low" art.

ADH-YOU: Agreed. So then what's the problem?

Well, just because my favourite song isn't as sophisticated as it could be doesn't necessarily mean that I'm an idiot.

ADH-YOU: Well, it doesn't make you a genius. LOL.

LOL, indeed! But perhaps I'm not interested in intellectual music; maybe I'm merely craving a tune that I can dance to, or that sounds pretty to my ears—in which case, is there anything wrong with my selection?

> **ADH-YOU:** Nope, and there's nothing wrong we me laughing at you for it either.

Nicely done. You can be amused by whatever strikes your funny bone. My suggestion, though, is that you go easy on the rest of us when you mock us in public. Not that you shouldn't give your brilliant opinion on the music you encounter, but when you treat the wrong tunes as an indication of a vapid soul, you may alienate some of your audience.

> **ADH-YOU:** Gosh, you really are closed to learning new things, aren't you?

Not as you much as you might think. In fact, you may be surprised to learn that I'm actually interested to find out why you believe X band kicks Y band's drums. But when you mock "uncool" musicians without explanation, your contempt seems hollow, as though it has more to do with wanting to fit in with the cool establishment than with justified musical criticism.

The Movie Snob

If you're a professional movie critic, you're probably a big fan of being a snob, and, to your credit, you provide some of the most creative demonstrations of ADH-SNOBBERY in the world today. Sometimes, of course, you have genuine and nuanced reasons for your critical opinions.

> **ADH-YOU:** If being nuanced is wrong, I don't wanna be right.

That's great to hear, YOU! Once again, though, you run into trouble when you try too hard to like/dislike a film to prove your virtues to your audience.

> **ADH-YOU:** When have I ever done that?

Well, for instance, if the film involves a topic you sense is politically significant, you may celebrate it regardless of its rendering. Or, in the opposite case, you might try too hard to dislike a movie because you believe its topic or genre is beneath you.

> **ADH-YOU:** Well, if letting the needs of my reputation influence my movie reviewing is wrong, I don't wanna be right.

Well said, YOU. But just keep in mind that, once again, you may find that your reputation dwindles as your audience realizes that your reviews are not actually an analysis of individual films' value, but instead are a demonstration of yours.

> **ADH-YOU:** Fine, I'll try to give unsophisticated movies a chance.

Fine words, YOU!

ATTENTION-REQUIRING-YOU

For someone as amazing as you, attention is like food, and you're always hungry.

Hijacking Attention (At Events)

Imagine that one of your friends has, just now, arrived in your neighbourhood tavern to announce that they have recently made a medical breakthrough; but let us also consider that you have twice before sipped from similar success. Would the conversation go anything like this?

> **YOUR FRIEND:** My friends, I'm pleased to announce that Malady X is now a thing of the past.
>
> **YOUR OTHER FRIEND:** OMG! You did it?!
>
> **ADH-YOU:** Of course he did. That's what we do for a living. Why don't people believe us when we cure something? It's liked last year, when I cured Ailments Y and Z in a two-week period, and no one believed me. It's like, "Um, yeah, people, this is what I do: I cure diseases."
>
> **YOUR OTHER FRIEND (redirecting to YOUR FRIEND):** So how'd you feel when you realized that you'd discovered the cure?
>
> **YOUR FRIEND:** At first, I didn't believe it. I was like, "No, that can't be right." So I called over my boss and he's like, "That can't be right, so—"
>
> **ADH-YOU:** That's funny: my boss didn't believe me when I found the cure for Ailment Y either. Because of his incompetence, the drug was delayed in getting to market by three days.

Okay, that's enough for now. Do you see what happened there?

> **ADH-YOU:** Sounds like a good conversation.

Excellent observation, YOU. Additionally, this is a case where it would actually be okay to allow someone *else* to enjoy the spotlight for a while. I'm sure your experiences are interesting and superior to your friend's, but because your friend's event has just happened, they and your mutual friends may want to focus specifically on their accomplishment for now.

> **ADH-YOU:** To quote Luke Skywalker, "You ask for the impossible."

Well quoted, YOU! I know this seems daunting, but in Chapters 2 and 3 you'll find lots of training on how to listen without dominating. Plus, you can take comfort in the fact that this task is actually one of the most daunting ADH-DRAGONS you will ever have to slay.

> **HINT:** Nobody expects a moratorium on sharing stories that relate to those of your friends (NON-ADH-SUFFERERS do that, too): we just want you to hold off until the immediate storyteller has finished celebrating their most significant details.

Hijacking Attention (In Pain)

One of the most significant and tragic symptoms of ADH-ME is attention-requiring hypochondria, which causes you to overpower your friends' injury stories with your own.

> **ADH-YOU:** Oh my God! I think I have that. My pain is always worse than my friends'!

I know. And please understand that it's not your fault. I would never blame you for thinking—upon hearing a feeble story of someone else's injury—about how much worse you've had it.

> **ADH-YOU:** Why would I think it was my fault that my pain is bad?

Right, fair enough. You shouldn't. However, within the NON-ADH-ME world there is a peculiar etiquette that dictates that the person who has most recently suffered a wound or catastrophe be given first dibs on the immediate attention. So, before you submit your story as a companion piece to theirs, please wait until they've had their turn.

> **ADH-YOU:** Well that sounds tedious.

It is, but unfortunately it's something we all have to do if we want to be seen as mature humans. If it makes you feel any better, I must confess that I, too, have been caught trying too hard to get credit for an injury. See the story, *Shouldering the Pain*, below for the evidence.

Shouldering the Pain

During my childhood, I was well known for my ability to injure myself. It was a talent that garnered me lots of attention. One day, though, as I was having a minor injury gushed over, I noticed that my father had cut himself. I asked him about it, but he told me that it was nothing to worry about. Strangely, I found his downplaying of an injury—one that deserved much consideration—to be classy. I therefore decided that I would be classy, too, and would not demand attention the next time I injured myself.

At school a few days later, I was attacked by a tree whose branch gave me a sharp poke in the shoulder. That night, I was true to my word and I did not announce to my family that I had an injury. Oddly, though, unlike my thoughtful observance of my father's refinement, no one spotted me being so classy. That was disappointing, so I was forced to help them out. I pulled my shirt off my shoulder so that my fresh wound was out in the open for people to notice if they wanted to.

"How was your day today?" my dad asked me.
"It was fine," I said with immense class.
"It looks like there's something wrong with your shoulder."
"Oh right," I said, "I forgot about that."

I then received some of the attention I sought, but somehow, my classy stoicism didn't feel as rewarding as I'd hoped.

Shock Val-You

So . . . you're an unusual cat, aren't you?

> **ADH-YOU:** Hey, I gotta be me.

Exactly, and the neat thing is that, in some circles, being seen as weird has a certain cachet. Am I right?

> **ADH-YOU:** I wouldn't know. I'm just being me.

Well put, I'm sure, but the trouble is, people don't always notice your kookiness, so sometimes you feel inclined to accentuate or even manufacture evidence that you're wacky.

> **ADH-YOU:** Well, if nobody notices me, they're missing out.

Right, and so you double down on your naturally unconventional tastes in hopes of helping more people to enjoy them.

> **ADH-YOU:** I suppose it is a public service, yes.

Well said, WACKY-YOU. But here's one thing to consider: while I'm sure you are offbeat in your own way, the majority of genuinely eccentric people are too caught up in their quirks to spend much time thinking about how to accentuate them. So, when you try to emphasize your weirdness either by forced behaviours or by insisting that people notice them (with comments such as, "I'm totally weird, aren't I?"), your efforts may ring hollow.

Musically You

One lovely example of your kookiness is delightfully enunciated by your tendency to sing and whistle when you're wandering about in public.

> **ADH-YOU:** Hey, I can't help expressing myself! Rat, tat, tat! ♪

And I'm not saying you shouldn't, but before you play it again, ADH-YOU, I want to point out that when you share your melody, you are deciding for the people around you (including strangers) whether they will be listening to you sing or not.

> **ADH-YOU:** Lucky them!

Yes, well put. And, if you are irreversibly confident that their day will be improved by your selection of music, then there's not much I can say to convince you otherwise, but if you're at all unsure, then maybe you could occasionally leave the public expressions of soulfulness to the professional musicians.

MALEVOLENT-YOU

The ADH-MALEVOLENT are the most elite and rare of ADH-ME sufferers—

> **ADH-YOU:** Sounds like the club for me!

I appreciate your enthusiasm, but to qualify for this diagnosis, it isn't enough to just to be self-focussed, you must also have a tendency to hamper the happiness of others *just for the fun of it*. Consider this story told to me by my high school history teacher regarding his wait in line for the epic *Star Wars* sequel,

Chapter 1: *Finding ADH-You*

The Empire Strikes Back, in which (spoiler alert!) one major character shocked the audience by revealing himself to be the father of another major character. While my teacher and his friends stood in a long line outside, anticipating what might happen to Luke Skywalker, Princess Leia, and Han Solo in their battle against the evil empire and Darth Vader, a group of fellows drove by and called out (urgent spoiler alert): "[X character] is [Y character's] father!"

Oh . . . my . . . evil!

You can only watch the sequel to *Star Wars* for the first time once, and you can only be startled by the above news that same once. My teacher and his friends didn't get to enjoy that first discovery because those drive-by Sith lords took it away from them—and not just because they were selfish, but because they actively wanted to deprive others of happiness.

> **ADH-YOU:** C'mon, it was funny!

Well caught, YOU. Similarly, I'm guessing you also enjoy keying people's cars, throwing insults at strangers when you pass them, and kicking your grandmother's puppy?

> **ADH-YOU:** Guilty: those things are hilarious, fun, and good exercise.

Fair enough. You are indeed an ADH-MALEVOLENT who enjoys causing your fellow citizens pain for its own sake. You probably also delight in ruining internet comment sections by saying vile things to strangers.

> **ADH-YOU:** Says the ugly man baby!

Good one, YOU! Indeed, there's no way I can reason you out of these malevolent behaviours by pointing out that you're a menace to the experience of others. You would need to be capable of compassion in order for that to matter to you, so I will only suggest that one day you may be in need of assistance from others, and you may be startled to find out that nobody wants to help you.

ADH-YOU: Yikes. Harsh much?

Good point. And your best chance to avoid this fate is to impersonate other humans by being nice, or at least as humane as possible, and you'll have a chance at keeping friends who might look out for you when you're in trouble.

Chapter 2

A General Theory of Listening For You

Conversation is likely one of your greatest sources of direct contact with people who aren't you. I'm sure you're already aware that it is a tool by which you can transmit information *about* yourself to others, but did you know that the medium can also be used to *receive* information?

> **ADH-YOU:** Of course I knew that! I just, you know, maybe forgot.

Don't be embarrassed: it is common for people with your affliction to believe that communication is for output only. For instance, I once went on a blind date with a woman who happily answered my many questions about herself during our two-hour conversation, but asked me zero questions in reply. While I didn't mind taking the inquisitive lead—

> **ADH-YOU:** What's wrong with that? Maybe she was more interested in *your* questions than she was in her *own* questions!

Nicely done, YOU! There is, of course, nothing wrong with her and your preference for answering questions, but in order to mingle well with the less interesting people of this world, it's important that you learn to share in the responsibility of conversational curiosity. So to help you to improve your conversation-receiving skills, we'll begin by teaching you how to be what's called a "listener" (which is sort of an audience member in a conversation).

> **ADH-YOU:** Sounds like work.

I know. It's going to be a challenge for you. Now, there are three main types of conversational presentation that your NON-YOU colleagues may attempt, (1) the expository essay, (2) the anecdote, and (3) the philosophical rant.

ADH-YOU: Oh, great, I smell a lecture approaching.

I know, and I'm sorry. But, unfortunately, it is important to understand the distinction between the leading types of conversational offerings, because—as a listener—you have different responsibilities in each case.

LISTENING TO DESCRIPTIONS

You're probably not particularly experienced with being the receiver of an expository essay; generally, that would require you to ask interested questions about a NOT-YOU's life. As we've already discovered, this is not an activity you have previously been involved in, but now that you're learning to look for opportunities, it's probably the easiest type of listening to pick up.

ADH-YOU: No need to patronize me, dude. Once you explain what the heck you're talking about, I'm sure I'll dominate this task like I do all others.

That's great to hear, YOU! I'm sure you will. So, expository conversations feature general descriptions of a person's life, or an aspect of that person's life, such as their work life, love life, or Barbie-doll-collecting life. Often expository conversations are led by one speaker; however, it is logistically possible to have an expository exchange where the two conversationalists compare details.

ADH-YOU: *But?*

But for now you should focus on letting your conversation partner lead a one-person exposition.

> **ADH-YOU:** Called it.

Well done, perceptive YOU! Now, in order to provoke a conversation starring someone else, you have two choices:

OPTION 1: Ask your conversation partner an exposition-provoking question. But that's pretty scary for you at this stage in your development, so you may want to start with

OPTION 2: Wait for your conversational teammate to slip into the dialogue something about themselves that sounds interesting, and then ask them about it.

To learn how to do this, we need to first remind ourselves how you would have responded to such information previously. Have a look at the following real conversation that you had with my brother on a first date:

> **SETH'S BROTHER:** I actually cycled down to San Francisco from Vancouver a few years ago.
>
> **ADH-YOU:** Yeah, I just don't like bike riding. I'd rather run for exercise.
>
> **SETH'S BROTHER:** Cool. Do you run often?
>
> **ADH-YOU:** Um . . . not really, no.

Do you notice the awkward pause that followed your last remark? That was because you didn't actually have much to say about your running regimen. So why did you segue to it?

> **ADH-YOU:** I dunno.

Don't feel bad. It was because your ADH-ME told you to! You heard a statement (that your date had cycled to San Francisco), so you searched your brain for the first thing you could think of about that subject that related to you. And the only thing you found was that you don't like cycling, and that, when you exercise, you prefer to run. Unfortunately, since you're not

Chapter 2: A General Theory of Listening For You

even that interested in the topic of running, the conversation was suddenly stalled.

> **ADH-YOU:** Well, maybe your brother should start with a more interesting topic for me to work with next time.

Great idea, YOU! But just in case he's unsuccessful in that pursuit, I'd like to propose a radical manoeuvre: occasionally, instead of responding to a conversational colleague's statement with a remark about how it relates to you, try exploring how it relates to *them*.

> **ADH-YOU:** Yikes, that sounds exhausting. How are they going to learn about me if I only talk about them?

I understand your concern. And I'm not saying that you shouldn't sometimes match your date, disclosure for disclosure. But I *am* suggesting that you pay close attention to what they're saying. When their voice illuminates something particularly unusual or personal—say, that they cycled all the way from Vancouver to San Francisco—try asking about it. Let's try again.

> **ADH-YOU:** Try what again?

Try responding to my brother's San Francisco trip with a wee bit of interest, and see if the conversation does any better.

> **ADH-YOU:** Okaaay, I'll try it.

ADH-YOU: Wow, you cycled all the way to San Francisco. How was that?

SETH'S BROTHER: It was pretty amazing, actually. Riding 7 hours a day, I started to clear my mind.

ADH-YOU: Yeah, I had a 7-hour flight once. I hated it, though.

SETH'S BROTHER: Oh, yeah? That sounds rough.

Okay, so you did really well there with that first question, but maybe fell off the wagon a bit with your long flight story. Keep practicing! If in doubt, simply ask a question about the last thing your companion said.

> **FUN TEST:** If you're still not sure if you're suffering from ADH-ME, ask yourself this: do your friends know every small detail about you, such as your shoe size, but you don't know vital information about them, such as if they have any siblings? If Yes, then I'm afraid you are severely stricken by ADH-ME.

LISTENING TO ANECDOTES

Stay On Target

As with expository essays, I know it's painful to listen to someone else's entire anecdote without relating it to your own life. Let's have a look at how you normally take on this challenge:

> **YOUR FRIEND:** So the weirdest thing happened to me at the grocery store this morning—
>
> **ADH-YOU:** I shopped at the grocery store yesterday. It was busy.

Do you see what happened there?

> **ADH-YOU:** Yeah, the grocery store was busy. I hate that.

True! Well spotted, YOU. But, also, notice that the point of your friend's narrative was not so much to compare shopping schedules, but instead to enunciate for you the details of a particular shopping occasion where something notable occurred in their existence.

> **ADH-YOU:** Your point, please?

Well, it turns out that, when someone is telling you an anecdote, they are offering you a piece of artwork, a nonfictional story, for you to enjoy. So your job, primarily, is to be the "listener" and to react to the plot developments (briefly, if you can).

> **ADH-YOU:** Awe, man.

I see your point, but the good news is that anecdotes are generally based on events that have *already* happened, which means they must have come to some sort of end! Just be patient—hold your stories until the anecdote is concluded—and then I assure you there will be a chance to show how you have an existence full of happenings, too.

> **ADH-YOU:** Nice! Can we do that now?

Soon, YOU! First, though, let's take another shot at that conversation, but this time, try focussing initially on the NOT-YOU in the interaction:

> **YOUR FRIEND:** So the weirdest thing happened to me at the grocery store this morning: I was at the till, and I realized that the check-out guy was that bully who used to pick on me in high school.
>
> **ADH-YOU:** I hate bullies.
>
> **YOUR FRIEND:** I know, right? So, anyway, I looked at him and ...

Not bad at all, YOU! Do you see how—by (A) waiting patiently for your friend to finish the premise of their anecdote before you made your comment, and (B) tailoring that remark to be somewhat in keeping with the substance of what they were saying—you managed to avoid leaving your friend's story stranded?

> **ADH-YOU:** I do! And I don't even hate bullies that much. I was just playing along.

Well done, YOU!

Hold Your Questions

Now, brace yourself: here comes a complicated and confusing part of listening to stories. Remember how, in the case of expository conversation, you did better when you asked a question?

> **ADH-YOU:** Don't remind me.

Well, shockingly, in the case of anecdotal stories, your questions can actually be disruptive to the narrative flow, and so should be reserved for essential curiosities and confusions. Consider this example in which I attempted to tell a classmate a story:

> **SETH:** I had quite the awkward experience at work the other day.
>
> **CLASSMATE:** You're still working at that bread store?
>
> **SETH:** Yup, so, you know how—
>
> **CLASSMATE:** Do you like it there?
>
> **SETH:** Um, it's okay. Pays the bills for now. So, this strange customer came in—
>
> **CLASSMATE:** Where is the store again?
>
> **SETH:** Um, it's on 6th Street, across from the Seventh Heaven Market.
>
> **CLASSMATE:** Is that the one that nearly burned down?
>
> **SETH:** No, I don't think so.

CLASSMATE: Which one was that?

SETH: I think that was up the hill. So, anyway, the customer came in, and told me he didn't like the flavour of bread we'd sold him. So I—

CLASSMATE: And you sell all types of bread, right?

SETH: Yeah, it's a discount outlet, but we get everything there. So, anyway—

CLASSMATE: Do you like your customers?

SETH: Um, sure. So, anyway, how are your courses going?

CLASSMATE: Good, thanks. I love my new Psych prof.

Okay, so you might notice that I gave up on completing my story. This might be because I got the impression that my classmate wasn't interested.

> **ADH-YOU:** Geez, they were just asking questions.

Yes, and I appreciated her interest. But my suggestion for you—if you're ever in the same situation—is that you save such questions until after the story is complete. That way, the story will be allowed to pick up some speed.

> **ADH-YOU:** Why does that matter?

Well, let's imagine that you're watching a movie. There may be many points in the plot that provoke your curiosity: *Where is that small town? Where did that bad guy get his haircut? Does the policeman like his job?* These are all good questions, but if you ask your neighbour every time such thoughts occur to you, both of you will likely lose track of the actual story.

> **ADH-YOU:** But you're not a movie when you're telling a story.

Right, sorry, that was meant to be an analogy. That is, similar to a movie plot, an anecdote's plot can get lost if it's oversaturated with tangential questions.

> **ADH-YOU:** But what if I need to know the answers in order to follow your babbling story?

Yes, fair enough. If you feel that the answer to your question is crucial to your understanding of the plot, then please do ask it. However, if you think you could follow the story without the answer, I suggest holding onto your query like a squirrel does a nut for winter; that way, when the conversation goes dry, you can come back to it.

> **ADH-YOU:** So many rules. So little time.

Yes, I know this is confusing. But all you really need to do is keep an ear out for when your friend might be sharing an anecdote. If you're able to determine that they *are* in the act of storytelling, then just imagine that they're putting on a min-play for you.

> **ADH-YOU:** Okaaay. And then what do I do?

And then please hold all non-essential questions until *after* the performance.

> **ADH-YOU:** So how do I know when an anecdote's over, so that I can re-take the conversation?

Excellent question, YOU. Generally, an anecdote will conclude with either something funny or surprising and then may be followed by a concluding statement, such as this:

> **YOUR FRIEND:** So I guess I'll never go water-skiing again.

Then the storyteller will often pause and wait for you to speak.

> **ADH-YOU:** Excellent!

Yes, that might be a good time to ask a few of those questions you have saved up.

> **ADH-YOU:** Awe, man.

Fair enough. If you prefer, you can switch to your own story now.

> **ADH-YOU:** That's what I'm talking about!

Yes you are. Congrats!

LISTENING TO RANTS

First Response

The philosophical rant is basically a hybrid between the expository conversation and the anecdote. It often features an incident which has led the speaker to go off on a philosophizing spree. They might be annoyed by something they saw on TV, or the treatment they received at the mechanic's shop, or perhaps they disagree with Einstein on a particular point in his dissertation.

> **ADH-YOU:** The Einstein one—that's me.

Impressive! In any case, just as when you are listening to an anecdote, it can be worthwhile to let the speaker unleash the heart of their frustration before you fully react.

> **ADH-YOU:** Great, more listening to someone blather.

Yes, I know it's hard. But the good news is once the basics of their argument have been shared, the philosophical rant can become a two-way interaction, much like an expository offering.

> **ADH-YOU:** And am I allowed to ask questions on this one?

Yes! In fact, it's recommended, especially if you focus on the catalyst or contents of their rant. And, if you feel a particular kinship with their diatribe, you might choose to officially agree with it by describing—in equally ranting detail—just how right they are (this could even be a good time to tell your own story of similar frustration).

> **ADH-YOU:** Okay, now we're talking.

Yes, you go, YOU! Just remember to wait till your co-ranter has finished describing the facts of their frustration before you take over.

> **ADH-YOU:** And now you're blocking.

Yeah, sorry about that.

Second Thoughts

If you want to disagree with your ranting friend, that's fine, too. In that case, though, given that your friend may be a wee bit worked up, you might want to be cautious at the start. Make sure you understand what they're ranting about before countering. When a person is already agitated, they can become particularly annoyed when someone makes arguments against them that miss the point of their diatribe. For instance:

Chapter 2: *A General Theory of Listening For You*

YOUR RANTING FRIEND: I think it's ridiculous when politicians' personal lives are used as reasons to kick them out of office.

ADH-YOU: So you think it's okay to cheat on your wife?

YOUR RANTING FRIEND: No, I just don't see how it's relevant to the running of a political office. There have been many great political leaders who had affairs.

ADH-YOU: How would you like it if your spouse cheated on you?

Do you see how the vein on your friend's forehead is about to burst?

> **ADH-YOU:** Well that's just because they can't stand it when I prove them wrong.

I'm sure you're right, as always. But, just for fun, let's consider another possibility. It's conceivable that the main reason your friend's annoyed is *not* because you disagree with them, but because your argument seems not to have considered the heart of their point.

> **ADH-YOU:** So I'm not allowed to argue *my* point of view?

No, no, your perspective is of course always welcome, and I'm confident your friend will be interested to hear a counterargument to their thesis. For instance, perhaps you think politicians are meant to represent us, and so must be held to a higher moral requirement than the rest of us, even when they're off-duty. Sure, go forth and argue that, YOU! However, by turning the discussion into a debate about whether adultery is good, you have made it seem as though your friend is opposed to fidelity.

> **ADH-YOU:** Well, if they're actually *opposed* to infidelity, how can they defend someone who takes part in it? Isn't that like playing for the baseball team you hate?!

Okay, let's try another example. Do you agree with free speech?

> **ADH-YOU:** Yeah, of course! I'm not a fascist.

Okay, great, and so I assume you would support someone's *right* to say something that offends you even though you might dislike said speech?

> **ADH-YOU:** Um, no, free speech doesn't include the right to be offensive.

Hmm, okay, I'm not sure we have the same understanding of free speech. Let's try a less controversial example. Do you like to drive?

> **ADH-YOU:** Yeah, I love my car.

Okay, but in order to have a vehicle that's affordable to individuals like ADH-YOU, unfortunately car manufacturers need to produce those cars at a massive quantity, which means, painfully, that lots of people get cars, and you have to drive in traffic, which stupidly slows you down! That's annoying, isn't it?

> **ADH-YOU:** Yeah, I hate traffic.

Exactly. So you agree that's it possible for you to love your car, even though you don't like some of the consequences of car culture (such as traffic and parking)?

> **ADH-YOU:** I guess. But I'm not going to stop hating traffic!

Fair enough. Similarly, sometimes unfortunately one's legitimate philosophical positions come with not-so-desirable associations and/or consequences, but that doesn't necessarily mean your friend must *like* those results in order to stand behind the principle that allows for them.

> **ADH-YOU:** If you say so.

Great, so watch for that. When someone's making a philosophical argument, try to listen to and understand the thrust of their opinion before trying to prove them wrong with tangential counter attacks.

Chapter 3

Listening Practice For You

Now that we've learned about the three major listening scenarios and gained some ideas for dealing with each, this chapter will provide you with some high-level tricks of taking in information.

LISTENING WITHOUT TALKING (IN CONVERSATION)

Do you ever get a vague sense that the person you're talking to is not really interested in what you're saying?

> **ADH-YOU:** Yeah, totally! Just the other day, I was telling this awesome story to my friend, Sam, and I totally felt like he/she wasn't listening.

Exactly. So, as a result of such non-thusiasm, did you find yourself either trailing off from what you were saying, or asking Sam if he/she heard you?

> **ADH-YOU:** I would never trail off when I was saying something awesome, but yeah, I did ask Sam if he/she was listening. And Sam claimed he/she *was*.

Okay, interesting, so now I'd like to offer a possible explanation of what happened there. The most common reason that we sometimes suspect our conversational colleagues are not following along is because, during our presentations, they're not giving us any minor-verbal or non-verbal feedback to indicate they're keeping up.

> **ADH-YOU:** What the hell is minor and non-verbal feedback?

Great question, YOU! Some people will use minor-verbal cues (such as, "Yeah," or "Right," or "Really?") and/or non-verbal indicators such as ("mm-hmm," or a nod) to demonstrate that they are keeping up with (and are interested in) the details of their co-converser's remarks.

> **ADH-YOU:** Why would I need a nod to tell me someone's listening. I know they have ears, don't I?

Excellent point, YOU. But, the thing is, most people *do* provide us with such non-verbal reactions, and so most of us have subconsciously come to expect from our listeners a certain level of nodding along. Consequently, if we don't receive it, we assume they're nodding off.

> **ADH-YOU:** Okay, I'm starting to taste what you're cooking. You're right: most people *do* nod at what I'm saying. So Sam totally threw me off when he/she didn't give me such replies the other day.

Agreed! Plus, beyond the psychological, I think it makes pragmatic sense for people to acknowledge you during your conversational presentations so you know you haven't lost them. A simple "Uhuh," or "Right," or "Word!" seems to do the trick.

> **ADH-YOU:** Word to that!

Hee, hee, well played, YOU. In contrast, if you don't receive the implied "go ahead" on a particular point you've made, you don't know if your listener is following along. And, with each successive statement you offer without receiving approval, you'll likely start to lose confidence that the audience is still with you.

> **ADH-YOU:** I'm glad to see you're finally on my side, but why are you telling me about this? I'm already aware that I deserve better listeners.

Well caught, YOU. Well, I would like to submit the possibility that your friends and colleagues would benefit from the *same* improved minor-verbal and non-verbal treatment from you.

> **ADH-YOU:** I knew this was too complimentary to be true.

Yes, you guessed it! It's time to add minor-verbal patter and non-verbal cues to your own listening!

> **ADH-YOU:** Fine.

> **HINT:** If you're going for an advanced listener's badge, then—in addition to demonstrating that you understand what your conversation partner is saying—you may want to give indications, via enthusiasm, that you are enjoying or are interested in the contents of their speech. For now, though, let's just start with basic demonstrations of understanding and work our way up to that.

LISTENING WITHOUT TALKING (IN AUDIENCE)

Rather excitingly, even if you're part of a group listening to a presentation, you can apply the same tricks of non-verbal enthusiasm.

> **ADH-YOU:** What for?

Excellent question, but if you don't mind, I'll show you how it works first, and then I'll explain my reason for suggesting it.

> **ADH-YOU:** Whatever, dude. It's your dime.

Thanks, YOU! So, have you ever noticed that sometimes a teacher or public speaker will seem to focus on just a few people in the audience?

> **ADH-YOU:** No.

Well, try watching for it. I promise you, once you look, you'll see such preferential speaking everywhere.

> **ADH-YOU:** No great mind shift, Sherlock. I'm sure they're just focussing on their mom who thinks everything they say is brilliant.

Great point, YOU. But it turns out that preferential speaking is not always the result of nepotism; instead it is most often caused by the fact that particular audience members are giving the speaker faces of interest (perhaps, smiling, nodding, smirking at their jokes, etc.), whereas others seem bored (perhaps playing on their phones, sleeping, and so on). You see, most presenters instinctively focus on those who seem to be paying them the compliment of attention. Consider the vignette, *Psychology Experiment*, below for an example of the length one speaker travelled to attain his class's consideration.

Psychology Experiment

When my mother was in university, she and her classmates performed an experiment on one of their psychology professors. If the instructor moved towards the window, they provided all the signs of good listening; whereas, when he drifted to the other side of the room, they did the opposite—they whispered to their neighbours, looked out the window, etc. The subject performed to this author's delight: he moved instinctively in the direction of where the listening cues were best, eventually travelling all the way to the side window ledge, and even sitting on it.

> **ADH-YOU:** That's funny, but what's it got to do with me?

Well, this is another suggested behaviour that's not required, but if you want to get bonus marks in your ADH-REDUCTION efforts, I recommend providing non-verbal feedback to presenters. You may be surprised to see they'll appreciate your evident interest, and may give *you* more attention as a result.

> **ADH-YOU:** I accept your terms.

STREAM OF INTERRUPTIONS

Standard

More often than not, conversations are communal engagements wherein the participants take turns at the helm. Unfortunately, it will be tempting in such situations to revert back to grabbing for every topic before your co-conversers have finished their thoughts. This mode of behaviour is called "stream of interrupting" and it is frowned upon because, strangely, it can be inadvertently belittling to your conversational colleagues.

> **ADH-YOU:** I'm beginning to feel like my opinion isn't welcome in the NON-ADH-ME world.

No, no, of course that's not true! Your thoughts are still the best we have in the universe today. And I'm not suggesting that interruptions must be exhaustively exiled from your conversational arsenal (when humans get together to chat, a certain amount of incidental overlap is inevitable). The question is: how do you avoid interrupting more than is healthy for a growing conversation?

> **ADH-YOU:** I dunno. Aren't you supposed to tell me?

Good point, YOU. I suggest the following two-step process:

STEP 1: Recognize your interrupting tendencies. For instance:

(A) Notice how your friends often say things like, "So, like I was saying..." after you've just finished pointing out something brilliant?

> **ADH-YOU:** Yeah, my friend did that to me the other day. What's the deal with that?

Well, because they were mid-stride on a point when you started yours, they probably felt a certain emptiness of soul that they weren't able to finish their thought.

> **ADH-YOU:** Wow, who's the narcissist now? Why does everyone have to finish all their thoughts?

I see your point, YOU. Nevertheless, please keep an ear out for that phrase so you'll at least have a better idea of when you're disrupting another person's conversational momentum.

(B) Do you see how a second friend in your conversations frequently follows up your rants by asking your first friend to *finish* their thought?

> **ADH-YOU:** Yeah, I don't get why they do that.

Exactly! Seems out of the blue, doesn't it? Why would your second friend want your first friend to continue a point after you've offered up an intriguing remark for everyone to ponder?

It may be that they noticed that your first friend was feeling cut off by your delightful elocution.

(C) If you watch closely, you might be surprised to see how often your statements begin while another person in your circle is still chattering away.

> **ADH-YOU:** And what does that mean?

Once again, that likely indicates that, in pursuit of sharing your brilliant ideas with the world, you have accidentally been starting your presentations in the middle of other peoples' offerings.

STEP 2: After recognizing your interruption-tendencies, try waiting for your opposing converser's contribution to come to a natural conclusion—a sort of pause—before you begin your excellent remarks. Moreover, if you want to get really advanced, when you *do* start up your voice, try using it to respond first to what the previous speaker has just said, instead of immediately taking the conversation in another direction.

> **ADH-YOU:** Good heavens. Why?

Well, you see, sometimes people feel pride in the ideas they put forth, and so, if—after they say something important to them—the only response they receive is your immediate transition to something else, they may feel frustrated that their idea didn't get its day in court: it's like being unable to complete a sneeze.

> **ADH-YOU:** I hate that.

I know. And it happens to all of us naturally sometimes, but if your voice is repeatedly the culprit, your friends may start to resent you.

> **ADH-YOU:** That displeases me.

I know, it's rough. But, keep reading, and we can reverse the trend together.

Now, perhaps the most interesting style of interruption is the result of what I like to call the "pause-provoked-overlap." Occasionally, that is, there will be an opening in the conversation that is available to anyone who wants to fill it, and so sometimes more than one person will go for it only to discover that another person has reached for the same conversational roll on the table. Three possible situations result:

(1) Most commonly, one of the applicants will politely offer the roll to the competing converser. Although, it probably won't be you, will it?

> **ADH-YOU:** Certainly not! I'm not going to stop talking just because someone else has a roll in their hand.

Right, understood.

(2) Second most often, both of the people reaching for the roll will be ADH-CONVERSERS like yourself and so will both assume that the other will stop to hear them, and so they will each continue proudly forth on their excellent statements expecting that the other will soon realize that it's not their turn. Does that sound familiar to you?

> **ADH-YOU:** I dunno. I don't remember that happening. But, if someone tried to talk over me, I would just keep talking till they shut up.

Well put. I've seen you do that. In fact, I've witnessed such simultaneous conversation go on for literally 5 seconds (which is a long time for polite society to endure) before either (A) the audience is forced to pick sides as you and your ADH-RIVAL separate into two groups of conversation, or (B) one of you finally gives up and allows the more unflappable person to continue.

(3) Least frequently, we have the strange occurrence, known as the "delayed overlap," which has baffled conversational researchers for centuries. In this case, there is once again an open space in the interaction. The vacancy provokes one converser to glance around, and upon noticing that no one else seems to want it, they grab the unguarded conversation roll, and begin their statement. There is then approximately a quarter-second moment in which another person can start their simultaneous transmission on the basis that they had already sent the signal to their mouth before they'd heard their predecessor. However, sometimes the first speaker will be well into their comment when suddenly another person in the group will realize that they *did* want to say something, after all, and so will reach out and take the roll out of the first converser's hand! Let's watch:

> **YOUR FRIEND (*concluding a joke*):** "Actually," Jimmy replied, "there's still a parachute left for both of us. That physicist, who said his brain is too important for humanity to lose, just jumped out of the plane with my backpack."
>
> *Everyone politely laughs, and then there is a small pause in the conversation.*
>
> **YOUR OTHER FRIEND:** That's funny—reminds me of a joke my father told me. This hypnotist is going for a walk and—
>
> **ADH-YOU:** I knew a physicist once: he was very much like the man from your story . . .

Oh my! Even as a fictional rendering, it still shocks me. Did you not see that your other friend had already started to respond to the joke? Why did you interrupt several moments into what they were saying as though the conversational space was still up for grabs?

> **ADH-YOU:** I dunno. I just wanted to tell that story. Why are you taking this so personally?

Very good, yes, I'm sorry. I do get a little agitated about this one. My apologies: as always, you have noble reasons for your actions. Nevertheless, in the future, please wait for the next conversational opening.

> **ADH-YOU:** Okay, I'll try, but I still don't get why it matters so much.

Fair enough. This one may not make sense until you have significantly reduced your ADH-ME. So, for now, please just try utilizing your eyes and ears to see if someone is already talking before you thunder into a conversation. If the sounds in the air don't help, watch the lips of the others in your group, and if they're moving, wait! Hesitate before speaking and once again you will spare yourself the silent rants of your friends.

> **YOU GOTTA ASK YOUR IMPENDING INTERJECTION ONE QUESTION, "DO YOU FEEL INTERESTING?"**

Interjections are usually not as off putting as interruptions: they're generally used as temporary tangents as opposed to full-scale takeovers of conversations.

> **ADH-YOU:** So I'm *allowed* to do them?

Yes! For instance, sometimes there are interjections that are time-sensitive and it can be tough to hold onto them until after the story/rant/exposition is complete. So it's okay to occasionally jump in if your point is time-sensitive, relevant, and/or significant to one or both of you. However—

> **ADH-YOU:** Here we go.

Well anticipated, YOU. The problem is it can be tricky for someone with your disorder to determine the above criteria, so your best bet is to avoid such diversions unless you're sure of them.

> **ADH-YOU:** I really have no idea how you want me to make that determination, bud.

Okay, let's consider some examples.

The "I thought You Said" Tangent

The following is a humourous but not-always-necessary interruption:

> **YOUR FRIEND:** So, I got into the casino, and I paid for my chips—
>
> **ADH-YOU:** You paid for Chip?
>
> **YOUR FRIEND:** No, I paid for *my* chips.
>
> **ADH-YOU:** Oh good, 'cause I was like, "Why would you pay for Chip? He can pay for himself." And then I was like, "I wonder if Chip's in financial trouble?"

This is called the "I thought you said" tangent and it is common even amongst those who aren't ADH-PATIENTS. It's actually a tricky one because sometimes when you mishear someone, the misunderstanding is funny, and so it justifies taking a quick break from the story to share with your speaker. Much of the time, though, a temporary misinterpretation is not really that entertaining, and so it's okay to keep it to yourself.

ADH-YOU: Well, why don't I just share it in case it's funny?

Well, you see, stories have a rhythm to them, and if they're disrupted too often—with every might-be humourous interjection—they will start to become tedious for both teller and listener. So if you're confident your "I thought you said" tangent is especially funny, then by all means, tell your friend about the fruits of your misunderstanding. However, beware of replying to everything your friend says with exactly what it makes you think of (legitimately, or by misunderstanding). Otherwise, you will kill your friend's story. In fact, on more than one occasion, I have witnessed a story accosted so severely by an "I thought you said" tangent that the conversation never returned to the tale.

ADH-YOU: The conversation never returned to the jail?

No, to the tale.

ADH-YOU: Whoops, sorry, I thought you said, "to the jail," and I was like, "Why would you be in jail?" LOL.

Hee, hee, yeah, that's funny.

Devil In The Details

Another instance of over-tangenting is when you test the validity of the small decisions within a person's story. For instance:

> **YOUR FRIEND:** So I had a very weird experience at the bank today—
>
> **ADH-YOU:** What bank do you bank at?
>
> **YOUR FRIEND:** Bank of Friendship.
>
> **ADH-YOU:** You shouldn't bank with them—they don't pay their employees well.
>
> **YOUR FRIEND:** Oh, okay, thanks. So, anyway—

> **ADH-YOU:** Don't you have a Bank of Union down the street from you? Why don't you go there?
>
> **YOUR FRIEND:** Um, I don't know. I've always gone to the Bank of Friendship.
>
> **ADH-YOU:** You really should go to Bank of Union. I know one of the managers there.

Do you see what happened there?

> **ADH-YOU:** I don't see a problem. I *do* know a bank manager at Bank of Union.

Yes, and that sounds like an interesting thing to talk about *after* you friend's story. But the trouble with bringing up such fascinating facts *during* your friend's story is that they're too interesting to be snuck in between beats of an anecdote. So, because the two conversations couldn't exist at the same time, yours took over.

> **ADH-YOU:** I can't help it if I'm more interesting than my friend is.

Fair enough. But, once again, I'd like you to try to give your friends a chance to show what they've got. So please hold your tangents as long as you can.

Stream-Of-Consciousness Listening

Meanwhile, some people who aren't you may feel annoyed when you interject during their story to let them know random details of your mutual surroundings that relate to your life, such as, say, the fact that you've just passed the store at which you purchased your umbrella.

> **ADH-YOU:** But the umbrella store's going to be out of view in a second!

Yes, fair enough: the source of your rain protection is time-sensitive if you're moving quickly past it, and so it is not necessarily conversationally illegal if your companion is interested generally in umbrellas and/or specifically in the one to which you're referring.

> **ADH-YOU:** Thank you. That's all I needed to hear.

However, if your friend is, in fact, not an umbrella connoisseur, it's probably okay to let the umbrella store pass without commentary, especially if they were telling you something important to them.

> **ADH-YOU:** I knew there was a catch. Always is with you.

I know. I'm sorry. But, you see, to your companion, such an interruption may sound something like this:

> **YOUR FRIEND:** I was so nervous. It was 10 years since I'd seen her. But it's my mom, so I didn't care what she'd done: she's my—
>
> **ADH-YOU:** That's the place where I once did something insignificant, but which I care more about than you or your emotional story.

I suggest avoiding that result, if you can.

The Circle Of Topics

A useful thing to remember is that topics that come around once usually circle around again, and so as vital as it may seem in the moment to segue from the middle of your friend's story to your thoughts about banking (because, after all, they brought banking up in their story!), it's likely that your opinion will keep until after their story.

> **ADH-YOU:** But what if I don't think of it when the story ends?

Yes, that's always a risk. But the thing is: if the point you're planning to interrupt with is important to you, you'll find an opportunity sooner or later to get it out. You're a master of that! Trust you!

> **ADH-YOU:** But what if I forget altogether?

Well, on the off chance you do forget, I promise you will have other bank-related conversations in the future to remind you again.

> **ADH-YOU:** They better. I'm going to hold you to that.

That's fair.

CONVERSATIONAL PATIENCE

Great Anticipations

When listening to a story, one honour you can bestow upon your storyteller is to let them tell the tale. Even if you think you can see the ending coming, it can be fun for the storyteller to be the one to describe it. Don't forget, as with travel, the fun is sometimes in the journey—not the destination. So listen with your ears, instead of your anticipations, and you'll do fine.

> **ADH-YOU:** I knew you were going to say that!

Very good, YOU! Thank you for waiting till I said it to let me know.

First Opinions First

When someone is sharing an opinion on an issue, your inclination may be to immediately respond by updating them with your opinion on the same. That's understandable. And I'm sure your ideas are worth investigating. Sometimes, however, the initially supplied opinion from your friend is rich enough to deserve some follow-up questions before you swarm in with your parallel contemplations. Let's go to a clip for illustration:

> **YOUR FRIEND (*to your other friend*):** Hey, Other Friend! I haven't seen you since you bought the time machine. Have you used it yet?
>
> **YOUR OTHER FRIEND:** Yup, I couldn't wait to see what the 1800s were really like.
>
> **YOUR FRIEND:** Cool, what *were* they like?
>
> **YOUR OTHER FRIEND:** Fascinating. Just amazing—people's attitude towards personal boundaries was totally different.
>
> **YOUR FRIEND:** Really? Like how?
>
> **ADH-YOU:** If *I* had a time machine, I'd like to visit the Dark Ages.

Good point, YOU. But do you see how, in this case, your friend has just had an amazing adventure about which they might have a lot to say, but you have overpowered their elaboration by focussing the conversation on your spontaneous contemplations about the topic?

> **ADH-YOU:** Yeah, that's because I have some pretty cool ideas about time travel.

Fair enough. That certainly sounds reasonable on the surface; nevertheless, I want you to consider the fact that you're not in grade 2 anymore. There, everyone was asked what their favourite colour was, and so there seemed to be real value supplied by each person simply announcing their preferred pigment.

> **ADH-YOU:** Actually, I would say I have two favourite colours. Blue in winter and red in summer.

Thanks for sharing, YOU! Indeed, the complexity of your colour preferences segues nicely into the point I was hoping to make. As we mature, many people become interested in the nuances behind their friends' thoughts, and so while I'm sure your selection of where in history you'd like to travel is exciting, it's okay to let the person ahead of you in the conversational queue go into detail about their selection first. And then, when it's your turn, you can go into the same level of detail. Yay!

SEGUES IN THE CITY (STARRING CARRIE BRADSHAW)

A famously successful means by which to take over a topic before your companion's thoughts have been fully explored was developed by Carrie Bradshaw, the lead character in the '90s drama-comedy TV series, *Sex and the City*. When her soul takes a particularly ME-BASED turn, she resets any conversation to be about herself in a manoeuvre known as the "Bait and Segue." Here's how it works:

STEP 1: Carrie responds to a friend's story or statement with apparent enthusiasm, but she demonstrates her interest by alluding to some juicy event that's happened in her own life—an event on which she knows her friend will want to comment.

STEP 2: Carrie waits for her friend to inquire about the passive tangent and *voilà*, we're talking about her! Let's watch in slow motion:

> **MIRANDA:** He left a message on my machine when I got home. He wants to go out this week.
>
> **CARRIE:** Hey, that's fantastic.

Good. To warm up the victim, our expert has offered a small, placating comment of pretend interest.

> **MIRANDA:** Well, it's too quick. I think maybe that kick in his head scrambled his brain.

At this point, Carrie spots the words "too quick" and sees how they could relate to the self-topic that she has in mind—namely, the fact that she recently went to bed with a gentleman on their first date.

> **CARRIE:** What's "too quick" is sleeping with him on the first date. That's too quick.

There it is—the bait! To the untrained friend, it sounds like Carrie's merely trying to make her companion feel better by comparing their folly to her own. But watch:

> **MIRANDA:** You both got excited and you went for it. Stop blaming yourself.

Wow! Carrie's now provoked her friend to switch the topic of the conversation to be about Carrie. Incredible work, Carrie!

> **CARRIE:** No, I don't blame myself, I blame the dress, the dress. The dress led me on, it had a life of its own. Then we went to this Chinese restaurant afterwards and you'll never guess who I ran into ...

And the change of topic is complete! The "Bait and Segue" is a brilliant technique for directing the discussion to the topic you're more interested in without much effort. The only trouble is Carrie's friends may slowly start to resent her ME-FOCUSSED conversation; they may eventually even notice the "Bait and Segue" and one day tell her off for it. That won't be so much fun for ADH-CARRIE, so I suggest you don't copy her.

Chapter 4

Talking You!

After all this cumbersome listening, you now get a chance to talk!

> **ADH-YOU:** Finally!

And, worry not, there are not as many responsibilities for the speaker as there are for the listener. The main (confusing) thing to remember is that conversation is a shared experience, and so, when you're talking, try to keep your listeners' (and nearby innocent bystanders') enjoyment in mind.

> **ADH-YOU:** I knew there had to be a catch.

CONVERSATIONAL HOSTAGES

One thing to consider when you begin a conversation with someone is whether they are in a frame of mind or location to engage in the length of chat you have queued up. While I'm sure your theories about free trade are interesting, if you run into your friend while they're carrying a large grocery bag full of soup because they're combatting a cold they've been warring with all weekend, maybe cut to the abridged version—a quick "Down/Up with free trade!" will do.

> **ADH-YOU:** Sorry, I don't get what you're talking about, mate. I really don't care about free trade, so I'm gonna need a better example.

Okay, well, one day, my mother-in-law was carrying a large and heavy tray of dishes between the cottages she co-managed and she was intercepted by a neighbour who delayed her delivery because he wanted to tell her about his current thoughts on cottage life. After several minutes, with my mon-in-law's weighted-down arms screaming for relief, our exhausted victim was forced to interrupt the meandering pontificator to announce that, sadly, she had to get to her chores.

> **ADH-YOU:** Why didn't she just say something earlier?

That's a helpful suggestion, I'm sure. But, unfortunately, for polite humans, when someone we know starts a heartfelt submission in our direction, it will feel inconsiderate to interrupt them in the middle. So our best hope is that the presenter will notice we're not in good position to be conversing, and let us off with a warning.

> **ADH-YOU:** Well, what if I don't notice they're busy? I'm not a mind reader.

Yes, fair enough. All that I'm asking of you is to take a peek at your intended receiver while you're chatting to see if there are any impediments or ailments that may put them in a not-so-ideal listening position. If they are encumbered, please move them along as quickly as possible.

ON THE PHONE; ON THE HOOK

Now let's have a look at your phone-based communication. When you're initiating a call, there are a couple of things to keep in mind:

Your Talk-Chewing

For many of us, listening to someone talk with their mouth full is an unpleasant experience (yes, I'm referring to you, gritty television shows that enjoy the realism of chew-and-talk characters—stop it, or I will remote-vote you off my TV). This trouble is amplified when the listener has a phone signal pushed up against their ear, so please avoid eating while on the phone. I know, sometimes you're the one receiving the call, and since you were mid-bite, you had no choice but to answer with a food-clogged voice. That's fine, but exactly what reason do you have for taking a chomp just before initiating a call?

> **ADH-YOU:** Hunger, obviously! What's the big deal? I don't mind the sound of me talking while eating.

I can't argue with that. But maybe the person you're talking to *does* mind.

> **ADH-YOU:** So? It's efficient for me to eat my lunch while on the phone.

Another excellent point, but surely you can pick something else (that doesn't grate against other people's ears) to complete your multi-tasking requirements. Maybe you could update your social media feed with your latest eyebrow selfies?

> **ADH-YOU:** Fine. I guess that could be fun.

Thanks, YOU. I'll go and click *Like* on your update right now.

Your Caller-Initiation Responsibilities

This one's strange, so don't feel bad if you don't understand it right away: when you call someone, it is—rather oddly—your job to start the conversation. That is to say, you're not allowed to do this:

> **YOUR FRIEND:** Hello?
> **ADH-YOU:** Hi.

> **YOUR FRIEND:** Oh, hi, YOU. How are ya?
>
> **ADH-YOU:** Not bad, you?
>
> **YOUR FRIEND:** I'm okay.
>
> *Short pause.*
>
> **YOUR FRIEND:** So was there anything in particular that you called to talk about?
>
> **ADH-YOU:** No, I just called to say, "Hi."
>
> **ADH-YOU:** Oh, okay? So . . . Hi?
>
> **YOUR FRIEND:** Hi.
>
> *Another pause.*
>
> **YOUR FRIEND:** Um . . . so how's work?

See how your friend seems to be hesitating? The reason for that is because they were doing something else before you arrived in their ear, so upon receiving your call, they assumed that the interruption had a particular point, and they answered in order to find out what it was and whether they could accommodate. But, when your reason for the invasion turned out to be simply, "Hi," they weren't sure what to do with that.

> **ADH-YOU:** I'm confused. Obviously I just want to talk. Why else would I call?

You make a good case as always, but before you start your victory dance, there are two points I'd like you to consider:

(1) Unless you have one of those kindred friendships where both sides are always assumed to be available to chat, your first responsibility when calling for an impromptu conversation is to assess your friend for availability. Try to remember that your friend might have been focussed on something else and so perhaps isn't in a good position to talk right now. So see if you can find it in your heart (or ADH equivalent) to ask them whether, in fact, they currently have time to chat.

(2) If your friend is available to gab, please consider the possibility that, since you initiated the chat, it's your job to provide the conversational kindling to get it started. Random conversation can be enjoyable when achieved amongst consenting adults, but since your friend wasn't the one who called in search of that chat, they may still feel a strange expectation that you will begin the proceedings.

Keeping (1) and (2) in mind, try this out:

> **YOUR FRIEND:** Hello?
>
> **ALTERNATE-YOU:** Hey, it's ALTERNATE-ME.
>
> **YOUR FRIEND:** Oh, hi, how are ya?
>
> **ALTERNATE-YOU:** I'm good, except I was thinking we haven't talked for a while, so I wanted to catch up.
>
> **YOUR FRIEND:** Good point—you've gone into exile since the party.
>
> **ALTERNATE-YOU:** Can you blame me?
>
> **YOUR FRIEND:** No, I guess not.
>
> **ALTERNATE-YOU:** So's now a good time to chat, or—?
>
> **YOUR FRIEND:** Sure, yeah, I have about 20 minutes before I have to go see my parole officer.
>
> **ALTERNATE-YOU:** Fair enough—so how's the legal system treating you?
>
> **YOUR FRIEND:** Funny you should ask . . .

Great work, ALTERNATE-YOU! Do you see how ALTERNATE-YOU took responsibility for getting the call going? And, now that it's started, the conversation has become a shared task.

If, however, you don't think you have the requisite energy to start such a conversation, I suggest waiting to call your friend until you have at least one question to ask or story to tell.

SMALL TALKING

As you may be aware, some circumstances call for a form of conversation known as "small talk."

> **ADH-YOU:** Groan.

I understand your irritation. But the good news is small conversing is fairly simple. If someone else starts the chat ("Nice rain we're having, eh?"), all you need to do is try to understand what they have said, and respond with agreement or gentle disagreement, per your preference ("Yeah, I love breaking out my new umbrella," or "I prefer a skin-scorcher, myself"). Also, I recommend confining your remarks to the point at hand for at least a sentence or two. You can then legitimately segue elsewhere if something strikes your interest ("Have you seen the latest *Rain Man* sequel?").

> **ADH-YOU:** Well, what if no one initiates the small-talking?

Great question, YOU! If another member of your small-talk gathering doesn't start the proceedings, then feel free to get things going with your own easy-going contribution.

> **ADH-YOU:** Gee, thanks.

I empathize with your sarcasm. And I know that leading the small-talk is an imposition. But, sadly, unlike when you were a kid, it's not always someone else's job to get the conversation going. So why not try out the role of catalyst? It can be fun—although, if you're the only one holding up the conversation, it can also be exhausting, so you'll probably be glad to find others who share in the responsibility, just as they'll be glad to find you.

ME-TAILS: RIDING VS. HIDING YOUR STREAM OF CONSCIOUSNESS

I love your stream of consciousness: it's fun, it's interesting, it's real! And I'm really glad that you have the self-esteem to share with the rest of us whenever something takes a ride on it.

ADH-YOU: Thanks. What's the catch?

Well caught, YOU. I do have another request in regard to your stream of delivery. As you know, we've already talked about cases where your co-converser is in the middle of telling a story, and you take over with your stream of consciousness—

ADH-YOU: How many times are you going to bring this up?

Yes, sorry, I mention it again because it transitions into an even more daunting challenge. I want you to consider subduing your stream of consciousness *even* in cases where you're the one talking.

ADH-YOU: But I thought it was my turn to talk! Shouldn't I finally be allowed to say whatever I like?

Good point, YOU! Of course you should express yourself freely, but if you talk a lot about little day-to-day details of your life that are not particularly entertaining or remarkable, you may have trouble keeping your co-conversers' eyes open. You don't want a sleeping audience, do you?

ADH-YOU: I guess not.

Great! So here are a few examples of topics that may star in your stream of consciousness, but aren't necessarily useful or interesting to your co-conversers.

Dreams

Don't get me wrong, dreams can be interesting, and for the right crowd (perhaps your spouse or your therapist), they can be a great way to get to know you.

> **ADH-YOU:** Thanks, yeah, last night I dreamt I was being chased by birds around a polka-dot mountain.

Interesting! But before you share that dream-cident with your friends, I have to point out that some people aren't even interested in interpreting their *own* dreams, so they probably won't be intrigued by yours either.

> **ADH-YOU:** How rude.

I know. Nevertheless, before you go into a *full* synopsis of your latest R.E.M. drama, watch the not-so-rapid eye movements of your listeners. If they're staring blankly at you, your dream description probably sounds to them like an incoherent series of details that never actually happened.

> **HINT:** Such dream dissenters likely see dreams as nothing more than random images projected onto our sleeping minds by the subconscious trying to clean up the day's memory. For these anti-dreamacists, talking about your sleepy-time adventures likely seems about as informative as discussing the sweat pattern on your shirt after a workout.

Your Bathroom Intentions

This one is controversial; I am aware of many people not afflicted with ADH-ME who nevertheless take part in this particular foible, so restricting it is optional. However, I will make the case anyway that, when you're hanging out with other adults and you announce, "I have to pee," you are offering more details than are strictly necessary, interesting, or polite.

> **ADH-YOU:** What else am I supposed to say?

Well, why not simply excuse yourself to visit the washroom and let your audience's imagination fill in the rest if it so desires? Would that be so hard?

> **ADH-YOU:** I dunno.

I understand. You're probably just making your "pee"-nouncement because it's common these days. But maybe you could restrict it in formal occasions? I have been amazed, at serious professional encounters, to find previously dignified colleagues announcing their specific plans for the nearest toilet.

> **ADH-YOU:** Wow, prude much?

I know, I know, I'm a fuddy-duddy with a stick up my receptacle: everyone has business to do in the washroom, so why hide it? My only answer is that, by convention, we as a society have segregated washroom habits from the common areas, and so polite manners seem to want to leave them there.

> **ADH-YOU:** But what if I'm on a date? Surely, my date will think me rude if I just get up and leave the table?

Good point, YOU. Yes, if you just wander off without explanation, your date will likely be confused. But that doesn't mean that you must provide your companion with an itemized list of your plans for the washroom in order to step away for a minute; instead, you can simply excuse yourself "to visit the restroom," and leave your companion to ponder your essence.

> **ADH-YOU:** But what if I'm at a friend's place? Surely, it's polite to ask if I want to use their washroom?

Certainly, but I can assure you—from my many years of generalized washroom requests—that I have yet to encounter the following interaction:

> **SETH:** May I visit your washroom?
> **HOST:** Whatever for?

If that *does* ever happen to you, you may instantly consider this book to be invalid, and discontinue following its counsel.

Directionless Directions

Sometimes when you're telling someone about a place you've explored and enjoyed, they'll ask about it. This doesn't specifically mean that they want to go visit that place, themselves. It may just be that they're interested because you are. So you don't necessarily need to go into a long description about how to get to your prized location unless they ask you to. Consider this common conversation:

> **YOUR FRIEND:** So where'd you end up going?
> **ADH-YOU:** Lake Waziabni. It was beautiful.
> **YOUR FRIEND:** Cool, did the kids like it?
> **ADH-YOU:** They had a blast! Have you been?
> **YOUR FRIEND:** No, I'm not much of an outdoorsman, myself.
> **ADH-YOU:** Well, you should go sometime. It's just outside of Filipland.

> **YOUR FRIEND:** Cool, thanks. I'll keep it mind. So how was the—?
>
> **ADH-YOU:** Do you know where that is?
>
> **YOUR FRIEND:** Um, no, but—
>
> **ADH-YOU:** Okay, do you know where Whitchita is?
>
> **YOUR FRIEND:** No, I don't think so.
>
> **ADH-YOU:** It's just outside of Winterland. Do you know how to get there?
>
> **YOUR FRIEND:** Actually, no, but—

And so on, until finally your friend is forced to pretend that they *do* know the name of a place that will yield the directions they're not interested in.

> **ADH-YOU:** Okay, so from Idler's Way you keep going along the highway until you get to Gonzo Smile Road where you turn left. Then drive till you hit Mill Brook Lane.

If you enjoy giving directions for your own entertainment, by all means, continue this habit, but if you're doing it for the benefit of your listener, be advised that sometimes while you're creating your large verbal maps, they'll be daydreaming about what they should make for dinner that evening.

THE ART OF RANTING

Sometimes things will happen to you that should provoke your friends' compassion. So it is certainly okay to release those problems into the ears of your closest compatriots. However, correct me if I'm wrong, but, when you chat with your friends, you have a tendency to dramatize your troubles with an angry tone-of-voice.

> **ADH-YOU:** What a cruel thing to say!

I know. And I apologize. Nevertheless, your melodramatization of your everyday struggles may sometimes exhaust your otherwise admiring listeners. Thus, where possible, I suggest trying not to lament every unfortunate circumstance with your full arsenal of rage.

> **ADH-YOU:** I have no idea what you mean.

Fair enough. Consider how you would normally deal with an annoying incident:

> **ADH-YOU:** So I was at the store and I wanted to return that rotten, stinky onion, but I forgot my receipt, so I told the woman in customer service that I'm a regular and I don't buy my vegetables anywhere else so I shouldn't need a receipt, but she was a total bitch, and said I needed a receipt, which is ridiculous because I shop there all the time! I was like, "Are you seriously gonna make me carry this rotting vegetable, that *you* sold me, all the way home?" And she looks at me and she's like, "Yeah." Total bitch. I hate people.

Do you see how your friend is pulling away from you a bit there with a less than sincere nod? I suspect that's because they find that your rage level doesn't coincide with the level of crime, and so they feel like you're a bit wild. Next time, I suggest adding some humour to your story. Maybe try something like this:

> **ALTERNATE-YOU:** So I was looking forward to making some nice onion tart—my favourite—after my long week at school, and so I chopped with delight into the vegetable only to discover that, OMG, there was a monster rotting inside the thing. Some people would have been turned off by onions altogether at that point, but not me, I was determined! So I set off to the store ... [etc.]

Notice how ALTERNATE-YOU has taken an annoying incident and made it light-hearted for your observer who can still empathize with your plight while being entertained by it simultaneously?

> **ADH-YOU:** I guess.

Well caught, YOU! And the good news is, when you rant with humour, your friends are more likely to support your diatribes, and you'll get more time on the conversational stage. Yay!

ARGUING YOU

Missing Their Point

When a conversation turns to argument (whether philosophical or personal), maintaining dignity can be difficult for a regular person, let alone for someone besot with your cruel affliction.

> **ADH-YOU:** I appreciate that. So there's really not much I can do then, right?

Close, YOU! It turns out that you can minimize negativity by taking time to listen to the other side of the dispute. As we talked about in Chapter 2, if you demonstrate that you understand what your adversary is saying, they are less likely to become agitated.

> **ADH-YOU:** Why? Treating them with kid gloves won't make them any less wrong.

Yes, of course, but at least they won't feel like you're mischaracterizing their point of view. Plus, if you can show that you disagree, but at least appreciate where they're coming from, I think you'll discover that they are more likely to do the same for you.

> **ADH-YOU:** Okay. But I should point out: I have no idea what you're talking about.

Sorry, let's look at an example of how you would normally counter argue:

YOUR FRIEND: I think John/Jane Q. Famous-Actor is overrated. He/she had that one great role, and so has been given lots of significant roles in good movies ever since, but I don't think he/she brings much to them.

ADH-YOU: How can you claim that Famous-Actor isn't successful? He/she's won an Oscar!

Now, if you look carefully, you might notice that your response there is missing your friend's point.

> **ADH-YOU:** But Famous-Actor *has* won an Oscar, *and* two Golden Globes!

Well spotted, YOU! Nevertheless, if you were to peer inside your friend's mind, you would likely learn that they don't dispute Famous-Actor's widespread acclaim; their point, though, is that they think Famous-Actor has gotten more appreciation than their skills warrant.

> **ADH-YOU:** So you're saying I'm not allowed to disagree with that? Geez.

No, no, excellent YOU, I'm not saying you shouldn't counter your friend's point, but I *am* saying that your above argument is not dealing with the claim they're making. Try this:

ALTERNATE-YOU: Yeah, I know what you mean. Sometimes actors get typecast as important actors because of one good role, and so they get more good roles even though they're not necessarily brilliant. But I don't think John/Jane Q. Famous-Actor fits into that category. His/her work in *The Bleeding Soul* was, for me, so subtle. The way he/she looked like he/she was going to cry so many times, but never did. I thought that was amazing.

Do you see how ALTERNATE-YOU is now taking on the content of your friend's argument, instead of a flimsy, straw version of it?

ADH-YOU: I guess, but that looks like more work.

It is. I know. But I promise you that the extra work will be paid off in fewer voice-raised arguments with your friends.

> **HINT:** Sometimes, of course, your attempt to understand your opponent's side of the argument won't be reciprocated, and instead your conversational foe will take advantage of your goodwill. When that happens, you are likely dealing with a fellow ADH-SUFFERER, and so you may be justified in reverting back to some of your expert change-the-subject strategies to pull out of the conversation. Feel free to use any of your old false segues to get out of there: they may be your best chance to avoid a major conversational collision.

Fixating On Incidental Mistakes

I've noticed that, when your side of an argument isn't doing so well, you sometimes attack tiny language choices in your opponent's presentation instead of the thrust of their argument. For instance:

YOUR INTERNET FRIEND: Dear YOU: I'm hurt that you stood me up for our date on Thursday evening. I had told you in advance that I would understand if you didn't want to go, but you insisted you were ready to meet. So I don't understand why you wouldn't show up without calling or texting me on your iPhone—or at least emailing me afterwards. I would appreciate an explanation.

ADH-YOU: I own an rPhone, not an iPhone.

Do you see how this latching onto one tiny point in your correspondent's message without acknowledging the greater thrust of their argument may send them in search of a therapist? Is their phone-identification error really relevant to this discussion? And, if it is, does it make the rest of their argument obsolete? If it does, could you maybe explain why?

ADH-YOU: Certainly. I own an rPhone, not an iPhone, which justifies me not showing up for our date because all rPhone owners have recently suffered radiation poisoning and so I was at the hospital.

Oh ... I see ... thank you for clarifying that.

ACCIDENTALLY MEAN YOU

You don't always mean to be mean.

ADH-YOU: But sometimes I do!

That's true, you do. In this section, though, I'd like to look at a couple instances where you may not intend to be cruel, but you succeed anyway.

ADH-YOU: Colour me intrigued.

So, for instance, you might find it harmless to occasionally use the name of certain oft-maligned groups as an insult to identify things you perceive to be silly.

> **ADH-YOU:** I'm not following you, bud.

Well, have you ever heard yourself describing something disagreeable as "retarded"? For instance:

> **YOUR FRIEND:** I forgot my password—again.
> **ADH-YOU:** Oh my God, you're so retarded!
> **YOUR FRIEND:** Hee, hee, I know.

Does that sound familiar?

> **ADH-YOU:** Sure, but it's just an expression. I mean no ill will towards retards.

I don't doubt that. But I wonder if you might consider the possibility that "retarded" carries with it an association with genuinely disabled people who were formerly identified by that word? You may or may not mean to insult those born with such troubles, but your word usage implies otherwise.

In fact, by utilizing "retarded" to illustrate the stupidity of your friend, you are employing exaggerated emphasis as your means of mocking. Kind of like when the referee in a sporting event doesn't see something that seems obvious to you, and you call out, "Hey, ref, are you blind?"

Of course, you know that the object of your teasing is not, in fact, blind, but the remark exaggerates the referee's alleged lack of vision for your comic effect. Very funny of you. (Indeed, it's especially funny to imagine a blind person applying for the job of referee.) I must ask you, though: if you were aware that there was a blind person nearby when you witnessed the incompetent referee, would you still shout out your blind insult?

> **ADH-YOU:** Obviously I'm not going to say that in front of a blind guy.

So it seems that in certain contexts you would be worried about how your language might affect certain members of your audience. Imagine, then, if the term "blind" had been used viciously in the direction of sightless people when they were growing up (in the way that "retarded" has been used as a slur against young mentally disabled people by their less friendly classmates). Might you not feel honour-bound to avoid using the term derisively even when blind people weren't around, just to avoid facilitating further cruelty?

> **ADH-YOU:** Okay, fine, I won't insult blind people.

Great, um, but ... so do you mind also avoiding "retarded" as an insult?

> **ADH-YOU:** This is so gay. But fine. Anything else?

Actually, yeah, I'm hoping this request is becoming antiquated these days, but I was also wondering about your use of "gay" as a general description for something bad.

> **ADH-YOU:** Here we go again. What's the problem this time?

Well, I'm sure—when you remark that something is gay—you don't necessarily mean to condemn homosexuality: instead, you may simply be using the choice insult of the day.

> **ADH-YOU:** Exactly, what's the problem? I'm not saying gay people are bad. I'm just saying that thing over there is gay, as in annoying.

I understand, but using the word "gay" as an insult is derived directly from the fact that many people think (or have thought) that being gay is, in fact, wrong. So calling something "gay" is basically saying, "That's as wrong as being gay." Even if you don't mean that connotation, it *is* the expression's basis for existence, so can we really blame a gay person for feeling insulted when you use "gay" as a general put down?

> **ADH-YOU:** I guess not, but I'm not sure what other word I could use to express that something's gay. If I tell my friend that something's annoying me by saying, I don't know, that it's "awful," how will they know I'm annoyed by it?

I know it's scary, but I promise you that over time your friends will come to understand your fancy new vocabulary.

> **ADH-YOU:** Fine, I'll stop using "gay" and "retarded" as insults if you stop taking me so literally all the time.

Fair enough. And, in honour of this deal, see the story, *Sorry Expression*, below for an example of someone using those terms without, I suspect, meaning any ill will towards the official groups in question, just as you've suggested.

Sorry Expression

One day, at the politically correct organization at which I worked, a young colleague arrived late for a meeting with me:

> **YOUNG COLLEAGUE:** Sorry, I'm late.
>
> **SETH:** That's okay—was the bus late again?
>
> **YOUNG COLLEAGUE:** Yeah, the transit system here is so gay.
>
> **SETH (*raising his eyebrows in surprise*):** Oh—

YOUNG COLLEAGUE (*backtracking*): Sorry! I meant that the transit system here is retarded!

Yeah, that was much better.

Chapter 5

Conversational Discretion & You

Freedom of speech is my favourite freedom, so please don't misunderstand me: with the verbal adjustments I suggest here, I do not mean to say that you do not have a *right* to say whatever you like, but instead I propose that you might *consider* curating how, where, and when you unleash your favourite ideas.

CONVERSATIONS TO CONSIDER AVOIDING (FOR OTHER PEOPLE'S ENJOYMENT)

Ridicooling

Music taste is probably second only to clothing choice when it comes to separating the cool from the not-so-much. Somehow, one's selection of tunes indicates the validity of the person listening to them.

> **ADH-YOU:** Well, if you don't want me to mock you, then maybe pick better tunes.

Well noted, YOU! And, if, by my enjoyment of the songs of Celine Dion, you infer a particular trait in me that you don't want to be around, then I support your decision to avoid me. However, when you're at a social gathering and are about to announce the irredeemable folly of certain musical performers, maybe you could consider that, within your audience, there may be a closet-enjoyer of the music for which you're vocalizing contempt.

> **ADH-YOU:** So I'm not supposed to say which music I dislike? Geez, anti-fun much?

Well teased, YOU. No, I don't mean to suggest that you shouldn't share your ever-valuable taste. Instead, I'm just arguing that if you treated your preference as simply that—a preference, and not an objective separator of the worthy from the unworthy—you could avoid making those who enjoy the wrong music feel as though they're unfit for society.

> **ADH-YOU:** But they *are* unfit for society—mine, at least.

Yes, but since they're there anyway, there's no need to kick them while they're dorky. The same goes for objectively dismissing behaviours such as science-fiction-consuming, crocheting, lisping, aging, video-game-playing, cat-collecting, and TV-viewing (which we'll talk about more in the next section).

TV-Eschewing

Now I have no objection to your contempt for television—

> **ADH-YOU:** I see no value in the drivel they put on TV.

Right, nicely said, YOU. Nevertheless, when your friend tells you about a TV program that *they* enjoy, I'd like to propose that you don't *always* have to point out that you "don't watch TV." Such a comment can be interesting if properly segued to, but when you bring it up any time someone mentions their TV preferences, it can accidentally come across as though you are announcing that those who watch TV are inferior to you. Thus far, you have been able to proceed happily with this implied thesis because it is a subliminal insult, and therefore difficult for the receiver to pinpoint for complaint. But I wonder what you would say if your friend questioned you on your announcement:

> **YOUR FRIEND:** I love *I Love Lucy*.
>
> **ADH-YOU:** I don't own a TV, so—
>
> **YOUR FRIEND:** So?

Chapter 5: *Conversational Discretion & You*

> **ADH-YOU:** So I just thought you should know.
>
> **YOUR FRIEND:** Why?
>
> **ADH-YOU:** Because you're telling me about a TV show and I don't watch TV so I don't know what you're talking about.
>
> **YOUR FRIEND:** Well you just spent half an hour telling me about your new girlfriend, and I don't date girls, so—
>
> **ADH-YOU:** That's different.

Yeah, it does feel different, doesn't it? Yet, I can't see a logical distinction. Instead, I submit that the reason we feel like there's a difference between those two cases is because it's more commonplace for someone to announce that they don't watch TV when told about a friend's television-viewing tendencies than, say, to interrupt their friend's favourite driving story to tell them that they don't have a car.

Just to be safe, then, maybe when someone tells you about their favourite television show, you could try reacting with inquisitiveness. If, however, you feel that you simply cannot contain your superiority over TV-viewers, then why hide it in irrelevant-seeming statements? Just be direct:

> **YOUR FRIEND:** I can't wait till the next *Mary Tyler Moore Show* comes out.
>
> **ADH-YOU:** You're excited about an un-evolved pastime that is beneath my interest. Please discontinue.

If that sounds to you to be inappropriately rude, keep in mind that it contains the same implied content you had previously invoked with your sudden, conversation-stopping statement, "I don't watch TV."

CONVERSATIONS TO CONSIDER AVOIDING (DEPENDING ON CONTEXT)

Meanwhile, there are some conversation topics that are perfectly friendly on their own, but which you might consider avoiding in particular instances.

Movie Twists

I know it can be fun to discuss the plot of a movie you've just watched, but if you give away the ending to someone who has specifically requested to be left out of the discussion so that they can watch the story unspoiled, then you are once again making a nuisance of yourself. Consider this example:

> **NOTE:** The names and plots of the movies mentioned have been changed to protect those who haven't seen them yet.

YOUR FRIEND: Yeah, I was totally shocked when Captain Hungry turned out to be a werewolf.

YOUR OTHER FRIEND: Me too, at first, but then I realized they'd given lots of hints—

ADH-YOU (*just arriving on the conversation*): What are you guys talking about?

YOUR FRIEND: *The Captain Hungry Chronicles.*

ADH-YOU: Oh, I want to see that! Is it good?

YOUR FRIEND: It was decent, but we shouldn't say too much because any details could accidentally give away the ending.

ADH-YOU: Thanks! Yeah, it's like *Cloud Walker*: I shouldn't say anything about that one, 'cause it'll give things away.

Chapter 5: *Conversational Discretion & You*

YOUR FRIEND: Yeah, that one was even more mysterious.

YOUR OTHER FRIEND: Oh, I wanna see that one, too, so yeah, please don't give anything away.

ADH-YOU (*to your other friend*): So did you like *Cloud Walker*?

YOUR FRIEND: It was pretty good, but I found the cloud walking to be unnerving.

ADH-YOU: Yeah, me too at first, but once they reveal that the whole thing is happening in the pilot's brain, it all makes sense.

YOUR OTHER FRIEND: Oops, that sounds like an important detail.

ADH-YOU: Oh, right! Hee, hee, sorry, I forgot you haven't seen it. Oh well, just forget that I told you that.

Now, while I'm sure you didn't mean to betray the plot of this particular movie, you were still negligent in your free-wheeling discussion of it in front someone who requested moderation. In future, please be a wee bit patient, and delay talking about such movies in detail until those who have requested spoil-protection-services have left the room.

> **ADH-YOU:** How am I supposed to know which details I'm supposed to be patient with and which I'm not?

Great question, YOU. Once again, my request is that you consider your audience: *would the plot point you're about to share harm their movie-viewing experience if you announced it?* If so (or if you're *at all* unsure), please hold it in as long as you can!

> **ADH-YOU:** Spoiler alert. I won't be able to hold onto it for long.

I understand.

Unsolicited Health Advice

When your co-worker, friend, or just-spotted celebrity is eating a meal that is not as nutritional as it is tasty, it is not necessarily your responsibility to point out the discrepancy to them. In spite of your helpful intentions, it is a fact of nature that such commentary will aggravate the unhealthy eater, leading to the following sarcasm aimed in your direction:

> **UNHEALTHY EATER:** Oh, thanks, I assumed deep-fried chocolate was good for me.

You may not hear them say so out loud, but trust me: they're thinking it. If you want to promote health in your friends and colleagues, then maybe you could just go about your healthy ways, and when others ask you about it, try your best to make it seem like a palatable option for anyone interested. For instance:

> **YOUR FRIEND:** Wow, that looks healthy.
>
> **ALTERNATE-YOU:** Yeah, it's actually got decent flavour, if you can believe it.

Not bad at all, ALTERNATE-YOU!

Politics And Philosophy (Rant Carefully)

Political issues can be a lot of fun to talk about, but the problem is that they often matter deeply to people. This—combined with the fact that one person's obvious political point can be another's ridiculous claim—means that it's easy to find two people on opposite sides of an issue that they both care about. Such a conflict can disrupt the flow of polite conversation if it isn't dealt with delicately.

> **ADH-YOU:** But I have so much to teach people!

Yes, good point. I know that your opinion is a beautiful dove that should always be shared, and I'm not suggesting that you don't honour your convictions by voicing them. I'm only proposing that there are certain times and places (such as work events or family reunions) where controversial discussions can overrule the friendly purpose of the occasion. So, if you feel an urge to say something politically contentious during such a polite circumstance, it might be worth framing your opinions with a gentle (almost tentative) air that shows you're not necessarily labelling those who disagree as stupid and/or immoral.

> **ADH-YOU:** But sometimes I want to get my rant on!

Well said, YOU! And, where appropriate, a passionate political diatribe can be great fun. However, to people who don't immediately recognize your intrinsic righteousness, your delightfully assertive rhetoric may make you seem like a bully (which I know you're not!).

Politics And Philosophy (On The Wings)

The above problem is especially pronounced in workplace cultures that tend to align specifically with one of the political wings.

> **ADH-YOU:** That's a lot of babble. What are you trying to say?

Sorry, thanks for reigning me in, YOU. What I mean to say is that just because you work for a food bank (which may tend to match up with left-wing viewpoints) or a financial bank (which may generally favour right-wing policies) doesn't mean that all of your co-workers are obligated to vote in those directions.

> **ADH-YOU:** I didn't say they were obligated, just that they were stupid and immoral if they didn't.

Fair enough, and thank you for the clarification. But to avoid making your politically outnumbered colleagues feel like pariahs, I'm going to ask you to allow for the possibility that, although your opinion is obviously right, not everyone has figured it out just yet. So, once again, gentleness in your presentation would be much appreciated.

> **CONVERSATIONS TO CONSIDER AVOIDING (BECAUSE THEY'RE NOT YOURS TO SHARE)**

Please consider the following real-world situation that my sister got herself into in fourth grade. One day, her friend gave her two bottles of perfume, which she, of course, immediately deposited in her pocket. Subsequently, during a skip-rope dominated recess, the perfume bottles collided with each other and broke. Thus, my sister acquired both a cut hand—when she put it in her pocket—and an outfit that smelled aggressively of perfume. After recess, the other kids in the class were not particularly delicate in their reaction to the aggressive smell.

> **KID 1:** Eww, what stinks?
>
> **KID 2:** Gross, what's that smell?

Such decorum-free commentary is understandable when it comes from kids: most humans go through many years of childhood-induced ADH-ME before they mature into adulthood. However, when my sister realized that she was to blame for her co-students' dissatisfaction, she hoped her (adult) teacher might be able to help.

> **SETH'S SISTER (*whispering for her own protection*):** Excuse me, Ms. ADH-TEACHER, I think the smell is coming from me—I broke these perfume bottles.
>
> **ADH-TEACHER (*loudly*):** Yes, Seth's sister, you may go home and clean up.

As my sister left the room, she could hear the teacher explaining her perfume-fed troubles to the rest of the class. This disconcerted my sister, who certainly wouldn't have whispered her plight to the teacher if she had wanted the news announced to the class.

CONVERSATIONS TO CONSIDER AVOIDING (BECAUSE THEY'RE NEEDLESSLY MEAN)

Body Remarks

Many people are sensitive about their physiques. So even if someone's physical features seem indisputable, I suggest not commenting on those traits (unless the person to whom you direct such comments has indicated to you that they're interested in your opinions on such matters).

> **HINT:** There are technically a few generally accepted comments on physical appearance, such as the excellence of someone's new hairstyle, but I think that may be a little too nuanced a distinction for you. So if you're hoping to say something nice to someone with whom you don't have a close relationship, I suggest applauding their non-appearance-based achievements instead.

(1) AGAINST WOMEN:

The entertainment industry appears to be populated by a variety of women who on average wear a much smaller dress size than those who are not on TV or album covers. And, yet in the rare cases that less thin women become famous (or formerly thin women remain famous), they often become comedic fodder for comedians and internet commentators.

> **ADH-YOU-TUBE:** I have a right to make jokes about anything I like.

Well defended, YOU! Yes, once again, free speech is perhaps the most important right of a free society. And I support your right to say whatever choose. However, if you would like the benefits of being considered a kind and/or respectful person, I'm afraid these jokes are severely hampering your application for that title.

(2) AGAINST MEN:

While the entertainment industry is probably harder on women who don't fit into the expected dimensions, I believe men are more likely to be picked on *in person* for diverging from standard proportions. Conventional wisdom assumes that men don't care about the structure of their bodies nearly as much as women do—

> **ADH-YOU:** Well, if being conventionally wise is wrong, I don't wanna be right. Dudes don't care about their bodies.

I'm sure you're right as always, but your claim dismisses the obsession that many men have with building muscles (sometimes via steroids). In fact, many men want to be called skinny about as much as women want to be described as overweight.

> **ADH-YOU:** No way guys care about their body size as much as women do.

Okay, I may be overstating this claim, but the spirit of the remark is, I believe, useful. Many men are sensitive about the shape of their silhouettes, too: they're just not socialized to admit it. Men, for instance, are allowed to say, "I need to lose a few pounds," but they're not expected to comment that they're worried about how they look in a particular outfit. So again, my request is that you avoid teasing people for their dimensions—even if stereotype tells you they won't mind.

Plus, those jokes are somewhat standard; surely you have some original humour you could employ instead?

> **ADH-YOU:** I've always got brilliant original material.

Perfect!

Chapter 6

Egos & You

I see little harm in having a biggie-sized ego. My only request is that, when you're puffing up, you avoid knocking others down in the process.

GRACE UNDER EGO

Listening Gracefully

In a former career, my spouse was a music historian. And more than once I witnessed her in the following conversation:

> **RANDOM PARTYGOER:** So what do you do?
>
> **SETH'S SPOUSE:** I'm studying music history.
>
> **RANDOM PARTYGOER:** That's cool. So what made Mozart so great?
>
> **SETH'S SPOUSE:** Well—
>
> **ADH-YOU (to Seth's spouse):** Have you seen *Amadeus*?
>
> **SETH'S SPOUSE:** Yeah, I love that movie. Although it does take some liberties—
>
> **ADH-YOU:** Well, what amazed me about that movie was that Mozart could play piano blindfolded when he was only five years old! I'd say he was a prodigy.

Very good, YOU! You sure taught her. Indeed, I have no doubt that your lecture was worthwhile, and that my spouse learned a lot from it; however, given her many years of studying the topic in detail, it might have been worth letting her finish her thought before you intervened with yours.

> **ADH-YOU:** So you want me to hide my superiority? I am what I am.

I know: it's not easy knowing and being good at everything. But there are little things you can do to allow others to feel as though they can provide a tiny piece of value to your conversations. I recommend the following two steps:

(1) Pretend for a moment as though the person you're talking to *might* have something interesting to say to you. Once you're in that frame of delusion, pause and let your co-converser finish their thought before you overrule it with your own.

(2) If by some fluke, they subsequently tell you about something you're unfamiliar with, then relax and enjoy taking in some new information.

Speaking Gracefully

If you are in the (well-deserved) position of being a presenter or workshop facilitator, be aware that it can be painful for your audience to be lectured on a subject of which they have significant knowledge—remember how much you hate it when someone does that to you! So try to keep your viewers' expertise level in mind. For instance, normally, ADH-YOU might say something like this to a gathering of hockey fans:

> **ADH-YOU:** In addition to being a great family man, I've determined that Wayne Gretzky was also a very good hockey player.
>
> **AUDIENCE MEMBER:** Yeah, I kinda knew that.

Do you see how your observer's reply seems snarky? This may be because you've inadvertently suggested that they—a hockey scholar, themselves—didn't know the most obvious of hockey facts.

> **ADH-YOU:** But I'm just trying to build an argument, starting with the simplest facts first.

That's understandable. Maybe we could compromise. How about something like this?

> **ALTERNATE-YOU:** As you probably know, Gretzky was a great hockey player...

Nice! See how ALTERNATE-YOU has managed to get your simple, premise-setting point across without implying that you were *teaching* it to your audience?

> **ADH-YOU:** Yeah, how the heck did ALTERNATE-ME do that?

Great question, YOU. All ALTERNATE-YOU had to do was acknowledge that your audience was likely already aware of the simple fact you were using as a starting point of your argument. It's actually an easy trick if you can remember it.

> **ADH-YOU:** Okay, yeah, it looks pretty simple, bud. I don't need a lecture on it.

Great, YOU! And, given your quick mastery of that technique, let's look at a more complicated scenario within the same genre. Sometimes, particularly at work, you have a tendency to lecture your colleagues on concepts that *they* brought up. For instance:

> **YOUR COLLEAGUE:** I think it would be a good idea to order one of each colour so that we're covered if the client isn't satisfied with their first choice.
>
> **ADH-YOU:** Well, it's important that we have variety. You never know when the customer might change their mind, right?

Yes, exactly! That's what your colleague was arguing. Why are you instructing them on this point as though you initiated it?

> **ADH-YOU:** Because I want to make sure everyone knows I already understood what my colleague was talking about. I don't want anyone thinking I learned it from them.

I understand. Well, then, if it's important for you to demonstrate that you comprehended a concept before your co-worker invoked it, then all you have to do is credit your colleague with saying it first, i.e.:

> **ALTERNATE-YOU:** I totally agree. It's so annoying when the client changes their mind and we're not prepared.

See how ALTERNATE-YOU has managed to support the point without claiming credit for the idea?

> **ADH-YOU:** I guess.

You guess right! Well done, YOU!

Answering Gracefully

Now, as you know, you're smarter than the rest of us.

> **ADH-YOU:** And, as *you* know, I am aware.

Well put, YOU. And this means that you'll figure things out faster than we ever could. Thus, when you notice something, you certainly cannot be expected to think that someone else could have spotted the same thing. So, when someone asks you a question in which they preface their inquiry with an acknowledgement of a fact that you are delighted to already know, you have a tendency to *explain* that fact right back to them instead of responding to their question. Consider this interaction:

> **YOUR FRIEND:** Hey, I know that in terms of saving money, it's always best to pay off my credit card debt first. But, given that I'm getting close to paying off my car, would it help my credit rating if I made a lump sum payment to remove that debt completely?

> **ADH-YOU**: Well, the interest on your credit card is highest, right? So it'll save you money if you pay that off first.
>
> **YOUR FRIEND**: Yes, I understand that. I'm just wondering if my credit rating would benefit if I got one thing completely taken care of first.

Do you notice how your friend has raised their voice? That's because, even though they clearly demonstrated that they knew X, and wanted to know Z, you still told them X.

> **ADH-YOU**: Yeah, what's their deal? X is a useful piece of information! I'm only trying to help them learn.

Yes, I'm sure you are, but if you were to spend just a few moments listening to people's actual questions, you may find that they, in turn, would be more interested in your answers. Win-win! (Your favourite.)

DOGMATIC YOU

I admire the certainty with which you state your convictions. You are assertive and passionate. Unfortunately, though, some people confuse those lovely traits for dogmatism.

> **ADH-YOU**: Well, if being strong is wrong, I don't wanna be right!

Good point, but there's just one small problem. In the rarest of occasions, you might make a dogmatic assertion that turns out to be a teensy bit incorrect. That could create a traumatic situation for you. After all, when you invest so much certainty in a claim that turns out to be false, you are forced into a painful predicament of choosing between either:

(A) backing down from your lofty statement (not your favourite thing to do), or

(B) defending a suddenly untenable position.

> **ADH-YOU:** I'll take option B. Backing down is for cowards.

I admire your consistency! And I've definitely seen you defending your weakest statements with full earnestness (against all facts). But, while I revere your passionate efforts to dance with the argument that brought you, I worry that such loyalty is hard on you. Consider your two most common means of protecting a factually troubled statement.

(1) THE "JUST GO WITH IT":

ADH-YOU: That idiot doesn't realize the earth *is* flat.

YOUR FRIEND: Hmm, I'm not so sure that it is flat. Those ships seem to be gradually disappearing into the distance. That would imply that the earth is round, wouldn't it?

ADH-YOU: Oh, well the fog must be blocking our view.

YOUR FRIEND: But it's a clear day.

ADH-YOU: Well the ships must have sunk, then!

YOUR FRIEND: But I'm still receiving messages from one of the captains.

ADH-YOU: Somebody's probably impersonating the captain. Man, are you gullible!

Your idea here is that you will defend your initial argument to any extreme necessary to avoid admitting you are wrong. You figure that, so long as you argue each point with conviction, then officially you haven't lost face. Well played. One thing you *might* consider, though, is that, while, yes, you never *have to* admit that you've made a mistake, you may lose more respect from those around you—for sticking to your untenable position—than you would have if you'd simply conceded an error.

> **HINT:** If you tease yourself for that initial mistake (as soon as possible), your friends will be more likely to forgive your initial blustering blunder than if you pretend that it didn't happen. Strangely, they'll appreciate your willingness to laugh at yourself.

(2) THE "BOB AND WEAVE":

> **YOUR CO-WORKER:** I think we're out of stamps: can you order more?
>
> **ADH-YOU:** Check the mail tray.
>
> **YOUR CO-WORKER:** I did. I don't see any there.
>
> **ADH-YOU:** Well, you have to let me know when you need more stamps. I'm not a mind reader.
>
> **YOUR CO-WORKER:** I know. That's why I asked you to order more just now.
>
> **ADH-YOU:** Yeah, I heard you—you don't have to repeat yourself.

Brilliant! Every time your opponent proves one of your points to be weak, you re-calibrate and attack them from a new (often contradictory) angle as though that was your point all along. The invention of this strategy is one of your great achievements: by being impossible to pin down, you become exhausting to argue against.

> **ADH-YOU:** Awe shucks, thanks for noticing.

That's what I'm here for, YOU! Although, once again, it's worth keeping in mind that, while you won't officially "lose" the discussion, you will surrender the respect of those around you.

> **ADH-YOU:** Why? I won!

I know you did! But, strangely, observers will see you as myopic in your defences because you seem only able to respond to the last thing said. This in turn gives the impression that you have no understanding of the overall debate.

> **ADH-YOU:** But I cannot risk seeming unconfident in front of others. If I don't believe in me, no one else will!

Right, good point. I understand you're not about to give up your celebrated confidence without a fight. But it might be worth occasionally admitting to the tiniest of errors so that your reputation can live to be celebrated another day.

BOASTING YOU

Regular Boasting

Some boasts are inextricably linked to insulting others. For instance, consider the following phrase:

> **ADH-YOU:** I'm far and away the best salesperson in this company.

While I'm sure you're right, that statement carries with it an implication that you're better than the rest of the salespeople, and so may offend some of your colleagues. In contrast, try this victimless boast on for size:

> **ALTERNATE-YOU:** I'm an awesome salesperson.

Not bad, eh? You can still announce your greatness without necessarily insulting others.

Chapter 6: *Egos & You*

> **NOTE:** You should be aware that, even after you've traded in your insulting boasts for non-insulting ones, some may still quietly laugh at you for your bragging. If you can live with that, so can they.

Quiet Boasting

Now, if you don't want people to see you as a braggart, you may also want to avoid trying to sneak your boasts in subliminally.

> **ADH-YOU:** Whatever do you mean?

Well, one of your favourite pastimes is to hide a boast within a seemingly innocent factual statement. For instance, compare these distinct ways in which ADH-YOU and ALTERNATE-YOU would indicate your childhood affinity with science:

> **YOUR DATE:** What were your favourite subjects in school?
>
> **ALTERNATE-YOU:** I was really into science as a kid.

Notice how ALTERNATE-YOU has identified your scientific interest without celebrating you for it. In contrast, watch how you would normally answer the same question:

> **ADH-YOU:** I won a national science award when I was ten. So, yeah, I was really into science as a kid.

While there's nothing wrong with pointing out your achievements in a particular field, such details can seem boastful when they are not required for the point you're making.

> **ADH-YOU:** But my science award was totally relevant to that discussion!

Yes, you're right: technically it was relevant. But since it wasn't *essential* to your presentation, it may have seemed to your

105

listener that you were forcing the complimentary fact into the conversation.

> **ADH-YOU:** But I just wanted to give them evidence of my science interest! Winning a science award shows a lot of interest, doesn't it?

So it does. My point, though, is not that you should never bring up your scientific greatness, but that your natural tendency to sneak it into cases where it's not necessary makes you and your understandably grand ego look silly. So, to avoid that result, your best bet is to be as cautious as you can with words that celebrate you unless you're certain that they're vital to the conversation.

> **ADH-YOU:** I still don't see what the big deal is if I occasionally point out little facts that happen to prove how awesome I am.

Fair enough. Such clandestine boasts are victimless and may not even always be noticed. However, if your companions start catching your hidden self-praise, they'll soon spot it everywhere in your conversation, and so will likely commence teasing you during water cooler discussions with their friends. If that doesn't trouble you, then feel free to continue quietly boasting whenever you have a craving to do so.

Meanwhile, to demonstrate the dangers of subliminal boasting, check out the following story, *Ego on the Range*, which stars one of your ADH-BRETHREN attempting to emphasize his brilliance.

Ego on the Range

I'd now like to call to the stage the ex-boyfriend of a friend of mine. I only met him once, but within seconds of meeting him, I could see that he'd been blessed with an impressive ego. Somehow our conversation turned to the subject of IQs, and the gentleman in question noted that he found IQ tests to be ridiculous because they were so inaccurate:

Chapter 6: *Egos & You*

WELL-EGOED GENTLEMAN: I've taken the IQ test twice. On one occasion I scored 135, and another time 150, so clearly they're unreliable.

Delightfully, our new friend of plus-sized ego had managed to sneak into that statement the obvious implication that, even though he didn't believe in IQ tests, he still had an impressive score (someone ranking between 135 and 150 would be considered an abundantly bright person). Yet, given his implied intelligence, he surely could have argued the inaccuracy of IQ tests—without noting his excellent scores—by simply pointing out the 15-point swing in his two tests. But he chose not to because, I surmise, publicizing his high scores was his main point. Sadly, that meant he was mocked in the lesser minds of those around him.

BLUNT YOU

You delight in "telling it like it is." As Jane Austen would say, you "are ever-celebrated for your frankness." And you're not about to change that for anyone! If people don't like you, they can "change the channel." Good, good, good.

But can I ask you one thing? Why? What is it about other people's emotions that you find so unworthy of your concern? I'm not saying, of course, that you shouldn't give voice to your opinion, but do you think there could be room for diplomacy in your delivery?

ADH-YOU: Ah, no, I'm not about to coddle someone who needs to hear the truth.

Well put, YOU. But consider this: I doubt you would tell a nervous child about to give a piano recital that their clothes are ugly, and I hope that I would criticize a maniacal dictator if I had their ear, so clearly neither of us is opposed categorically to politeness/bluntness. It's just a matter of where we mark our thresholds.

So I suggest a compromise. Would you consider moving your line to a slightly more sensitive point? I don't want to undermine your passion, but I would like you to reign in those occasions when your bluntness has no moral value, but has a good chance of insulting an innocent bystander in the process. For instance:

> **ADH-YOU:** Internet dating is for losers.
>
> **YOUR COLLEAGUE:** Well, I guess that makes me one since that's how I met my wife.
>
> **ADH-YOU (*shrugging*):** I calls 'em like I sees 'em.

Chapter 7

Patronizing You

While arrogance is harmless on its own (since self-delight doesn't require a victim), speaking in a patronizing tone takes your preference for ADH-YOU and belittles those who aren't.

> **ADH-YOU:** I'm sorry, pumpkin, but you're speaking in code. I'm gonna need some specifics on this one.

Fair enough. To my ear, your greatest weapon in your pursuit of condescension is your expert use of subtly belittling language.

> **ADH-YOU:** So what's the example, sport?

Right, sorry. Below is a list of phrases (and one system of phrases) which you expertly use to talk to down to your fellow citizens.

> **HINT:** You may find that you use some of these phrases as clichés without necessarily meaning them in their literal sense. In that case, just to be safe, I would double check that your receivers are taking them in the non-insulting way that you intend them.

"IF YOU THINK ABOUT IT..."

Consider this conversation:

> **YOUR FRIEND:** I've decided I'm going to vote for the Purple Party. I like their X, Y and Z policies.
>
> **ADH-YOU:** Well, if you think about it, their policies are actually going to do more harm than good.

I believe the origins of (and perhaps your intention for) this lovely phrase is to note that, whereas conventional wisdom is X, *if one really thinks about it*, Y has some merit as well. But when your conversation partner believes they *have* thought deeply about a point already, you may be inadvertently giving them the impression that you believe your thoughts on the subject are automatically superior to theirs.

> **ADH-YOU:** But my thoughts *are* superior.

Well, yes, you know that, and I know that, but as Sheldon's mom tells Sheldon in the television sitcom, *The Big Bang Theory*, "People don't like it when you point it out." And since your adversary may annoyingly believe that they have the same right to the intellectual floor that you do, they may think it's unfair for you to announce that your thoughts automatically overrule theirs.

> **ADH-YOU:** I don't see the problem. I'm just trying to help them learn.

I'm sure that's true, and I'm not arguing that your brilliant thinking can't aid others. But perhaps instead of suggesting that people learn from thinking the way you think, you could simply let them know *what* you think and see if it compels them. Try this:

> **YOUR FRIEND:** I've decided I'm going to vote for the Purple Party. I like their X, Y and Z policies.
>
> **ALTERNATE-YOU:** Yeah, I like those policies, too, but I'm not convinced that they'll follow through with them because of the way they handled the incident with their own party members.
>
> **YOUR FRIEND:** Really? What would you have had them do differently?

See how your friend is intrigued instead of offended? By presenting your case as simply your take on something as opposed to the universal truth, ALTERNATE-YOU managed to pique your friend's interest. Well done, ALTERNATE-YOU!

"NO, IT'S X."

This is a subtle one. There is little wrong, in itself, with stating that something is one thing or another. However, when your conversational companion has an opposing opinion, for you to announce unilaterally that your side is the correct one may again give them the impression that you think that your take on something is automatically better than theirs. For instance:

> **YOUR FRIEND:** I remember that game well; it was my best game ever. I couldn't believe I got five goals.
>
> **ADH-YOU:** It was four goals.
>
> **YOUR FRIEND:** I'm pretty sure it was five because—
>
> **ADH-YOU:** No, it was four.
>
> **YOUR FRIEND:** But I remember Anderson kept boasting that he had assisted on all five of my goals.
>
> **ADH-YOU:** Anderson wasn't there. You're thinking of a different game.
>
> **YOUR FRIEND:** But it was St. Patrick's Day—I remember Anderson wore his green shirt.
>
> **ADH-YOU:** No, it was Valentine's Day.

Do you see how, at every turn, your friend is trying to make an argument for their side, clearly indicating that they think the matter is still up for debate?

> **ADH-YOU:** Yeah, I see that. Why aren't they just taking my word for it?

Well, rather strangely, they don't necessarily believe that you're the arbiter of fact in every situation.

> **ADH-YOU:** But I'm totally positive I'm right. Do I really need to hide the truth from them?

Unfortunately, your counterpart in this discussion seems to be similarly confident in their opposing answer. Therefore, a neat way to show respect for them is to converse in a hypothetical model of the matter where you both pretend as though the truth is still unsettled. So you might say:

> **ALTERNATE-YOU:** I feel confident it was four goals because I remember writing it in my diary.

Good! See how ALTERNATE-YOU has shown respect for your opponent by indicating confidence, but not omniscience, thus allowing both sides to present their cases to each other's juries without one of the parties announcing that their conclusion is automatically better than the other's?

> **ADH-YOU:** I guess. I don't really see the point in pandering when I'm positive, but I'll try it.

Thanks, YOU. I'll take it.

"THAT'S RIGHT."

During Presentations

This is another one that's context-specific: sometimes the phrase "that's right" can be perfectly legitimate; consider this interaction at a dog behaviour presentation:

> **ADH-YOU-AUDIENCE-MEMBER:** Is "pack mentality" an important part of dog obedience training?
> **DOG BEHAVIOUR EXPERT PRESENTER:** That's right.

I doubt many would feel irked by that kind of "That's right," wherein an expert politely utilizes it to confirm the speculation of a non-expert. Yet sometimes the expression is not so benign. Consider the opposite case:

> **DOG BEHAVIOUR EXPERT PRESENTER:** Pack mentality is an important part of dog obedience training.
> **ADH-YOU-AUDIENCE-MEMBER:** That's right.

In this case, the confirming "That's right," might be irritating because—

> **ADH-YOU:** I'm just letting the presenter know they're on the right track. What's wrong with that?

Well, by announcing that the speaker has gotten something right, you seem to be putting yourself in the position of the presenter's superior on the very matter about which they're lecturing. This, I submit, extends your high self-esteem to the point of accidental condescension.

> **ADH-YOU:** Okay fine. But how come the "expert" can say that something's "right," but I can't? Aren't they being condescending, too, then?

Good question, YOU. I submit that in the former case there is a social contract in place that allows the presenter to take the position of know-it-all about the topic on display. However, in the latter example, when the alleged expert is making their presentation, you are in no such position. For you to authorize their individual points is condescending (and unnecessary) because it implies that they need your approval to continue on a path for which they have already paid their dues.

> **ADH-YOU:** Can I let you in on a little secret? The reason I tell presenters that they're right during their presentations is not really for their sake—it's so that everyone *else* will realize that I already know what the so-called experts are telling us.

Well clarified, YOU! I see now that you're providing your "That's right" interjections for a noble purpose, known as "know-it-all" signalling.

> **ADH-YOU:** Thanks for understanding.

Nevertheless, I still request that you halt this behaviour because it often has the effect of irritating your presenters as well as your fellow audience members (who will be distracted by your competing bids for attention).

> **ADH-YOU:** Fine. I won't tell people that they're right if they're an "expert."

You're very kind, YOU!

In General Use

Once you've dealt with presentation-based know-it-all signalling, please consider also taking on everyday versions of the same, as in this example:

> **YOUR COLLEAGUE:** It turns out Socrates's friends tried to rescue him, but he refused to hide from his fate.
>
> **ADH-YOU:** That's correct.
>
> **YOUR COLLEAGUE:** Oh, I guess you already knew that.

See how your friend seems shut down by your interjection?

> **ADH-YOU:** I guess. So you're saying I can't let people know when they're telling me something I already know?

Close, if someone starts telling you something you already know, then feel free to inform them so they don't continue unnecessarily. But I submit that there is a way to do so without undermining the pride of your conversation partner. Try this:

> **YOUR COLLEAGUE:** So Nixon is the new President of the United States.
>
> **ALTERNATE-YOU:** Yeah, I heard about that. Isn't that amazing? Finally an honest guy in that office!

In this case, ALTERNATE-YOU is admitting that you already knew the factual piece of your colleague's story, but is simultaneously demonstrating that you are nevertheless still interested in hearing what your colleague has to say about the general topic. No easy feat. Well done again, ALTERNATE-YOU!

"JUST DO X."

One step beyond know-it-all signalling is know-it-all claiming to have solved another person's nuanced problem by offering a statement of apparently obvious solution:

> **YOUR FRIEND:** I can't decide whether to quit. I love my job, but I hate my boss.
>
> **ADH-YOU:** Well, just tell your boss off.

I'm sure this is wonderful advice from you as always, but the situation is likely more complicated than you make it seem, and so it might be worth (A) hearing your friend out before you present your solution, and (B) offering your remedy tentatively. Such caution will demonstrate that (i) you recognize that this is a tough choice for your friend, and (ii) you don't necessarily think you're so much smarter than they are that you can instantly solve an issue over which they've spent a long time struggling. So how about this?

Chapter 7: Patronizing You

ALTERNATE-YOU: When I've had horrible bosses, I've found them easier to deal with when I [insert your brilliant suggestion here]. Do you think that would be feasible in your situation . . . or?

What do you think, ADH-YOU? Could you say something like that, or . . .?

> **ADH-YOU:** I don't know. It sounds kinda corny. But I like that you recognized my brilliant advice, so I'll think about it.

Thanks, YOU!

> **". . . RIGHT?"**

In Disagreement

> **NOTE:** My investigations have found that there is zero ADH-PATRONI-ZATION present in the increasingly popular expression, "I know, right?" because it is a cheerful way of emphasizing agreement. For instance:
>
> **YOUR FRIEND:** I can't stand bathroom humour.
>
> **CHEERFUL-YOU:** I know, right? It's awful!
>
> Approved. However, that expression is distinct from the "Right?" used for educating that I would like to focus on next.

When, in your wonderful wisdom, you are taking a contrary position to another person, I notice that you sometimes follow your disagreement with the apparent question, "Right?"

> **ADH-YOU:** What's wrong with asking a question?

117

Well, that's just it. In your particular use of "right?" you rarely seem to wait for a reply, so your alleged question seems to be more rhetorical than genuine. In fact, it sounds more like you're *teaching* your co-converser with a "right?" that's meant for them to have a quick think about your brilliant point before immediately realizing that they have been offered a batch of indisputable truth. Let's go to a clip for illustration:

> **YOUR FRIEND:** I don't like the current government. I don't think they've done enough to reduce X bad thing.
>
> **ADH-YOU:** Well, there's not enough tax revenue this year to make any changes, right? So there's nothing they could have done, I'm afraid.

The fact that your friend thinks the government *could* have done better shows that they clearly *don't* agree with your contention to the contrary. Thus, when you "ask" for your friend's confirmation of your contrary point without letting them reply, you are behaving as though you are their teacher who is in charge of educating them with the undeniable truth of the matter.

ADH-YOU: What's wrong with that? I *am* trying to teach them.

Well, here's the tricky thing: since you're not technically your friend's teacher, they may feel disrespected by your assumption that your ideas automatically trump theirs. Just when they thought they were in a discussion with an equal, you help yourself to a teacherly expression that pronounces yourself the superior in the conversation. How would you feel about saying something like this next time?

> **ALTERNATE-YOU:** Yeah, I would have liked more done about X, too. But the argument that I've heard in defence of the government is that, because of the recession, tax revenue is so low right now that they couldn't afford to do much.

Chapter 7: Patronizing You

See how ALTERNATE-YOU has made your case without a teacherly tone that tells your friend that their teacher has overruled them?

> **ADH-YOU:** Nah, ALTERNATE-ME is just using a lot of babble merely to explain that you can't get blood from a stone.

Fair enough. You don't have to be so longwinded about it, but the key is, if you speak as though you respect your conversation partners' opinions, they're actually more likely to consider yours. (And then you'll win them over more often. Yay!)

As Solution

Another popular way to employ "Right?" is as a means of emphasis when you once again simply and suddenly solve the apparent problem within your friend's personal struggles:

> **YOUR FRIEND:** My husband/wife is driving me crazy: he/she keeps—
>
> **ADH-YOU:** Well, you can always get a divorce, right? You need to get out of there.

Your use of this rhetorical "right?" doubles down on the condescension you utilized in your "Just do X" advice earlier in this chapter. Not only are you suggesting that you can easily solve your friend's problem, you're punching home the condescension with a teacherly tone that says, "And now you've learned something, haven't you?"

> **ADH-YOU:** Well excuse me for being helpful.

Thank you for your sarcasm. I understand you're just trying to help. But I once again suggest wording your suggestions tentatively, even if you're certain that you have in your possession the perfect solution. Try this:

> **ALTERNATE-YOU:** I was once in a difficult marriage, too. This may not work for you, but I ended up separating myself from the situation, and it was the best decision I ever made.

"M'DEAR" AND BEYOND

Similarly, the words "m'dear" (and sometimes "sweetheart," "hon," "sport," and "bud") can be condescending when they follow a point of correction that you've just made to a friend. Please desist.

> **ADH-YOU:** Wait a minute, cupcake: I see parents using "sweetheart" and "bud" to correct their kids all the time.

Well spotted, YOU! Indeed, coaches and parents alike have successfully utilized such friendly nicknames with kids for a long time. And that's precisely why such terms are condescending when they are employed in conversations between two adults. Suddenly the wielder of the "sweetheart" or "bud" is putting themselves in the metaphorical position of the wise parent or coach, just as the "right?" user—in the previous section—was putting themselves in the role of teacher.

"YOU'RE ONLY SAYING THAT BECAUSE YOU'RE X GENDER."

You may occasionally like to tell people that part of the reason they're wrong is because their sex, race, or sexual orientation is getting in their way. Consider these two statements that you may have previously voiced:

> **ADH-YOU:** You're just being an irrational female.

Or:

> **ADH-YOU:** You're just saying that because you're a guy.

Unfortunately, while I'm sure you're right in everything you say, when you use a person's sex, race, or sexual orientation to discredit them, you are (accidentally, I'm sure) taking part in bigotry.

> **ADH-YOU:** Well, how else am I supposed to discredit someone who's clearly wrong?

Great question, YOU! If you believe your opponent is being unreasonable, then all you need to do is articulate the basis for your objection. Noting their sex in the process is as silly as telling someone who has just dropped their umbrella, "Ha! Your big ears strike again."

> **ADH-YOU:** Wait a minute, sport. This is different. Obviously the big ears had nothing to do with the umbrella drop. But I believe that one's gender does have a general effect on personality and perspective.

I see your point. I was oversimplifying. But, since you agree that the trends of one's gender are general and not universal, there's no way for you to know whether an individual's argument is influenced by that generality or not. So, once again, you're best off just treating each person as an individual and assessing what they have to say on that singular basis instead of as a function of their sex, race, or sexual orientation.

> **ADH-YOU:** Fine, you got me on a technicality.

Deal!

YOUR SOCRATIC METHOD

Finally, beyond your condescending phrases, you also have a talent for accidentally patronizing your audience/friends/opponents when you ask them to make your case for you.

ADH-YOU: I'm quite sure I don't know what you mean.

Sorry, allow me to clarify. When you're in a teacherly mood, you have been known to achieve condescension by posing questions for which you already have answers planned. For instance:

> **ADH-YOU:** If you think about it, all language is arbitrary.
>
> **YOUR FRIEND:** How do you mean?
>
> **ADH-YOU:** Well, think of it this way: what does the word "house" mean?
>
> **YOUR FRIEND:** Um, it's a dwelling where people live.
>
> **ADH-YOU:** Right, but is there anything about the sound of the word "house" that automatically makes it the perfect word to represent the notion of a dwelling?
>
> **YOUR FRIEND:** No, definitely not. I see what you're getting at. All words, themselves, are arbitrary.
>
> **ADH-YOU:** Right, and what about the word "definitely"? Is there anything intrinsically "definite" about the sounds that make up the word "definitely"?
>
> **YOUR FRIEND:** No, I get it.
>
> **ADH-YOU:** So you see now that all words are arbitrary?

You make a compelling case as always, but did you really need to express it via this teacherly lesson?

ADH-YOU: How else am I going to teach my friends?

Well, given that you are technically *not* their teacher, maybe instead of treating them like they're your students, you could simply present your argument, and see what they think.

Chapter 8

A Friend in You?

Chapter 8: *A Friend in You?*

Making friends may seem easy to you.

> **ADH-YOU:** Yup.

Nevertheless, I have a few ideas to help you ensure you don't accidentally alienate friends you'd like to keep, or scare off potential friends you'd like to acquire.

HANDSHAKING YOU

The perfect handshake is more complicated than it sounds—

> **ADH-YOU:** I've never found it to be difficult, and no one ever complains, so I think we can skip this one.

Well, the trouble is because handshakes are a convention of polite society, it's awkward for participants to voice their objection. So let me point out the three ways you might be getting your handshakes wrong:

(1) THE FINGER-GRABBER

In this troubled handshake attempt, you intercept your opposite's fingers before the rest of their hand can make it into the traditional palm lock.

> **ADH-YOU:** So? We're still shaking hands.

I see your point, YOU. Indeed, this is the least troublesome of the leading handshake errors as it's not far off the goal; however, because the finger shake is not engaging both participants' full hands, it can give the receiver a faint sense that there is something missing in the purveyor of it. And, given that you are someone who is already stigmatized for your ADH-ME, you don't need any additional negative first impressions to impede your ability to connect with people.

> **ADH-YOU:** Fine.

(2) THE BONE-CRUNCHER

In this case you squeeze your new friend's hand so intensely that they notice their pain sensors are firing.

> **ADH-YOU:** I like it: I'm sending them a message about who's the boss!

And well done, YOU! But, unfortunately, I'm going to have to ask you to desist. You see, regardless of your noble ends, it's considered rude in our polite society to intentionally cause someone pain without their permission.

> **ADH-YOU:** OMG. Prissy much?

I'm afraid so.

(3) THE CLAMMY-CALAMITY

This one is the opposite of the bone-cruncher. Instead of over-squeezing, you're under-utilizing your hand muscles such that your receiver senses only a soft imitation of a grip, which can feel like a ghost's handshake, and thus a wee bit creepy.

> **ADH-YOU:** Wait a minute! If I'm not allowed to squeeze tightly, then gripping softly is my only choice!

Brilliant observation, YOU, but I'm afraid there is an additional option. You know how, when you grab a door handle, you're able to grip it tightly enough to keep hold of it, but not so aggressively that you strain your hand muscles?

> **ADH-YOU:** Yeah. So?

Well, in turns out that you can use a very similar level of pressure when shaking a hand.

> **ADH-YOU:** Hmm . . . I have to admit: that's not bad. I like to think of people as inanimate objects, anyway, so that could work.

Great, YOU!

FEELING FOR FEELINGS

It turns out that NOT-YOU people are weak: they possess these strange mental states called "feelings," which can be injured if you treat them unkindly. To get along with such sensitive creatures, your best bet is to avoid insulting them. Of course, you rarely *mean* to offend—you're simply ever-celebrated for your frankness. You call 'em as you see 'em; you are who you are, and you never say anything that isn't the complete truth. These are wonderful traits, but polite society suggests that you tread less aggressively.

> **ADH-YOU:** But how the heck am I supposed to know when emotional simpletons are going to overreact to my truth?

Try this: before you speak, see if you can think of a person or puppy in your life whose face is dear to you. Now imagine that face (and its associated feelings-holder) will be the beneficiary of your delightful observation. If it occurs to you that your favourite would grow sad because of your remark, then resist! Bite your tongue (literally if necessary) and save the comment for your diary.

Let's try an example. Imagine your friend's cat is missing. What's the first thing you would say if you encountered them putting up signs around the neighbourhood?

> **ADH-YOU:** What's the big deal? It's just a cat.

Good self-awareness, YOU! I've definitely heard you say that. So now I want you to think of something that's precious to you, perhaps your own pet, or your model airplane, or your personal autographed picture of you. Let's say you lost it, how would you feel?

> **ADH-YOU:** Sad! That would be awful.

Right! So now I want you to imagine that your friend would have similar feelings in regard to the loss of their cat.

> **ADH-YOU:** But it's just a cat. They should grow up.

Right, of course. Except, even though you and I know that they're being silly about their sadness, they don't know it. So for now, when you talk to other humans, I'd like you to pretend that their emotional states are worthy of your consideration.

BUST YOUR INSTINCTS

When Reacting To Others' News

Responding to a NOT-YOU person's hopes and dreams in life seems, on the surface, to be one of the most time-wasting activities possible. Unless they're sharing their winnings with you, why should it matter to you if your friend has acquired a new job? The answer will, at first, seem contradictory: it should matter to you because it matters to them.

> **ADH-YOU:** What does the one have to do with the other?

Excellent question, YOU! This is tricky stuff, so don't beat yourself up if you don't get it right away. You know how, when you have a big success, you want to tell your friends about it? Especially those friends who are likely to be excited for you?

> **ADH-YOU:** Sure, I don't mind a little adulation on a Saturday night.

Right, well, it turns out that your friends often appreciate the same enthusiasm from their compatriots.

> **ADH-YOU:** Well, aren't they selfish!

I know. It seems greedy of them to take up space in your spotlight, but once again part of your task in reading this book is to learn to imagine that your friends deserve some attention, too.

> **ADH-YOU:** Fine, they can hog some of my glory.

Generous work, YOU! Now, brace yourself: things are about to get even weirder. Once you have completed this book, you will not only be expected to share the spotlight, but also on occasion to be the bearer of that light, yourself.

> **ADH-YOU:** How could I possibly do that?

Great question, YOU. Consider the following conversation that you have previously had with a friend at a restaurant:

> **YOUR FRIEND:** So my boss loved the design, and he/she's thinking of giving me my own account next month.
>
> **ADH-YOU:** Oh ... cool. Where's the waitress? I'm getting hungry.

First of all, you should congratulate yourself for being so polite about the mundane topic your friend offered up. Yet, oddly, I think that your companion may have been disappointed by the shortness of your reaction.

> **ADH-YOU:** Why? I said it was "cool." That's a compliment. Shouldn't that be enough? I'm hungry! Where's the waitress?

Well, you see, the truth is your friend might have enjoyed sharing not only their good news with you, but also some of the details of how it happened and where it might lead. Try this:

> **YOUR FRIEND:** So my boss loved the design, and he/she's thinking of giving me my own account next month.
>
> **ALTERNATE-YOU:** Wow, that's exciting. You got your wish!
>
> **YOUR FRIEND:** I know. But I'm nervous—now I have to have the ideas to back it up.
>
> **ALTERNATE-YOU:** Right, that's the hard part, isn't it?
>
> **YOUR FRIEND:** Yeah, I don't know if I can do it.
>
> **ALTERNATE-YOU:** How come?
>
> **YOUR FRIEND:** Well, I just find it so hard to be creative on demand. That probably sounds weird.
>
> **ALTERNATE-YOU:** No, I know what you mean: it's easier to be creative when people aren't expecting it.
>
> **YOUR FRIEND:** Yeah exactly. The expectation is intimidating.

> **ALTERNATE-YOU:** If only you hadn't done such a brilliant job on that campaign, they wouldn't be expecting more creativity.
>
> **YOUR FRIEND:** Well, I don't know about that.

See how your friend is smiling? I suspect they're expressing such merriment because they feel like ALTERNATE-YOU is following their details with interest (and a little humour), and is responding specifically to what they were saying. Great job, ALTERNATE-YOU!

> **HINT:** Even though the goal of this book is to help you smile sincerely when, for instance, you hear a friend's good news, don't feel discouraged if that doesn't happen right away. For now, just focus on pretending that you care and gradually such nonsense will start to feel natural.

When Reacting To Others' Projects

Now let's try a more complicated example:

> **YOUR FRIEND (*smiling*):** So I've built this chart to track my workouts. Every time I complete thirty minutes of exercise, I get to fill in one square in this cartoon dumbbell. And if I have the whole dumbbell filled in by the end of the month, I've completed my goal and I get a piece of cake.
>
> **ADH-YOU (*chuckling*):** You have too much time on your hands, my friend.

I see you nodding with a giggle at your clever remark, because it seems clear to you that your friend has indeed spent a silly amount of time developing a tracking system for their exercise regimen. LOL! Nevertheless, what I want you to consider is that your friend is excited about tracking their efforts, and, in fact, is actually feeling good about them. The moment you define such a project as the result of "too much time on their hands," you are indicating that their efforts are pointless. Thus, in spite of the fact that your comment was hilarious, your friend may feel belittled by it.

> **ADH-YOU:** Why? I was just making an observation. In fact, it was a compliment of how much free time they have. I wish I had time to waste like that.

Nice re-frame, YOU! But there's still a small problem. It turns out that most people are hoping that the way in which they spend their time is *not* a waste.

> **ADH-YOU:** Then why are they wasting their time on silly things?

Good point. Think of it this way: imagine something that matters to you and which you spend a lot of time on. Now how would you feel if your friend diagnosed this as the result of you having too much time on your hands?

> **ADH-YOU:** That's different. I'm doing something that I particularly enjoy. It relaxes me. How could that be a waste of time?

An intriguing point, YOU. However, you may be shocked to discover that your friends feel the same way about their own personal projects.

I don't expect you to understand this one fully just yet. For now, I suggest removing from your lexicon the phrase, "You have too much time on your hands," along with its wicked sister phrase, "You have no life." Instead, your assignment is to take note of when your friend is excited about something and then—regardless of the silliness of their efforts—pretend for their sake that you're interested.

When Inviting Yourself Over

Friendship, I'm told, carries with it certain tacitly agreed-upon expectations on all sides. And, each friendship has its own unique set of unspoken guidelines that can either keep it afloat or sink it when they are not met. You're welcome of course to suggest any expectations you like to go in your friendship arrangements, but don't be alarmed if some of your friends don't always concur with your ideas. For instance, while you may prefer your friends to be available to you any time you have a hankering for their company, some of them may prefer optional participation.

> **ADH-YOU:** Okay, I've let you babble for long enough, now. Time to get to the point.

Okay, well not long ago, I heard several talk radio discussions featuring pundits decrying the allegedly anti-social nature of my home city of Vancouver. According to a survey of our population, we Vancouverites were diagnosed as neither friendly with strangers nor social with friends. In response, many superior locals called in to the radio shows boasting of their methods of increasing interactions with their friends and neighbours.

One man said he was so fed up with his friends' anti-social tendencies that he'd started a program in which he baked cookies and then took himself on missions to visit his friends at their homes. His goal, he explained to the soothing verbal nods of the radio pundits, was to give his friends a break from whatever project they were working on. *Who, after all, didn't have fifteen minutes to talk and maybe share a cup of tea?*

"About 50% of them didn't like that I'd arrived unannounced," he said, "so no cookies for them."

Despite the cookie sanctions, this cookie fairy was lauded by the radio hosts for showing merry creativity in his efforts to reconnect with his world. Moreover—

> **ADH-YOU:** I agree with the radio hosts! Who doesn't like cookies?

Well said, YOU. But let me ask you, dear cookie-fan, are there any times when you *don't* want to socialize?

> **ADH-YOU:** No, I'm always the life of the party.

But what if you were just getting ready to take a shower after a long bike ride, or were planning to watch a movie with your spouse after a hard day at work? How would you like it if your friend arrived on your door step just then, informing you that it was time to socialize?

> **ADH-YOU:** I'd tell them to get lost. I'm busy.

Nicely done, but imagine if your friend showed up with cookies and a request for tea: might you not feel obligated to let them in? And let's be honest: it's not going to be a fifteen-minute morsel of time. Instead, it'll be at least an hour before you'll be allowed to get back to what you had planned for yourself. Wouldn't you prefer that your friends just phoned (or Tweeted) ahead to see if you were available?

> **ADH-YOU:** Obviously.

So why are you lauding the Cookie Fairy for arriving to socialize without checking first?

> **ADH-YOU:** Well, when I show up to visit my friends, I like it to be a surprise. Plus, by not calling ahead, I don't get their hopes up in case I change my mind.

Well played, YOU. For now, I'll take your acknowledgement that you wouldn't like it if people did the same to you as a compromise.

PUNCTUALITY NOW

In modern self-help mythology, we're not supposed to sweat the small stuff. And so, when you're delayed, it might seem unnecessary to rush; after all, that would be sweating the *small* fact that you'll be late. However, when there is someone waiting for you on the other end of your snail's pace—say, you're meeting a friend for a play that's about to start—it might be worth sweating just a little to get there sooner.

> **ADH-YOU:** But going to plays is supposed to be fun, not stressful.

Good point, YOU. But, eventually, as you progress through this book, I'm hoping you'll learn to consider your friends' fun, too, and so you'll want to be as close to on time as you can because that would make them happier.

> **ADH-YOU:** Well that's all fine and dandy, but it's a moot point because lateness is an act of fate. If something unexpected happens to make me late, I can't very well teleport myself into being on time!

Well said. Sometimes random things out of your control might cause your delay. However, there are people who live in the same random world that you do who still manage to be punctual most of the time.

> **ADH-YOU:** How the heck do they do that? They must have no life!

Close. But I submit that there is another difference between ADH-YOU and those watch-watching people. According to experts, being consistently on time is mostly a matter of planning.

Few people expect you to be perfectly punctual in every instance, but if you *try* to be, you'll succeed in most cases.

> **ADH-YOU:** Wait a minute! How am I supposed to plan around things that I don't expect to come up?

Great question, YOU. When something unexpected tries to get in the way of appointments with other people, the perpetually punctual will—in most instances—excuse themselves from the delaying item's path (vowing to deal with it as soon as they can). And, in the rare situation that the distraction is too crucial to ignore—

> **ADH-YOU:** Yeah, in my case, the thing that holds me up is always vital.

Of course it is. Okay, in that case, there are two things I'd like you to do from now on:

(1) Please make a significant effort to contact the person-in-waiting to let them know of your delay.

(2) Given the unavoidability of the urgencies that commonly impede you, please always aim to arrive half an hour early for any scheduled interaction. Thus, if something interferes with your travel, you will not be late. If that doesn't consistently work, then try 45 minutes, and so on.

> **ADH-YOU:** Why? Who am I trying to impress with all this?

Well, symmetrically enough, the benefit of these habits is the same one that you receive when your friends are on time for you: you create the impression that you believe their time has value.

Chapter 9

Funny You

In many ways humour is subjective, so I won't claim to have a roadmap for what's funny and what's not. However, I do suggest that when your humour reduces the happiness quotients of those around you, it may be worth double checking with yourself whether it's beneficial to apply in every case.

IS THERE REALLY A WINNER HERE?

A former colleague of mine once sheepishly described to me this horrific tale of "humour." Her ADH-MALEVOLENT boyfriend had acquired from a novelty shop some fake lottery scratch tickets that, when scratched, pretended to be winners. He unleashed one such duplicitous ticket as a prize at a gathering of his and my colleague's friends.

> **TICKET RECEIVER:** Oh my God! I think I won! Oh my God! Can somebody check it?
>
> **ADH-MALEVOLENT (*holding back his amusement*):** Yup, it clearly says you've won $10,000.
>
> **TICKET RECEIVER:** Oh my God! I can't believe it! This is gonna change my life. I can finally pay off my student loans. Maybe I'll quit the restaurant. Oh my God! I never win anything!
>
> **ADH-MALEVOLENT:** I guess Lady Luck's been saving up for you.

This cruel conversation continued for several minutes before my colleague finally persuaded her empathy-free boyfriend to tell the truth about the gag. The results were predictably tearful. When you bring someone's hopes up that high, the resulting fall is going to hurt.

And yet, in spite of the clearly devastating outcome of his joke, my colleague's vicious boyfriend plied his dreadful comedy again two weeks' later. This time, his victim called her mother to tell her about the news of her win before the soulless jokester informed her that she would not be able to afford her dream vacation, after all.

> **ADH-YOU:** That's terrible, but it's pretty funny.

Interesting statement, YOU. You might be an ADH-MA-LEVOLENT, yourself.

> **ADH-YOU:** Hey, I'm not saying I would *do* the joke—I'm just saying it's funny.

Fair enough. You may just have a tinge of MALEVOLENT blood in you. So, even if you wouldn't have been the bearer of that evil joke, you may nevertheless have been involved in smaller "comedic" crimes against compassion.

> **ADH-YOU:** What's that supposed to mean?

Well, any time that you derive your laugh from giving someone hope that a desired-by-them outcome has occurred when it actually hasn't, your comedy has a victim. For instance:

> **YOUR FRIEND:** I know I had them an hour ago—I don't know where I could have put them.
>
> **ADH-YOU:** Found them!
>
> **YOUR FRIEND:** Really?! Awesome—God, I would've been in so much trouble—
>
> **ADH-YOU:** No, just kidding, it's a paper clip—see?
>
> **YOUR FRIEND:** Oh. So you were just pretending you found them?
>
> **ADH-YOU:** Hee, hee, yup.

Please don't do that.

"NO" HUMOUR

This next one is tricky, because I know you're just trying to be playful; indeed, a large percentage of humour (excluding the lottery ticket viciousness above) is meant in friendship. However, I do want you to reconsider the humour of the following real-world interaction brought to us by my brother, who spent many years working at a coffee-selling chain:

> **ADH-YOU-FUNNY:** Oh, hi Seth's Brother. You on a break?
>
> **SETH'S BROTHER:** Yeah, I have to run over to the bank. Can I order a coffee first, though?
>
> **ADH-YOU-FUNNY (*holding back your giggle*):** No.
>
> **SETH'S BROTHER (*trying to play along with this played-out joke*):** Oh, okay, I guess I'll skip the coffee.
>
> **ADH-YOU-FUNNY (*grinning*):** Yup, sorry: we're out of coffee.
>
> **SETH'S BROTHER (*waiting for the joke to be up*):** Oh, okay. See you, then.
>
> **ADH-YOU-FUNNY (*giggling*):** No, no, I'll get you a coffee.
>
> **SETH'S BROTHER (*relieved, but bored*):** Great, thanks, can I get it with almond milk, please?
>
> **ADH-YOU-FUNNY:** Nope, sorry!

And so the comedy begins anew. Now, I have three points to help you reconsider this brand of humour:

(1) It is not original. In fact, my brother estimates that, when he tried to order a drink from his own store, he received a "No" about 25 percent of the time. Clearly it's a reflex joke that doesn't require any planning or creativity, so it might not actually be as funny as it feels in the moment. Meanwhile, to the receiver it tends to be annoying, as they are left with little to do until you agree to move on from the joke. This is especially the case when:

(2) You redo the joke every chance you get—this reduces the humour for your victim even further as there are only so many ways they can play along with your fake "No." Thus:

(3) If you're certain you want to go ahead with "No" humour, please let the receiver off the hook as soon as possible:

> **YOUR FRIEND:** Hey, can you pass me a napkin?
> **ALTERNATE-YOU:** Nope.
> **YOUR FRIEND:** Oh—
> **ALTERNATE-YOU (*giggling*):** Kidding—here you go!

See how this way you got your funny in without leaving your victim writhing in awkwardness for too long? Nicely done, ALTERNATE-YOU!

LITERAL YOU

Sometimes, you may discover, your friends will make jokes, too.

> **ADH-YOU:** Groan.

I sympathize with your suffering, but if we prepare you for the struggle, you should be able to handle it with panache.

In General

You are not obligated to enjoy all flavours of humour, but it is polite to at least try to recognize the comedic intentions of those making jokes in your vicinity.

> **ADH-YOU:** What if I find the joke to be offensive?

Worry not, acknowledging that someone is joking is not the same as condoning the joke, itself. If, however, you choose to take someone's joke literally, then the punishment you are imposing is much greater than their crime of failing to amuse you. You see, most jokes contain an element of the ridiculous and so, in order for the humourist to have actually meant such silly words seriously, they would have to be either a jerk or an idiot. For instance, I once attended a gathering for opera novices wherein we learned about the plot of *Madame Butterfly*, in which the pitiful heroine, Butterfly, falls in love with a cad, Pinkerton (whom I dubbed "Finkerton"):

> **OPERA TEACHER:** Pinkerton told Butterfly that he wanted to capture her like a real butterfly and pin her to a wall.
>
> **SETH (with saccharine sarcasm):** Isn't that nice?
>
> **FELLOW STUDENT:** Is it? Seems pretty awful to me.

Oh my baffled! For me to have actually thought that the metaphor of pinning one's girlfriend to a wall was sweet I would have to be a sadist. And, given that I'd already labelled the butterfly-catcher with the nickname, "Finkerton," I felt it should have been obvious that I was only sarcastically approving his ugly suggestion.

> **ADH-YOU:** Well I couldn't tell you were joking either.

Fair enough. If you truly don't realize that someone is joking, then it's hard for you to do anything but take their words sincerely. Nevertheless, if someone says something that seems ridiculous or idiotic (or sadistic), and the purveyor of it is not otherwise known for such traits, it might be worth consulting the comedy centre of your brain to see if they might be joking.

Here's another real-world example: after watching with our neighbour the playful "family-friendly" movie *George of the Jungle*, in which various primates spoke sufficient English to advise

George in his adventures, my adult siblings and I entertained each other by assessing the movie for biological authenticity:

> **SETH'S SISTER:** That was really good, but I didn't think it was very realistic.
>
> **SETH'S BROTHER:** Yeah, I agree: I don't think chimps can actually talk.
>
> **NEIGHBOUR** (*without a hint of humour*): C'mon, guys, it's a kids' show.

On another occasion, this same neighbour asked my brother to help fix her TV, which had gone fuzzy. So he spent some time behind the device adjusting a few cords. Thinking he might have mended it, he returned to the front of the screen to see if he'd succeeded, but he was surprised to discover he'd actually made the problem much worse.

> **SETH'S BROTHER:** Ta da! All fixed.
>
> **NEIGHBOUR** (*looking seriously at the screen*): No, it's still fuzzy.

Now, once again, I'm not suggesting that—

> **ADH-YOU:** Well I'm not going to pretend something's funny when it isn't.

Right, I'm not suggesting that you're obligated to falsify your amusement, but it would be nice if you could pay such attempted humourists the compliment of not assuming they're idiots.

> **ADH-YOU:** So you want me to lie?

No, I know you're a beacon of honesty. So I wouldn't want you to be dishonest and fake a laugh, but maybe you could play along with the humour. A simple, "Perfect!" would have done the trick in the latter case.

Over Ego

One arena of humour that is often taken literally by its alleged receiver is that of pretending to possess a giant ego. I may be biased here, as I myself am a practitioner of large ego humour. That is, I often exaggerate my confidence by saying arrogant things for the delight of my fans. For instance:

> **SETH'S CO-WORKER:** Nobody's perfect.
>
> **SETH (*shrugging*):** Speak for yourself.

In this case—

> **ADH-YOU:** That really wasn't that funny.

Fair enough. It wasn't a brilliant joke. But the point is, when you take an ego-humourist's joke literally, the punishment you're providing is again much more significant than they deserve for not being as funny as you.

> **ADH-YOU:** I still don't really understand this supposed humour. So you're saying you're not actually being arrogant when you claim you're perfect.

Yes, let's try another example. During a science class that my sister attended in university, the professor had on display a complicated chart of formulas.

> **PROFESSOR:** Don't worry, you don't need to memorize this stuff.

My sister sighed her relief, while her seat-neighbour and friend, Ben, smiled and shrugged his shoulders:

> **BEN:** Too late.

My sister laughed and told me the tale later to my additional giggles. And see how—

> **ADH-YOU:** What if your sister didn't find the joke funny? Should she still have laughed?

Well queried, YOU. My sister was under no obligation to enjoy her friend's comic show of ego; however, she was obligated, I believe, to recognize his humourous intent. In contrast, when you respond to ego-humour by taking the pretend-egotist literally, you are bantering below the belt. Let's watch how you would've handled the same joke:

> **BEN:** Too late!
>
> **ADH-YOU:** Seriously? You expect me to believe you could have memorized that in two seconds? Sorry, you're just not that smart.
>
> **BEN:** Oh ... um ...

I don't deny that there are cases where one's humour can leave the receiver stuck for reply, and so the comedian must accept some risks when they engage in jest. Nevertheless, is it possible that sometimes your humour-free reply is more the result of laziness than genuine misunderstanding?

> **ADH-YOU:** No, I just don't feel like playing along with stupid jokes.

Thank you for the clarification. I understand your irritation. But, before you take a large-ego-humourist's jokes literally, please consider less cruel options first. You will do much for the emotional health of those nearby if you try.

Chapter 10

Apologetic You

In an episode of the American version of the great British television comedy *The Office* (wherein many ADH-MOMENTS and retaliations are played out), the workplace hero, Jim, offers his nemesis, Dwight, a sincere apology while Dwight is making a critical announcement. Without pausing to consider, Dwight immediately says, "Apology rejected!" and moves on with what he was saying.

It is a delightful moment of comedy for those of us who have come to enjoy Dwight's always earnest and sometimes startling decisions. Beyond the comedy, though, I think Dwight's statement brings forth a useful concept. Not all apologies are good enough to be accepted. So even if you've said "sorry"—

> **ADH-YOU:** That's not fair. I said I was sorry. What more do you want from me?

Great question, YOU. According to most etiquette experts, a genuine apology should both:

(A) acknowledge to the receiver that you realize you have made a mistake, and

(B) express regret regarding the negative effects the error has had on them.

If you always aim to convey those two ideas, you should do fine.

> **ADH-YOU:** Good enough. Can we move on? I hate this topic.

I know you do, but first let's give it a try. Imagine you borrowed your friend's car without asking. Let's hear your best apology:

> **ADH-YOU:** Sorry I borrowed your car. But you weren't here, so I figured I could use it.

Great effort, YOU! That was very close to a full apology! Indeed, there's nothing wrong with offering an explanation for why you did something (in fact, your victim may appreciate it). But it's important that you also get across that, in spite of your explanation, you now realize you shouldn't have performed the offending action. For instance, let's see how ALTERNATE-YOU takes on an apology about a missing ring:

> **ALTERNATE-YOU:** I'm sorry. I shouldn't have taken your grandmother's wedding ring. For what it's worth, I was desperate because Jenny was expecting a ring, so I grabbed it, stupidly thinking you probably wouldn't notice it was missing until I could return it. I'm an idiot. Sorry. I had no right to take it.

An impressive effort from ALTERNATE-YOU. Imagine you were the one receiving that apology. Even though you might still be angry, it's harder to feel as much rage at the offender when they both acknowledge that they were indeed wrong *and* give you a glimpse into why they thought that it was okay in the moment. Such a combination contextualizes the apologist's untoward behaviour without excusing it.

In contrast, then, let us look at some of the leading "apologies" that cause more offence than they repair:

EMPTY APOLOGY

If you apologize for a behaviour that you have no intention of discontinuing, then—when that behaviour recurs—your contrition will likely feel retroactively hollow to your victim. My suggestion, therefore, is that you avoid making apologies that you can't keep. If, that is, you truly don't think you did anything wrong, then don't make a particular point of apologizing for it. However, on the off chance you *do* think you did something wrong, then maybe you should stop doing it.

Chapter 10: *Apologetic You*

CONDITIONAL APOLOGY

As you may be aware, the "if...then" apology is rarely popular with its receiver. For instance:

> **VICTIM:** I can't believe you stole my wallet at gunpoint.
>
> **ADH-ROBBER:** If my AK47 scared you, then I'm sorry.
>
> **VICTIM:** So you're not admitting that you did anything wrong. You're simply saying that if I happen to be bothered, then you're sorry that I feel bad. You're not sorry for what you did!
>
> **ADH-ROBBER:** Yes, what's wrong with that? If I didn't scare you, then why would I be sorry?
>
> **VICTIM:** Because the act was wrong, in itself, regardless of my feelings. It makes it seem like you're not really sorry—you're not taking responsibility for the intrinsic wrong of your behaviour. You're just saying, 'Oh, if that bothered you, then I regret it.'
>
> **ADH-ROBBER:** Exactly! I don't see a problem here!

I'm not going to push you too hard on this one. The punishment here is in the reaction. My only suggestion would be that, if you're going to make a conditional apology, you may want to check to see that it is indeed valid. Ask yourself: *Is this truly something that would only be a misstep if it happened to trouble the victim, or is it the sort of universal no-no that deserves a "sorry" regardless of results?*

> **ADH-YOU:** I never do anything that's universally wrong! I just use the "conditional apology" to placate the weak-minded.

Fair enough. In that case, I suggest you check to see if the placating is going as well as you intended.

ADH-YOU: What do you mean?

Well, you may be surprised to discover that the conditional apology is causing you more unpopularity than it's curbing.

"SORRY YOU FEEL THAT WAY" APOLOGY

This one's only a problem if you're claiming it to be an apology:

ADH-YOU: I'm sorry you feel that way.

In this case, your "sorry" just means "sad" or "disappointed," which are perfectly valid emotions to identify as long as you don't claim later (when apology-status would benefit you) that you apologized. Just remember, inserting the word "sorry" into a sentence does not mean that you've delivered a legitimate apology.

BLAMING APOLOGY

Please note that the following is also not an apology:

ADH-YOU: I'm sorry that happened, but I wouldn't have had to use your credit card without asking if you'd lent me the money when I needed it.

Once again, there's nothing wrong with feeling bad that something happened, and yet not feeling responsible for it (and, in fact, blaming the other person for it). So you're welcome to combine the phrase "I'm sorry that happened" with a justification of why someone's feelings are not your fault. However, please be advised that you are once again prohibited from later claiming that this use of the word "sorry" counted as an apology.

STORY IN LIEU OF APOLOGY

Sometimes you may have a good explanation for why you deflated the tires of another person's happiness. Unfortunately, though, this doesn't necessarily mean that, along with your story, you shouldn't also quickly apologize out of respect to the aggrieved party. So, when arriving late for coffee with your friend, instead of:

> **ADH-YOU:** Hey, the bus broke down.

Try:

> **ALTERNATE-YOU:** Hey, sorry I'm late! The bus broke down.

Nice! While ALTERNATE-YOU may not have had any control over the delay-causing bus, see how ALTERNATE-YOU has nevertheless begun with a direct apology before explaining that context.

> **ADH-YOU:** Sorry if this question proves you wrong, but isn't this context stuff the same as the conditional, blaming, and "Sorry you feel that way" apologies that you've just told me I can't do?

Well caught, YOU. I must admit: there is a similarity. In each case, the "apologizer" seems to be attempting to ameliorate their moral responsibility. However, I believe there is a distinction. The conditional, "Sorry you feel that way," and blaming apologies are enemies of contrition because they are insulting their victims by suggesting the apology receivers are overly sensitive, or are to blame for the problem incident. Such implications are unlikely to make your victim feel better about the situation for which you are allegedly apologizing.

> **ADH-YOU:** But what if the apology receiver *is* to blame?

And, of course, I'm sure they are in most cases. I'm only saying that indicating so in an apology undermines your claim to having made an apology. So my suggestion is this: if you don't owe an apology, then don't apologize. But in the rare cases that you *do* think an apology has been earned, then please try not to faux-pologize.

> **ADH-YOU:** Fine! But why then do you get to faux-pologize with your beloved context?

Right, thank you for getting us back on track. In the case of providing context, I believe that such clarification does not necessarily override the goodwill of the apology. Instead, I submit that the context-providing apologizer is explaining what happened so that the apology receiver can see that the infraction wasn't done as maliciously as it may seem. Does that make sense?

> **ADH-YOU:** If you say so, but what if the "plus context" isn't very compelling?

Well noted, YOU. I see you have much experience in these matters. When your story doesn't, in fact, justify your behaviour, it really should come in conjunction with a full-bodied apology that indicates a plan to do things differently in future.

Chapter 10: *Apologetic You*

MARTYRING APOLOGY

In spite of your disorder, even you probably recognize that this isn't really an apology:

> **YOUR FRIEND:** Did you really take Billie and Jenny to an illicit drug dealers' convention?
>
> **ADH-YOU:** Yeah.
>
> **YOUR FRIEND:** I can't believe you did that!
>
> **ADH-YOU:** Are you actually mad at me for that? Geez, I'm sorry for trying to give your kids new experiences.

Clearly, because "providing kids new experiences" is normally a good thing, you are, in fact, boasting about your efforts under the cover of a sarcastic apology.

> **ADH-YOU:** Thanks, Captain Obvious.

Well teased, YOU! That was indeed a self-evident point. Nevertheless, I have witnessed ADH-LEGENDS, who have retroactively claimed their obviously disingenuous apology was sincere. Let's watch:

> **YOUR FRIEND:** Do you really think a drug dealers' convention is the sort of new experience that kids would benefit from?
>
> **ADH-YOU:** I already said I was sorry! What more do you want from me?

Clever. Your desire to get sincere credit for your sarcastic apology is understandable. You really hate sincerely admitting fault. And since you *can* point to having technically said the word "sorry," it would save a lot of time and mortification if that were sufficient. Unfortunately, it isn't. Victims of this faux-pology will likely find it maddening, so I suggest using it only when you want to enrage your friends and eavesdroppers.

"I SAID I WAS SORRY" APOLOGY

When you notice that, in spite of your "sorry," your friend still seems to be expecting further apology, it may be that one of the above not-quite apologies has irritated them.

> **ADH-YOU:** O.M.Me. I said I was sorry. Do they want a pound of my flesh, too?

I understand your irritation. It's annoying when people keep pestering even when you've said "Uncle," isn't it?

> **ADH-YOU:** Exactly!

Nevertheless, before announcing reproachfully that you already stated that you were sorry, it might be worth double-checking your apology for crimes against conciliation. And, to be honest, if you truly *are* sorry, then isn't it up to your victim to determine whether or not to forgive you? If they are not satisfied, then wouldn't you want to find a way to help them get there, perhaps by continuing to acknowledge your culpability?

> **ADH-YOU:** Groan.

Yes, I know multiple apologizing is not fun. But, if you do your best to prove your remorse to the person you've wronged, you have a much better chance of acquiring their forgiveness.

"AREN'T I GREAT FOR APOLOGIZING?" APOLOGY

This one may be my favourite of your faux-pology strategies. When you're a famous moralist such as a politician or radio psychologist, and you've made a moral blunder—such as falsely accusing someone of a crime—you have been known to offer the following apology:

> **ADH-FAMOUS-YOU:** I've always said that, when you make a mistake, you should own up to it. And so that's what I'm doing now. I'm taking responsibility for my actions. In my zeal to fight child abuse, I made a bit of an error and might have, by accident, named someone who was innocent. I am taking ownership of that statement. I'm not ashamed to stand up and admit when I've made an oopsie in the name of fighting those who would hurt our children.

Now, I must admit that, hidden deep within this celebration of your integrity, you have sort of admitted you did something wrong, but just barely. Your mini-capitulation is so overpowered by your re-framing of your apology as a demonstration of your strength of character that it seems like you're actually feeling pretty good about yourself.

> **ADH-YOU:** But you said I should take responsibility for my actions. Isn't that a good thing?

Great point, YOU. Yes, genuinely taking responsibility for your actions is a virtue, but telling people that your apology makes you virtuous counteracts that very responsibility taking. It's like telling people that you're truly humble and unaware of your own talent: the moment you make such a claim, you invalidate it.

ADH-YOU: But what if people don't realize for themselves how great I am for apologizing?

I know—it's scary. Nevertheless, your only shot at redeeming an error is to straight up apologize for it without pointing out how awesome you are for doing so. But, if you sound sincere, people just might admire you for it.

APOLOGY ACCEPTING

If, meanwhile, you are a "sorry" rejecter, it may be worth double-checking to see if, in fact, the apologizer has made a worthy effort at an apology. Have they directly referenced the content of their mistake and shown a willingness to accept responsibility for it? If so, then maybe it's time to let them off your hook.

ADH-YOU: But I'm enjoying their grovelling.

Well noted, YOU. I know it can be difficult to accept an apology because sometimes, when someone is sorry, you smell blood and you want to attack for more. Unfortunately, such a tactic can be unnecessarily cruel to the apologizer. I have witnessed cases where an apology-receiver has cast aside an apologizer's sincere contrition and mined them for more by wielding accusations of just how right they were to apologize. In these cases, the apologizer has had to resist their inclination to retract their apology in favour of self-defence. So be careful of taking too much advantage of someone's apology—or at least, if you kick a person while they're sorry, don't be surprised if you never receive another apology from them.

ADH-YOU: So I just have to accept every apology sent my way?

No, you're not obligated to gracefully approve every apology that is offered (indeed, if the crime being apologized for is particularly flagrant, you may not feel that *any* apology can redeem the culprit); however, if in doubt, I'd say it's best to accept the sorry and reject the next one if the person repeats the offence.

Also, when you're deciding whether to accept a friend's apology, try to distinguish between their intentions versus the consequences of their actions. For instance:

> **YOUR FRIEND:** I'm so sorry. I tripped on the way over here.
>
> **ADH-YOU:** OMG—you ripped my jeans!
>
> **YOUR FRIEND:** I know, I'm sorry. I'll replace them.
>
> **ADH-YOU:** They're my favourite jeans.
>
> **YOUR FRIEND:** I know. I'm so sorry. Someone honked and I took my eyes off the sidewalk.
>
> **ADH-YOU:** I can't believe you ripped my jeans. I shouldn't have lent them to you.

Correct me if I'm wrong, but there seems to be implied within your critique an assumption that your friend intentionally sullied your beautiful clothing or at least was grossly negligent.

> **ADH-YOU:** You're damn right that's what I'm saying.

So, would you consider the possibility that the damage was caused by either a fluke of fate, or an understandable mistake?

> **ADH-YOU:** I don't follow.

Well, imagine that you received evidence that the error was one that even you could have made. How would you treat your friend then?

> **ADH-YOU:** I'd still be mad. Those're my favourite jeans. They're impossible to get.

Fair enough, but how would you think you deserved to be treated if the situations were reversed?

ADH-YOU: I don't borrow my friends' jeans.

Right, of course. But, if you were ever in a situation where you borrowed something from a friend and tripped while carrying it, I submit that you might feel some value in forgiveness. Again, this is not to say that no one ever commits mistakes that are so negligent that they are worthy of your contempt, but until you have a specific reason to think your friend has earned such a response, I suggest reacting with caution rather than rage.

Chapter 11

Electronically Communicating You

Social media provides seemingly infinite opportunities for ADH-BEHAVIOUR. For instance, Twitter and Facebook give people the chance to publish their every passing contemplation without considering whether their words will be valuable or entertaining to their audience. Indeed, the practice of exclaiming mundane self-details ("Just took a shower. Liked it.") with a straight face(book) is now so common as to seem legitimate in that arena. Given, then, that social media may at this point in its evolution be a humility-free zone, I think it's fair for you to consider it your narcissism sanctuary.

> **ADH-YOU:** I appreciate that. Thank you.

You deserve it. So, in this chapter, I will focus instead on a few email etiquette examples (since electronic email is a medium of more traditional conversational interaction). If you'd like to go far in your quest to free your ADH-SOUL of its most self-involved tendencies, then feel free to apply these ideas to other digital forms of communication. However, if you prefer to keep posting random tweets regarding your latest realization about your toenails, I won't try to stop you.

CAPITAL OFFENCE

As with other venues, you can be anything you want to be while using email, and so if you choose to write without conventional grammar or spelling, that is certainly your right. Indeed, perhaps in your particular social group, you find that you enjoy allowing the letters to fall where they may without the fascism of "correctness."

> **ADH-YOU:** Thank you! Me and my friends dont care about that stuff.

Excellent. However, I think it's worth noting that following *some* rules of language can be a way of showing respect to your email recipients, which is especially important in formal or professional situations.

> **ADH-YOU:** Shouldn't I treat everyone the same no matter what the situation?

Well played, YOU. But consider this: out in the non-electronic world, you probably sometimes alter your behaviour depending on context, do you not?

> **ADH-YOU:** When?

Well, for instance, while you might accentuate your best burp during a bachelor/bachelorette party, you probably wouldn't do the same during the subsequent wedding dinner. Similarly, in electronic correspondence, the more formal the interaction is, and the less you know someone, the more such burps of grammar and spelling highlight to your readers that you don't respect them enough to do them the honour of an occasional spell check.

In contrast, if you have a casual relationship with someone in which you enjoy competing for loudest burp, then by all means, go ahead. Just be aware of this decision and consider it carefully before implementing it with everyone. For instance, I know you enjoy removing capital letters from all of your correspondence—

> **adh-you:** yup, i gotta be me. lol.

Fair enough. I must admit that your lowercase letters look undressed to me, but if in your personal correspondence that is how you are most comfortable, I won't try to stop you. What I do demand, though, is that you add capital letters back in to your repertoire when you correspond formally. I have, to my horror, witnessed applications for jobs written without capitalization! Can you really expect a professional agency to take you seriously when you correspond with it as if you are exchanging text messages with your best friend?

> **adh-you:** i dunno. it wouldn't bother me.

Yes, I'm sure you would be very tolerant. Nevertheless, many professionals are not as open minded as you. So, if you'd like to be considered for a job, please *shift* your thinking on this one.

> **ADH-YOU:** Groan.

Fair enough.

COMING UP SHORT

Social niceties in email are like a referee in a sport. You may not always appreciate them when they're present, but, when they're gone, the difference is obvious.

Curt vs. Courtesy

Although you may think you're just being efficient by skipping social softeners in your messages—

> **ADH-YOU:** Exactly. Efficiency or bust, bud.

Yes, efficiency is grand. But, on email, I suggest extra caution when employing it. You see—whereas in person you can soften your efficient language choices with a friendly tone of voice—in email, your recipient can't hear those friendly vocal stylings, and so you may come across as impolite when you're not meaning to be. Consider the following email interaction between you and your friend:

> **YOUR FRIEND:** I'm so sorry again about losing your qPOD-7! I've thought of three ways to make it up to you. (A) I can buy you a new one right now, and then I'll help you get all your songs back. (B) I'll lend you my qPOD-8 for now. Then, when the qPOD-9 comes out, I'll buy you that one, and it'll be easier to replace those songs. Or (C) You can finally let me give you my old Y-BOX and all the games that go with it. What do you think?
>
> **ADH-YOU:** The third one.

Given that your friend clearly spent a lot of time coming up with and then describing those options, do you see how your short reply seems rude?

> **ADH-YOU:** Why? They gave me three choices. Why shouldn't I just pick one?

Well interrogated, YOU. The reason, I submit, is that as humans we've come to expect from conversation a certain level of softening social niceties, and so—since writing is a first cousin of conversation—when those polite details aren't in attendance, your communication can seem curt, whether you mean it that way or not.

> **ADH-YOU:** What are you talking about?

I see you're not convinced. Okay, let me try to explain by showing you how ALTERNATE-YOU might have handled that communication:

> **ALTERNATE-YOU:** Wow, thanks for thinking so much about it. That's really nice of you. I guess Option C would be fair.

Do you see how with an easy couple of sentences, ALTERNATE-YOU has demonstrated goodwill towards your friend's gesture?

> **ADH-YOU:** What if I don't have time for all that coddling language?

Fair enough, I'm sure. So, if you're in a rush, there is one thing you can do to simulate the friendly face that you would use in the real world to soften an otherwise curt-seeming reply.

> **ADH-YOU:** You mean emoticons?

Hey, no peeking! :(But yes. Please compare the following two possible reactions to this email request from your co-worker:

> **YOUR CO-WORKER:** Dear YOU: I'm sorry I wasn't able to get the report ready for you today. Would it be okay if I got it to you by Monday? If that's a problem, I'll stay late and make sure I get it done tonight.
>
> **ADH-YOU:** Monday will do.

Versus:

> **ALTERNATE-YOU:** Monday will do. :)

What do you think?

> **ADH-YOU:** That's your big advice? Use an emoticon?

Yes! Impressive, isn't it? Do you see how, in the above scenario, that simple little smiling punctuation let your co-worker know, "Don't worry—it's fine" without you having to say it? Indeed, if you only have time to emoti-communicate and run, then go for it: most of time that will significantly reduce your chance of provoking resentment. :)

> **ADH-YOU:** Wow, I never would have thought of that.

Thank you. But can you try that again without what I'm guessing is a sarcastic tone?

> **ADH-YOU:** Wow, I never would have thought of that. :)

It's better, but I still suspect you're being sarcastic. In fact, my uncertainty here segues nicely to my conclusion on this subject. Given that emoticons can't fully capture in-person facial and vocal expressions of cheerfulness, it's usually preferable—if you have time—to reply with a simple, but substantive explanation of your position:

> **ALTERNATE-YOU:** Hey, Co-worker: Not to worry. It can wait till Monday. Thanks for offering to stay late to work on it tonight, though. Cheers, ME

See how the content of this message clearly lets your co-worker off your hook? And it really didn't take that much effort from ALTERNATE-YOU, did it? Just a couple of friendly sentences.

> **ADH-YOU:** Fine, I'll do it. But what if I *want* to be curt because they've seriously messed something up?

Well noted, YOU. I didn't mean to suggest that you should always appease your co-workers' blunders. I only mean to say that if you don't *intend* to sound annoyed with them, maybe it's worth taking steps to ensure that your cheerfulness is evident in your message.

Subject-Lining

A service you could add to your emails to make them seem warmer is to always fill in the subject line.

> **ADH-YOU:** Why? I don't start conversations in real life with a subject.

Fair enough, but—

> **ADH-YOU:** Like, I don't say to people, "CONVERSATION ON THE WEATHER: Hey, friend, what do you think of the weather these days?"

That's very funny, YOU! Well put. But every form of communication has a variety of conventions, and not all of them apply to each. With email, an introductory subject is the common practice both (A) to give your reader an idea of what they're getting into (and thus to help them prioritize the order in which they read their messages), and (B) to help them to keep track of the many strands of communication they receive from you and others. So when someone receives a "No Subject" email from you, it can—by its contrast with the rest of their inbox—seem urgent or angry.

> **ADH-YOU:** I can't help it if people misinterpret me.

I see your point. But again, if you're not *intending* to express either of the above sentiments, I suggest providing a subject line just to be safe: a simple "Re the book loan" would suffice.

IGNORING IS BLISS

From your point of view, it may seem passive to ignore people, but strangely, such behaviour will often feel aggressive to them.

> **ADH-YOU:** Um, so you want me responding to SPAM?

Oh, no, sorry, throughout this section, I'll be referring to people with whom you have an established communication.

> **ADH-YOU:** If you say so.

Thanks, YOU!

General Evasion

In general, when someone asks a direct question in an email and you choose not to answer via various avoidance techniques (most commonly by ignoring the message), you may again begin to heat their blood to the point of boiling. Of course, if you have a reason to create that particular enemy then go ahead. However, if you're not currently seeking a new adversary and instead you just don't like the question they're asking or don't feel like answering it, I suggest that you respond anyway.

> **ADH-YOU:** But their question is so stupid!

I know, but once again I promise you that the time you will save in not having to repair troubled relationships will easily cover the time required to reply.

Question Evasion

A clever technique that you use to ignore legitimate questions is substituting them for queries you weren't asked. To illuminate this delightful style of ignoring, please consider this email correspondence between you and your co-worker.

> **YOUR CO-WORKER:** After Andre's mishap yesterday, I'm trying to determine whether I should send a memo reminding people of X policy. Do you mind checking your files to see if we've already sent such a message in the past?
>
> **ADH-YOU:** You shouldn't send that memo.

Now, if you could imagine your co-worker's face, you would see a glare emanating in your direction. That's because you have answered a question that they didn't ask ("What's your opinion on sending such a memo?") instead of answering the one they did ("Do you mind checking your files [for X information]?").

> **ADH-YOU:** I don't see a problem.

I understand. Here's the problem: your co-worker is deciding whether to do something that is in their purview, and they've asked you for some information that is appropriate for you to share with them.

> **ADH-YOU:** But I don't *want* to share it, because I think their reasoning is stupid.

Yes, and I am confident, of course, that you know more about your co-worker's job than they do and so are perfectly correct when you suggest that there is no point in them following their course of useless action. Nevertheless—by not answering their request and instead stating that their pursuit is not necessary—your reply says out loud that you think you know your co-worker's job better than they do.

> **ADH-YOU:** What's wrong with that? I'm helping them.

Great question, YOU. It's a problem because it is belittling for your co-worker to be overruled by a colleague on a decision that is theirs to make. If you feel that it's important to share your preference, try something like this:

> **ALTERNATE-YOU:** Hi Colleague: I've attached the information you requested. For what it's worth, I would suggest letting this one slide because I spoke to Andre after he committed the error with X policy, and I think he realizes his mistake. And I don't think anyone else would make the same error so it could come across as piling onto Andre. But I leave it with you. Cheers, ME

See how ALTERNATE-YOU offered a suggestion instead of a dogmatic pronouncement to your co-worker?

> **ADH-YOU:** Man, this is a lot of work.

Beautifully put as always, YOU, but I can assure you that the work of considerate emailing will save you much in ANTI-YOU gossip around the water cooler.

GETTING FORWARD

This one's not always a symptom of ADH-ME, but I point it out in case you're not aware that when you forward jokes or inspirational stories, compiled by strangers, to your friends and family, you may be irritating some of your favourite people. Some people love such random offerings, of course, but others in your acquaintance may find them disruptive and yet—because they like you—they may feel obligated to open and even respond to such messages.

> **ADH-YOU:** What I am supposed to do about such a failure of taste?

Well, I suggest carefully curating your e-ddress book to determine who's most likely to enjoy such forwarded messages. One way to create a collection of happy receivers is to begin by forwarding candidates directly with introductions such as "Thought you might like this." If they aren't enthusiastic in response, you may have found someone who's not interested and thus worth taking off your forward list. Their loss, am I right? ;)

THE HOSTILITY OF SUDDEN CC-ING

In General

This is another one that's more about being aware of what you're doing than discontinuing the behaviour. Let's imagine that you're engaged with a co-worker in an email correspondence that contains a disagreement or confusion between the two of you. In such a circumstance, your decision to suddenly CC other possibly interested parties on the email thread—without your co-communicator's consent—may be perceived by your original correspondent as hostile.

> **ADH-YOU:** Why? If they were willing to say what they did to me, why won't they stand by it in front of our other co-worker?

Well, you see, when they were emailing you directly, they may have been typing under the assumption that the communication was limited to the two of you, and so they may have said things in a way that they wouldn't have if they'd known there was going to be a bigger audience.

> **ADH-YOU:** I don't care. In a professional situation, you've always gotta assume your email could be read by others at any time.

You might be right about that. However, sometimes in work-correspondence, it can be counterproductive to always write each word with the politically corrected tone that assumes that everyone in the company could read it. So, when emailing just one person, many of your co-workers will likely try to save time by not triple checking every word for how it might be received by *every* person in your organization. While you technically have a right to share such correspondence, when you do so, you might be causing unnecessary friction between your co-workers.

So, in general, I suggest avoiding sudden CCing unless (A) the to-be-CCd correspondence is exhaustively benign, (B) you've asked permission from the other member(s) of the email thread, or (C) you feel the behaviour contained within is too egregious not to escalate.

To Their Boss

Similarly, one of your favourite colleague-warfare techniques is to CC your rival's boss in the middle of a correspondence as a sort of threat that implies: "Let's see whether you'll still agree with yourself when your boss is watching."

> **ADH-YOU:** Yup. Works every time.

Well played. This may be a legitimate practice in particular circumstances where the enemy is flagrantly mishandling or abusing a situation. However, much of the time, the hostility of such a move is greater than the crime you're attempting to curb. Again, do so if you must, but be advised that you may be creating a lifelong enemy in the process.

Chapter 12

Out In Public You

When you were a baby, people probably played a game with you wherein they hid their face and pretended they'd disappeared. For kids it generally takes around ten months to realize that the world keeps on ticking even when they're not aware of it; for you, however, this realization may have never come. Thus, you may still believe that, unless you're around them, other people's lives stop until your next encounter with them. Fair enough. It's not your fault that your parents didn't give you existential philosophy lessons. My bigger concern is that, even when you *are* in the direct vicinity of other people, you still often act as though you're the only one there.

THE "BE YOURSELF" FALLACY

You've got a big personality that's always itching to get out of its cage. Sometimes this means you'll shake a rickety suspension bridge in hopes of thrilling the strangers who are traversing the expanse with you; other times, you may be at a restaurant and possess an unusually big laugh such that diners at neighbouring tables must pause their own stories until you've finished your overpowering chuckle; and still other times you may simply enjoy heckling the comedian at a comedy club.

ADH-YOU: What are you babbling about?

Well, correct me if I'm wrong, but I think you might be under the spell of the popular notion that "being yourself" is always the right way to go.

ADH-YOU: Hey, I gotta be me!

Well put, as always, YOU. But, unfortunately, this generous claim that you can't go wrong with being who you are is the consequence of a self-esteem-is-supreme error known as the "always be yourself" (or ABY) fallacy.

> **ADH-YOU:** You know: calling something a fallacy doesn't make it so.

Well said, YOU. But, tragically, the universality of the ABY-platitude is immediately disproven when one realizes it would justify the behaviours of serial killers. You see, it turns out that even one's most instinctive inclinations can sometimes be more harmful (to you and others) than beneficial.

> **ADH-YOU:** Hmm, I guess I see your point. Is there any way around the problem? "Always be myself" is my favourite aphorism.

Sorry, I just don't see a way to hold onto ABY as a universal platitude.

> **ADH-YOU:** Man, I'll have to think about it, then. I'm not sure if I can give it up.

Yeah, give it some thought. And don't feel bad that you fell for the notion of always being yourself. It's not your fault that you've been cruelly seduced into thinking that anything you do—so long as it's done with your sincerest intentions—cannot be wrong.

> **ADH-YOU:** Thanks, yeah, um, so am I the only one that's been duped?

Actually, there are plenty of other ADH-CITIZENS who have taken comfort in the "always be yourself" aphorism and have been hurt in the process. Consider the story, *Noisemakers*, below. It features some fellow ADH-TRAVELLERS who fell for the fallacy and lost.

Noisemakers

After a long drive, my dad, my uncle, and I settled into a campsite which required its guests to lower our volume at 10 p.m. My father and uncle played their guitars until this sounds-out point, and then we settled into our tent and read or whispered till we fell asleep. A few hours later, a group of twenty-somethings arrived with much enthusiasm to set up their own camp. They were not concerned with the many people sleeping nearby, and instead constructed their tents at full volume. They slammed their car doors, bickered with each other, and generally had a loud old time.

The next morning, our group was up before theirs, and since there were no other campers still asleep nearby, my uncle found himself with extra reasons to go in and out of his car and slam its doors. Moreover, some rocks found themselves in an empty beer can, which then seemed to find its way into my uncle's kicking path throughout the morning.

When the youngsters arose from their disrupted slumber, they exited their tents and glared at our unnecessarily noisy group. Sadly, they did not realize that they were actually glaring at themselves.

Swearing On Swearing

One interesting form of communication that you and your big personality may choose to share with strangers in public is colourful language that some consider profane and/or offensive.

> **ADH-YOU:** Prudes.

You're right, of course. And I believe in your right to add whatever linguistic seasoning you believe is vital to your discourse. However, that doesn't mean you must *always* say every word that crosses your delightful mind.

> **ADH-YOU:** If I don't speak my mind, no one else will.

Well said, YOU. But my argument here is not that you shouldn't express yourself. As you know, profanity is simply an arbitrary set of words that we as a culture have set aside to indicate vulgarity. Consequently, profanity rarely expresses anything unique that could not have been captured without your devil-may-care vocabulary. So, to avoid using it in certain contexts does not necessarily restrict your ideas, but instead stops you from sounding like you're not concerned with being polite.

> **ADH-YOU:** Up yours. I love spicing up my language.

Fair enough, and thank you for that helpful intervention. Indeed, maybe you're a particular connoisseur of vulgarity, and I don't want to suggest that you should restrict it completely. However, I do think you would be a nicer person to be around if you were to quarantine it to locations where it will cause the least irritation amongst those around you. You see, there are certain arenas where such rudeness is less rude than others. For instance, some locker rooms may contain a culture of language that approves of crass language, whereas in some dining situations, the opposite may be true.

All that I ask, then, is that you pay attention to the effect you may be having on those around you and decide whether that's actually what you want. I know, for instance, that when you've been on public transportation with your friends, you have heretofore enjoyed freely enunciating your thoughts with four-letter emphasis. Before you continue do so, it might be worth glancing around to see if there are people nearby who might be disgruntled by your vocal stylings, and if so, ask yourself if it's worth it. Would speaking without those commonly winced at words really cost you any meaning or enjoyment in your conversation?

> **ADH-YOU:** Yeah, sorry, bud, those words are part of who I am. I gotta be me. But, for the sake of argument, how would I possibly remember which words are okay, and which aren't?

Good point. Memorization is tricky. Instead, I suggest simply asking yourself what language you might censor from your lexicon if you were in a job interview or making a speech at a wedding, and then try out subtracting those words from your general public performances. And then see if you miss them. If you truly do, then feel free to put them back. But if you don't pine for those edgy points of emphasis, then maybe cut them indefinitely from your out-in-public vocabulary. And, voilà, you will have turned yourself into a less obnoxious public participant. Congrats, YOU!

The Trouble With "Performance Laughing"

More than once I have attended a comedic play in which certain people in the audience were personal friends of the performers. These spectators thus took it upon themselves to laugh extra loudly at the funny parts of the show, but their guffaws were so loud and oddly timed (as they were provided in anticipation of the jokes instead of following them) that the rest of us couldn't fully hear the very punchlines that the laughter was meant to cheer on. Thus, if these ADH-AUDIENCE-MEMBERS were intending to celebrate and accentuate the performers, they failed. Instead, my overall impression of the show was lessened since I wasn't able to take it all in.

> **ADH-YOU:** Nice story. What's your point?

Well, if I were a snarky man, I might suggest that the over-laughers were taking part in a long-celebrated pastime known as "performance laughing." Such laughter is utilized to demonstrate something about yourself as opposed to illustrating something about the show. In this case—if my snarky reading is correct—the performance laughers were hoping those nearby would be impressed that they clearly *knew* the star performers on stage.

> **ADH-YOU:** I can relate to that. Sometimes people don't realize that I'm associated with someone important, so I like to give them a nudge.

Well said, YOU! And, correct me if I'm wrong, but I notice that you don't just do this to demonstrate your access to friends, but also to complex ideas.

> **ADH-YOU:** I don't follow you.

Well, consider your tendency—when attending Shakespeare's comedies—to laugh harder than the humour necessarily deserves.

> **ADH-YOU:** Ah, yes, William is very drôle.

Well noticed, YOU. And, if I'm right, then at least some of your overly enthusiastic chuckles at his jokes are meant to indicate to your companions that you *get* the supposedly high-level Shakespearian humour (unaware, perhaps, that many of Shakespeare's jokes were meant to satisfy the lowest common "groundlings" of his time).

> **ADH-YOU:** Well, I just like people to know that I know the bard.

I understand. But I'm sorry to say that many in your hoped-for audience are seeing through your performance. The truth is you would probably earn more respect from those around you if you were to let your genuine amusement define your laughter levels. You see, as with most of your noisy attempts to garner appreciation from those nearby, the harder you try, the harder they sigh.

Belchingly You

I'm told that everybody burps—

> **ADH-YOU:** Yeah, we do!

Right, so you have no reason to be ashamed of your participation in this natural human function. Nevertheless, at some point in our culture's development, the noise that goes with the behaviour was determined to be undesirable. As a result, most courteous citizens attempt to muffle such outbursts when hanging around in polite society.

> **ADH-YOU:** I have no interest in polite society, so why should I be expected to stifle myself around such snobs?

Fair enough, but I request that you at least don't inflate your belches to be bigger than they need to be.

> **ADH-YOU:** Whatever do you mean?

Well evaded, YOU, but we both know you do it. You've practised this skill during friendly burping competitions and so are well-equipped to let 'er fly on command when you want some extra attention.

> **ADH-YOU:** It's true, I *am* the champ!

Yes, and congrats. But, unfortunately, the truth is that the notoriety you are acquiring—when you practise your craft in non-competition areas—is not as favourable towards your reputation as you may have been anticipating. Instead, those around you will probably dismiss you as a child possessing an adult's belching power who has no other means of attaining confidence than pressing air out of their mouth in a noisy way.

> **ADH-YOU:** That's mean.

I know, and I'm sorry.

SMOKING MAD

Tobaccy

Even though I am a dedicated non-smoker (I was never tempted to try smoking, myself, and have yet to acquire the taste for the secondhand stuff), I feel a little sorry for smokers in the urban world. They seem to have progressively fewer places to ply their gradual suicide. Nevertheless, I think smokers can, in many ways, thank themselves for their shrinking freedom.

> **ADH-YOU:** What did *I* do?

Well, I'm afraid you haven't always been a considerate nicotine ingester. For instance, if you're a smoker who's waiting in a lineup, those downwind from you are captive breathers, and so I think it's fair to expect you to separate yourself from the group, or butt your carcinogen out. Similarly, when you're at a concert, I don't think you have a right to force the rest of the crowd to smoke with you.

> **ADH-YOU (*coughing*):** Relax! Concerts are supposed to be fun.

Well argued, YOU. In fact, I've heard some NON-ADH-CITIZENS take your side on this one. For instance, after attending my first concert as an adult and breathing in others' tobacco—regular and wacky—I arrived at work on Monday morning full of criticism of the smoky concert goers; but I was laughed off my soap box by my co-workers, who felt it was a music-given right to smoke at musical gatherings.

> **ADH-YOU:** Exactly! Why are you such a buzz kill?

I see your point. Nevertheless, I wonder if it's reasonable for those with poisonous habits to impose them on non-consenting strangers during a poorly ventilated three-hour show. It seems to me that, for the sake of the employees of the concert hall alone, attendees should be expected to rely on a nicotine patch for the evening.

> **ADH-YOU:** What if the musicians, themselves, are smokers?

Cleverly put, YOU! Yes, even if the musicians you're witnessing are smoking-culture promoters, their fans do not immediately acquire the right to smoke wherever they're enjoying their music. You see, most musicians are humans, and so, as with most humans, they likely possess a vice or two, but that doesn't give one set of their fans the right to impose every such weakness on another set of their fans.

> **ADH-YOU:** You know what, champ, breathing in car fumes is just as bad, if not worse, so until we ban driving, we cannot ban smoking.

Another cleverly coughed-out argument, YOU. But, unfortunately, the harms of one bad thing do not justify those of another. Even though it may be environmentally desirable to eliminate (or at least limit) driving in urban areas, it is not currently feasible. And, even if we could reasonably ban car fumes, the fact that we have failed to take action on one problem does not morally justify you contributing to another. Sadly, then, in order to cure your ADH-ME, I'm afraid you'll have to be a considerate smoker even if the cars around you are not.

Wacky Tobaccy

Regardless of whether pot is illegal in your area or not, I suggest that gentleman and lady tokers attempt to be as considerate as we expect smokers to be with regard to sharing their favourite drug with innocent passersby.

> **ADH-YOU-TOKER:** Oh, c'mon, man, Mary Jane is supposed to relax us.

Yes, I understand: thinking about how you're affecting others certainly isn't what you had in mind when you decided to inhale. So I'd like you to contemplate your toking in this way: imagine in your mind's nose the smell of a farm. Now, the next time you toke up, be advised that your flavoured air is as aggressive to some of your neighbours as manure is to you. The only difference is that cow fumes don't also play hopscotch with peoples' brains.

LITTER BY LITTER

Sharing Your Garbage

This one confuses me: some ADH-ME-AFFLICTED people believe it's okay to discard their garbage anywhere they like instead of depositing it in the designated waste collectors. On the surface, this behaviour seems like simple laziness, but given how easy it is to hold onto one's garbage until a trash can comes along, I suspect something more sinister. It strikes me that the free-range dropping of garbage without regard for the mess it creates may be the work of either an ADH-ATTENTION-RE-QUIRING person (who is attempting to impress their friends with their bad-ass lack of concern for our communal habitat) or an ADH-MALEVOLENT who doesn't care what matters to the rest of us.

If you are one of the latter litterers, please note that, in your quest to achieve the best for yourself, such malevolent behaviour might cost you the respect of a witness who might have otherwise benefitted you in the future.

> **ADH-MALEVOLENT-YOU:** How?

Hmm, yeah, I was hoping you wouldn't ask. Well, maybe they, as your friend, would have one day recommended you for a job, but tragically, they could never get the image of you tossing your trash on the grass out of their brain sufficiently to promote your cause.

> **ADH-MALEVOLENT-YOU:** That's weak, bud.

Fair enough, but given that it's so easy to use a garbage can, I suggest that even a small chance of hurting yourself in the above way is worth considering?

> **ADH-MALEVOLENT-YOU:** I guess.

Whew, thanks MALEVOLENT-YOU!

Meanwhile, if your reason for littering is that you're ADH-ATTENTION-REQUIRING—

> **ADH-ATTENTION-REQUIRING-YOU:** Yeah, I kinda just like to throw garbage in the park to shock my friends. I get a lot of respect for it.

I see your point. But consider this: while your friends and hoped-for paramours may *seem* to think you're cool for using the street or park or someone else's front yard as your personal garbage can, you may be surprised that some of them may, in fact, think you're an idiot, but feel awkward pointing it out.

In contrast, if you were to choose to deposit your garbage in a trash receptacle, I doubt any of your friends would condemn you for it. The upgraded behaviour is so common that they might not even notice it. And, if they do, what exactly what would their argument against you be?

> **YOUR FRIEND:** What an idiot—he put his garbage in the garbage!

Moreover, someday you might come to an ethical epiphany that causes you to regret your previous lack of consideration; and I must tell you, it's not much fun to realize you've been a jerk. So the sooner you stop your obnoxious behaviour, the better for your ego later.

> **ADH-YOU:** Fine, but in future, please leave my ego out of this. It's very precious to me, and I will not have you use it against me!

Fair enough, YOU.

Butting In

Now, I understand that it's difficult to safely dispose of cigarette butts in garbage receptacles, so I don't think the tendency to use the ground as the garbage can for your butts is necessarily an indication of ADH-LAZINESS. Nevertheless, smoking is your choice, and so, if you've selected it as your favourite addiction, it is still your duty to dispose of the evidence respectfully.

> **ADH-YOU:** But smoking's not just about the flavour. It's also about the lifestyle.

Well noted, YOU. Yes, I realize that part of the mystique of smoking is the attitude of "I don't care what others think of me." Nevertheless, if you want to cure yourself of ADH-ME, you'll need to find a way to reconcile the fact that the ultimate "cool" behaviour—tossing your cigarette buttocks on the ground to be smothered by your cowboy boot—is actually raising a middle toe to the rest of society.

Marking Your Territory

I realize that it's funny to imagine aliens flying by our planet, and upon seeing humans cleaning up after the dogs' messes, concluding that we're the inferiors to the canines.

> **ADH-YOU:** Exactly! Why should I clean up after my dog? I'm not his servant.

Well, I'll let you in on a little secret: we clean up after our dogs, not for them, but for other humans. You see, our society believes that animal offerings don't belong in the public space, and so if we want to keep an animal in that arena, we need to find a way to remove their inevitable output from the common area. So I must ask you: who's job do *you* think it should be to deal with your canine's bounty?

> **ADH-YOU:** Not mine!

Good for you for standing up for yourself. It's not a fun job, is it? But have you ever inadvertently stepped on a dog's treat?

> **ADH-YOU:** Yeah, I hate that.

So if *that* dog's owner had cleaned up his mess—

> **ADH-YOU:** No, that's not going to work this time. The number of times I've been able to skip cleaning up after my dog far outweighs the number of times I've stepped in it.

Fair enough; it sounds like you've got a bit of ADH-MA-LEVOLENT blood in you on this one. So the only way I can try to persuade you is by virtue of reward/punishment. Here goes. Once again, don't forget that every time you indulge in this behaviour, you risk getting caught in your act of canine graffiti by someone whose opinion matters to you (perhaps that attractive person you've had your eye on?).

> **ADH-YOU:** Hmm, he/she *is* cute, but I'm getting a little tired of you using other people's opinions of me against me.

Yeah, fair point. I'll try to only do that when I have no other option.

OUT OF BOUNDS

When you ski out of bounds, you put rescuers at risk and cost society money to pay for your recovery.

> **ADH-YOU:** But I didn't plan to get lost!

Yes, I figured. Instead, you probably decided you could handle whatever dangers you might encounter, and so you genuinely didn't think you would be risking the lives of any rescuers. Your crime, then, is more accurately one of over-confidence.

> **ADH-YOU:** Well I don't know about that. But skiing out of bounds is just an awesome challenge, that's all. My parents always taught me I could do anything I put my mind to. You wouldn't want me to doubt myself, would you?

Well spun, YOU. I would never want to put your high self-esteem in jeopardy. But, given that *everyone* is being limited by the out-of-bounds sign, maybe you could make an exception in this case?

> **ADH-YOU:** I don't know. If I don't believe in me, no one else will.

Beautifully put, as always, but I'd like to point out that many of your adventurous predecessors—who were just as confident as you are now—discovered that they, like their own fore-rule-breakers, were subject to the cruel machinations of increased risk.

> **ADH-YOU:** But I'm smarter than they were!

I certainly can't argue with that. Nevertheless—

> **ADH-YOU:** I'm just trying to have some fun here, bud.

Good point. But the reason you're going out of bounds is for the thrill, am I right?

> **ADH-YOU:** No, it's for the educational experience. Ha, ha, of course it's for the thrill.

So maybe you could select thrills that won't endanger rescuers when you make a mistake. That way you can enjoy the true thrill of taking a risk without a net made out of other people.

Chapter 13

Moving Around You

Chapter 13: *Moving Around You*

Sadly, as you move yourself around in the world, you may discover there are other beings interested in borrowing some of the space you have reserved for yourself and your kin. It's annoying, but with a few tricks, you can build harmony with the villains who get in your way.

SIDEWALKING YOU

Walking on a sidewalk may seem easy to someone who doesn't suffer with your affliction, but for you it is a challenge every day because—unlike travel by driving—there are no clear guidelines, and so you are left to guess at how to proceed.

> **ADH-YOU:** Thank you for acknowledging my pain. But, sorry, what are you talking about?

Well, for instance, when you and your friends are walking by yourselves, I know you enjoy taking up the full width of the sidewalk.

> **ADH-YOU:** Ah, yeah, what do you want us to do, tiptoe along it?

No, when there's no one else nearby, there's no problem with you and your friends using as much of the pedestrian lane as you would like. But what do you do when you pass people going in the opposite direction?

> **ADH-YOU:** Um... keep walking just as we were?

Well observed, YOU. That is what you have been doing. But here's the thing. Have you noticed that the people trying to cross your path seem strangely perturbed when you steer them off the sidewalk so that you can maintain ownership of its full width?

ADH-YOU: Oh, yeah, totally! Why are they so grumpy?

Okay, to help you traverse this confusing path, I want you to imagine that the sidewalk is a two-way roadway. So, if pedestrians are approaching in the opposing direction, then please move yourself (and your friends) to the right side of the path so that you don't collide with the approaching travellers.

ADH-YOU: I guess I can do that.

Nice, YOU! Now here comes an even more difficult situation; imagine someone faster than you comes up behind you.

ADH-YOU: Yeah, how am I supposed to deal with that, smart guy?

Well, this time, I want you to imagine that the sidewalk is one side of a divided highway, and so both lanes of your sidewalk are currently going in the same direction.

ADH-YOU: Okay, got it.

So, in that case, maybe you and your company could move to the slow lane (the right side of the path) to allow traffic behind you to pass.

ADH-YOU: That's it?

That's it! If you can follow those two easy metaphors, you won't be stepping on any sidewalk toes in the future.

ADH-YOU: It seems too simple to be true, but I'll try it.

Excellent, YOU!

Meanwhile, to give you a better idea of why you should follow these guidelines, please consider the story, *Little Gods*, from my journal of personal battles with ADH-SIDEWALKERS.

Little Gods

It has come to my attention that little kids and their parents surpass even young punks when it comes to feeling possessive of the sidewalks. On numerous occasions, I have been walking on the sidewalk in the direction of some little kids and their owners, and in many such cases, I have found that neither the kids nor their accompanying parentage were interested in making any effort to share the sidewalk. I can forgive the children for their lack of social sidewalk graces (since apparently they have been worshipped as rulers of the planet since the moment they were unveiled), but I find it disturbing that their parents seem to be so impressed with their "mini-me"s that they think nothing of bumping others out of their way.

In particular, when I walk up the hill to my bus stop, I often encounter a clump of kids and their parents reserving all lanes of the sidewalk, thus forcing me to go around them in order to maintain enough speed to catch my bus. In such a circumstance, I have two choices when veering off the sidewalk: the first is going left and treading on someone's lawn, and so I usually choose the second, and I move onto the neighbourhood road to pass the clog obstructing my journey.

One day, as I was speeding my way to my bus, a family merged suddenly onto the sidewalk immediately in front of me without signalling. As always, I prepared to veer onto the road so as to maintain my bus-catching speed, but, unfortunately, there was a car parked on the road beside me, thus blocking my access to a non-lawn-based fast lane. I was in a hurry, though, so I sheepishly stepped left onto someone's nicely manicured greenery and sped ahead.

However, as I passed that self-absorbed family of four plus stroller, a conscience-cleaning breeze came over me—it was their *lawn that I had stomped upon in order to get past them! All was right with the world.*

UMBRELLA REASONING

You may like to use an umbrella to shield yourself from the rain.

> **ADH-YOU:** Ah, yeah, I don't like being rained on, thanks very much.

Well put. That seems reasonable. Please consider, though, that when you're walking along a communal path with your large overhead protector, you're now taking up more space than you normally do. So when approaching other sidewalk dwellers, you may want to adjust the position of your umbrella so that they don't have to dodge around it.

> **HINT:** And don't forget that your umbrella may have rain on it, so try to tilt it in a way that won't pour water on those nearby.

THE LEASH YOU CAN DO

I love dogs as much as the next human who grew up tossing tennis balls for his four-legged friends. And I think leashes are an excellent means of keeping you attached to your dogs in public so they don't hurt themselves or others. But when you walk along a well-populated sidewalk with your leash outstretched to give Rover lots of freedom to sniff about, your ADH-ME is showing. Please pull Rover closer to you when NON-YOU strangers are approaching your space, so they don't have to walk wide around you and your best friend.

Meanwhile, if you have one of those wind-up leashes that can extend its thin (almost invisible) wire many leagues ahead of you, but you don't shore up the leash when others are crossing the space between you and your animal, you are a tripping hazard.

> **ADH-YOU:** Totally! My neighbour tripped on Captain Four Paws' leash the other day. Watch where you're going, people!

Well put, YOU, but I was actually meaning that you and your extenda-leash are a danger to others.

> **ADH-YOU:** Oh. But what am I supposed to do? Captain Four Paws wants to roam!

Well, consider this hypothetical situation: what if someone tripped *you* with a thin wire, and you fell and broke your arm. What would you do?

> **ADH-YOU:** I'd sue, of course.

Right, so what if your neighbour thought more like you.

> **ADH-YOU:** Everyone should think more like me.

That's the dream, of course, but then if more people were as litigious as you, and you were to continue walking with that long-range tripping wire, you might eventually be sued for clothes-legging.

> **ADH-YOU:** Hmm. I see your point. I don't like your point, but I see it.

That's all that I'm looking for, YOU!

SLOW-WALKING

Standard

In general, I have found "slow-walkers" to be an inconsiderate lot. Many of them find a way to meander in the middle of the sidewalk, staircase, or aisle such that they leave *just not enough* room for people to pass on either side of them.

> **ADH-YOU:** Relax. What's your hurry?

Yes, I'm aware that you usually prefer a leisurely pace, but recall for a moment those rare cases when you yourself have been in a hurry, but were caught behind snail-impersonating citizens who did not allow for easy passage beside them.

> **ADH-YOU:** That's different. I couldn't afford to be late those times!

Yes, of course, I am sure you had an excellent reason to be in a rush in each case. Nevertheless, since you acknowledge there are times when you are annoyed by slow-moving citizens, I want you to consider the possibility that—when you are in the role of the dawdling pedestrian who veers along the center of the sidewalk—you might be creating unnecessary pain to those hurrying behind you.

> **ADH-YOU:** Well, what the heck am I supposed to do about that? I'm just walking here.

Brilliant question, YOU! I suggest that you keep your surroundings in mind at all times. If there are people in your rearview mirror, pick one lane or the other so that such followers can get past your excellency without fantasizing about your demise. Moreover, if you're getting on an escalator or staircase and there's already a sluggish-walker on board, maybe you could plod directly behind them instead of blocking the "passing lane" by travelling beside your fellow slow stepper.

In Grocery Stores

If you're shopping in a grocery store and are pushing a shopping cart (or baby stroller), please note that the extra volume of space that you are taking up puts some responsibility on you to avoid obstructing the aisles.

> **ADH-YOU:** That makes no sense. Bigger things take up more space. Deal with it.

I see what you're saying. It is difficult to reduce your total volume. But that doesn't mean you can't keep in mind where you are, who is around you, and how your cart—on its own or in conjunction with another person's—might create a pedestrian traffic jam in the middle of the store. Just by adjusting your mini-vehicle's position a smidge, you, too, can help reduce grocery store congestion!

SUDDEN STOPPING

When you're walking in public and you realize you want to put on your brakes to have a good think or to check your pockets for something, try not to stop suddenly. This may leave the person just behind you stuck, or might even cause them to run into you. Instead, when you need to check the contents of your bag (or your thoughts), try shoulder checking to see if there is anyone directly behind you; if there is, please move to the side so that they can continue smoothly past you.

ADH-YOU: Why?

Great question, YOU. Once again, let's call upon the metaphor of traffic etiquette to illustrate this point. If you were driving, and realized you needed to check the trunk, would you suddenly stop in the middle of a thoroughfare to make sure the person you'd kidnapped was still sufficiently tied up, or would you pull over to perform the task?

ADH-YOU: I guess I'd pull over.

I think you would. I really do.

ESCALATOR STANDING

I must admit that I do not comprehend the motivation of most escalator-standers. Why would a healthy individual interrupt their day (in which, I'm told, time is precious) to wait for a slow machine to carry them to their destination, given that the device offers the option to move at double its speed by simply walking?

ADH-YOU: Because I like to relax sometimes, obviously.

Fair enough. If that is your preference, there is nothing on the official ADH-SYMPTOMS list that I can utilize to suggest that you desist. *Nevertheless,* I request that you at least not stand in the way of those who would choose to walk the escalator freely. Stay in your lane, and nobody gets glared at.

ADH-YOU: Fine. But, if I'm with my spouse, we like to stand next to each other.

Well observed, YOU. Yes, I have noticed that you and your teammate will merrily stand side-by-side, blocking anyone behind you from using the left lane to move past you.

> **ADH-YOU:** Sorry, bud, there's not much I can do there.

Well put, as always, YOU... Wait a minute! I have an idea. What if you and your companion were to stand single file just for those twenty seconds, like everyone else?

> **ADH-YOU:** That's not very romantic.

I'm sure you're right, but neither is the stare of contempt coming from a long line of people behind you who would've liked to have kept moving.

Chapter 14

Commuter You

Chapter 14: *Commuter You*

This chapter's going to be a tough one for you. I'm going to ask you to consider the possibility that, just because a rule doesn't benefit you in a particular commuter situation, doesn't mean you automatically get to break it.

> **ADH-YOU:** I'm not following you.

Well, for instance, as we talked about in the prologue to this book, if you're in a lineup to board a bus and you realize that you might not get a seat, you don't get to jump the queue.

> **ADH-YOU:** Yeah, I still don't get that. What if jumping ahead in the line is the only way I'll get a seat?

That's a fair point. You are utilizing your understandable faith in your supreme importance to justify skipping the obstructions that the serfs have to endure. Plus, if they're not smart enough to think of jumping the queue, that's not your problem, am I right?

> **ADH-YOU:** Exactly! So we're in agreement? We can leave this one alone?

Well, unfortunately, once again, as the ADH-POPULATION grows, this habit of a select few judging themselves superior to commuter conventions will not be sustainable. (Once any lineup reaches a critical mass of people who bypass it, the system will fail, and the lineup structure will evaporate altogether, and will be replaced by chaos-style boarding, which will diminish the experience for everyone—even YOU!) Therefore, tragically, I'm going to have to ask you to stop with the commuter elitism.

> **ADH-YOU:** I have no idea how I could possibly do that.

Not to worry, I will give you some examples that I hope will make the process as painless as a snowflake landing on your cheek.

> **ADH-YOU:** I like snowflakes!

Great! Here they come.

GETTING ON TRANSIT

Your First Lineup

Let us look at the proper way to enter a transit vehicle. We'll take our cue about how to queue from the lectures of Bus School (an imaginary institution invented in my dreams), where students discover that, before boarding any bus or train, one lets the exiting passengers go first. (It's like they have a green light, while yours is red.) This practice, Bus School professors fondly explain, allows us to avoid a clog of people going in two directions. To facilitate the complicated manoeuvre, learners are requested to line up slightly to the side of the entry doors until the original bus passengers have completed their exodus.

Now, while the above system is an efficient way to exit and board transit vehicles, there's one small problem with it.

> **ADH-YOU:** Let me guess! I'm doing it wrong?

Nailed it, YOU! Yes, ADH-CITIZENS such as yourself have been known to arrive at a bus stop, where a lineup of hopeful bus-goers are holding for the former residents of the vehicle to finish their exit, and you assume that the waiters are waiting for YOU, and so you merrily take the first position in the queue.

> **ADH-YOU:** What's wrong with that? If they leave a spot for me, why shouldn't I take it?

Another great question, YOU. It turns out that the wait-for-prior-passengers-to-exit-before-boarding system is not actually a gesture of deference to ADH-YOU. And so, when you take advantage of others' compliance with it, you damage your fellow travelers' faith in the rule, which in turn reduces their own interest in following this passenger protocol that benefits everyone.

> **ADH-YOU:** So you want me to be a sheep and do what everyone else is doing?

Nicely re-framed, YOU. I know it's dull to follow convention, but this is one of those cases I told you about wherein you've only been able to get away with the advantage of cheating the system because so many others don't cheat. So I—along with the hypothetical Bus School instructors—am going to have to insist on this one: no more abuse of queue.

Space On Bus; Space On Brain

There is a common and troubling occurrence on most city buses: when a large crowd boards the vehicle, an ADH-TRAVELER or two will stop in the aisle (like a pair of escalator-standers) and block the following masse from moving towards the spacious back. This means that just past the well-packed front half of the vehicular hallway, there is often a glorious walk-in closet's worth of room—and even empty seats! Nevertheless, ADH-YOU and your fellow ADH-AISLE-BLOCKERS will stay put as the bus driver turns away new passengers (because no more passengers can fit in the crammed front).

> **ADH-YOU:** Well, what do you want me to do about it? I like the middle of the bus. It's closer to the exit doors.

Yes, thank you for pointing that out, YOU. I understand that you have your preferences. But if you want to indulge them, then—for passengers' sake!—please make room in the aisle for those who would like to move into the glorious space behind you!

> **ADH-YOU:** Geez, why are you yelling at me?

I'm sorry. I didn't mean to shout at you. As always, you are understandably distracted by your focus on you.

> **ADH-YOU:** Exactly. Plus, why should it matter to me if other people catch the bus?

Good question. The only answer I can offer that might persuade you is that, one day, you may want to board a front-packed bus, but you will not be able to get on because your ADH-BRETHREN are blocking the aisle.

> **ADH-YOU:** That sounds stupid. I want on!

Yes, it is stupid. However, the more you contribute to a culture that closes its eyes to the needs of its fellow passengers (by blocking the aisle when you're on the bus), the more likely it is that you will one day be the one on the outside not getting in.

Space-Invading

When you're on a crowded bus, please be careful of taking up more space than you need to.

> **ADH-YOU:** I haven't the foggiest idea what you're talking about.

Sorry for the confusion, YOU! Let's go to the two leading examples of unnecessary space domination for illustration.

(1) BAG-SPREADING:

Feel free to bring your bags with you on transit.

> **ADH-YOU:** Done and done.

However, when the vehicle you enter is crowded, please try to make yourself and your collection of accessories as compact as feasible.

> **ADH-YOU:** How?

Well, for instance, if you're standing in a crowded vehicle with your backpack, instead of keeping it strapped to your back—thus creating a double-sized you, who inadvertently bumps into strangers nearby—I suggest that you remove the weapon and put it on the floor between your legs where it'll take up less of the communal space. Meanwhile, if you have a few bags, instead of creating a wide perimeter around yourself, please bring them in as close to you as possible, perhaps stacking them, and even putting one or two between your legs. Again, this will create less passenger congestion on the vehicle.

Perhaps most importantly, remember that—except in extreme baggage circumstances—the bus seats are meant for humans, so instead of taking up a bus seat or two with your bag(s), please call your lap into service and fill it up so that a human can have access to the spot next to you.

> **ADH-YOU:** But what if the bus isn't busy?

Well asked, YOU. If there are lots of bus seats available, then feel free to let your bags share a chair. However, the downside of that plan is that it comes with responsibility to watch the bus for signs of crowding. If the seats are starting to run out, then I'm afraid it's time for your bags to cozy up to your lap.

(2) LEG-SPREADING:

> **NOTE:** The following tackles the issue of certain transit passengers taking up extra room for themselves via excessive leg-spreading. A popular term for this behaviour is "man-spreading," which is clearly a sexist expression. Nevertheless, even though the phrase crudely demonizes all men for the actions of a few of them, those few may still be worth criticizing.

Often during transit travel, one must sit next to strangers. And sometimes the bus seats will be so small that people will be nudged up against each other. Such touching in that particular circumstance is unavoidable. However, my concern here is with those ADH-FOLKS who spread their legs so far apart such that their knees travel into the leg space of the people on either side of them. If you are one of these people, I must ask you, why?

> **ADH-YOU:** It's more comfortable to sit that way. I'm a large person, after all.

Well said, YOU! Indeed, I recognize that some people are bigger than others, so I understand that sometimes you might take up more space than your neighbour. My confusion is with why you expand your size even more by angling your legs outward in a diagonal direction. When you do so, there is suddenly a huge area not being taken up between your legs, while the space next to your legs is occupied by both you and the person next to you (who had assumed that space was intended for *their* legs).

The result is that the person next to you is either banished from their leg space or forced into a leg-pushing war with you. I don't see the benefit of such a conflict, given that you could simply use the space directly in front of you that is already allotted for your legs.

> **ADH-YOU:** Yeah, but it's more comfortable to spread my legs, because ... you know ... I'm a man, and ...

Oh. I see. So, correct me if I'm wrong, but I think you're defending the comforts of a great and revered creature that lives *between* your legs; and you spread your legs wide to give it space to breathe.

> **ADH-YOU:** Yup.

Okay, so let's assume for a moment that, indeed, your leader does prefer such a roomy dwelling. Do you see that, by definition, when you push your male neighbour's legs inwards, you are costing him the very space for his advisor that you feel yours has a right to?

> **ADH-YOU:** So?

Well, once again this book requires you to consider that everyone deserves consideration, and so, in a case where two people would like as much leg room as possible, I submit that they should each simply take up as much room as their hips require, and then send their legs ahead in a straight line from that point. Thus, neither of you is costing the other space just because you happen to be more aggressive than your neighbour.

Moreover, even if you're sitting next to a person with no such impediments, I still think they deserve to keep their designated leg room—and not have to scrunch away from you—regardless of your luxury hopes for your champion.

> **ADH-YOU:** But I need the space or I'll be crushed!

I understand, but cruelly, I'm skeptical that your impressive tenant is really that much more comfortable with your legs spread *that* widely. Instead, I suspect that your insistence on this behaviour represents a (subconscious?) attempt to tell others that you have an important friend that needs a lot of space to go about its daily business.

> **ADH-YOU:** But what if I'm not spreading out to impress anyone? Maybe I just find it more comfortable to sit that way.

Fair enough. There are, I'm sure, lots of spread-eagle sitters who do so not because they're trying to prove that their centre of gravity resides in their pelvis, but instead because they genuinely find it to be more comfortable to sit that way.

> **ADH-YOU:** Like me!

I believe you. Nevertheless, when you sit in such a way that your knees continually invade your neighbours' leg room, then you are elevating your luxury comfort requirements over the basic comforts of the person next to you. Please stop that.

Loud And Proud?

Now we move from the sharing of physical space to the sharing of sound space. As you know, anything you say out loud has the potential to invade the ears of those nearby. That works well when you're hanging out with friends at your place because, in that setting, you want to involve everyone in the conversation. However, when you're on public transit, the strangers around you may have other things to do beyond listening to your conversation. That's why most transiting adults will adopt a lower tone of voice that is loud enough to be heard by their group, but not so loud that it's hard for the strangers nearby to concentrate on their own activities. I'd like you to aim for that, please.

> **ADH-YOU:** Sorry, could you speak up? I couldn't hear you. You're too quiet.

Hee, hee, good one, YOU!

> **ADH-YOU:** Hee, hee, thanks. But seriously. I don't really see a problem with making noise while on the bus. We're in traffic. It's gonna be noisy.

Yes, I agree: noise is inevitable. But I want you to imagine those times that you have been by yourself on a bus and wanted to read a book or do your homework or contemplate your next vandalism. Have you ever found the noise of those nearby to be especially shrill and thus disruptive?

> **ADH-YOU:** I guess.

Well if you have, then brace yourself: you have been irritated by your own behaviours!

> **ADH-YOU:** I would never find me annoying. Regardless, we can't outlaw conversation just because it annoys people.

Well put, YOU. I'm not arguing that we prohibit conversations. But, unfortunately, the work of curing your ADH-ME asks you to go beyond doing what's legally required and asks you to do what's considerate.

> **ADH-YOU:** Oh, right, I always forget. I'm expected to be Pollyanna.

Good call, YOU. Now, I will admit that managing such noise pollution is trickier when you're a youth interacting with your peers, because generally they will be loud, so if you want to join in the conversation, you too will have to be loud (and perhaps expected to fill your language with profanity). So, to limit such noise, I suggest teasing your group for its volume. Simply look at your compatriots and say:

> **SMIRKING-YOU:** Hey, why are we yelling?

> **ADH-YOUR-FRIENDS:** I dunno. We're just talking here.
>
> **SMIRKING-YOU:** I think everyone on the bus can hear our conversation.

I don't know if that'll subdue the noise of your particular crew, but I do think it gives you an opportunity to object without losing your cool. Instead, by teasing the behaviour, you may allow your companions to see just how silly it is. And, even if they don't acknowledge it, I suspect they will find it difficult to come up with a rebuttal that proves your argument to be stupid.

Your Food And Fumes

Excessive noise isn't the only way to take up more than your share of sensory space. Perhaps you enjoy using your time on transit to make use of your nail polish remover, or fill your mouth with an onion-scented hamburger, or, if you're especially daring, maybe you like to sneak in a cigarette break. None of these activities are inherently inappropriate in public, but on transit, where the air space is confined, you are imposing aggressive aromas on those nearby.

In some cases, the rules of the transit system will prohibit the partaking of these substances for precisely that reason. But even if the rules don't forbid you from eating your dinner on the bus, do you not see how forcing your favourite fumes into the undefended airways of your fellow travelers might be discourteous?

> **ADH-YOU:** But why should their comfort be more important than mine?

I see your point. I don't mean to say that you must limit yourself only to those behaviours that will in no way disrupt anyone else, but I think that your fellow passengers have a reasonable expectation of freedom from your avoidable pollution. If in doubt, avoid any behaviour that would annoy you if it came from a NOT-YOU.

Your New Friendship

When you're on transit and you decide to make friends with your neighbour, please pay special attention to cues from those would-be pals which might indicate they're not as interested in starting up a companionship as you are.

> **ADH-YOU:** Why *wouldn't* they want to be friends with me? I'm delightful.

You certainly are! But it turns out that many people have busy lives, and they may think of their transit time as a precious opportunity to read, or think, or play Candy Crush. Plus, some people are introverts, which means that they are not energized by socializing and instead can actually be drained by it.

> **ADH-YOU:** What an unfriendly lot.

Brilliant point, YOU! Except that introversion isn't necessarily synonymous with unfriendliness. When I'm on the bus, I'm happy to give directions, or give up my seat to someone whose physical needs require it more than my own, but once those friendly interactions are taken care of, I like to read or put in my headphones and listen to talk radio. In contrast, I've met many ADH-STRANGERS who have decided that I would be better off chatting with them while we traverse the city. Rarely have I found such conversations to be fulfilling. Perhaps that's because I was enjoying my book or radio program, but it may also be because the process of getting to know a stranger is a stilted business, and so, if we're not destined to be great friends, we're doing the hardest part of socializing without the payoff.

> **ADH-YOU:** So you're saying I'm not allowed to talk to people on the bus?

No, no, there's nothing wrong with offering people your conversation, but if they don't seem interested, it's best to leave them be.

> **ADH-YOU:** Why? I'm just trying to get to know them. Isn't that nice of me?

Right you are! Nevertheless, I must ask you: have you ever been part of a conversation that was stilted, boring, or obnoxious?

> **ADH-YOU:** Ah, yeah, people bore me all the time.

And have you ever wished that, even though someone was being nice to you, that you could just go back to reading your book, or listening to your music, or strategizing for your next belching contest?

> **ADH-YOU:** Totally! It's so annoying when people don't get the hint that I'm enjoying some ME-time.

Exactly, and it turns out that those who will not give into your clear preference to entertain yourself are a species of extroverts known as socialization supremacists.

> **ADH-YOU:** What an annoying lot, they are.

Well put, YOU! But here's the thing: when the situation is reversed and you talk over someone *else's* preference for their transit time, you are condoning the socialization supremacists' plans to take over your transit time in future.

> **ADH-YOU:** Hmm. That displeases me.

Exactly! So try to remember that not everyone (including you!) wants to interact directly with other people all the time.

Chapter 14: *Commuter You*

> **ADH-YOU:** But how else am I going to make friends in this huge city?

Good question, YOU. The pursuit of friendship can be difficult. But, if that's your aim, why not participate in recreational sports, clubs, conferences, or volunteer endeavours? These are all fertile contexts for friendship-making that don't require you to impose yourself on the nearest stranger.

> **ADH-YOU:** Fine. So what are the stupid hints I'm supposed to watch for to tell me someone's not interested in socializing?

Well, for instance, if they give you only one-sentence replies and then attempt to return to what they were doing, you're likely dealing with someone who already has plans for their commute time.

> **ADH-YOU:** Fine.

Way to go, YOU.

YOU'RE DRIVING

Emergency Vehicles

You know how, when you're the victim of a life-threatening situation such as a car crash or an armed robbery, you find yourself cheering for paramedics and police officers to arrive quickly? This is likely based on your theory that early response times save lives, and you wouldn't mind if yours was given the best possible chance.

> **ADH-YOU:** OMG! So now you've got a problem with me *not* wanting to die?

No, no. I support your preference for living. But given your intuitive understanding that rescuer-speed saves lives, I'm curious to understand why—when you are not intimately involved in an emergency, but are in the path of those attempting to attend to it—you don't always make the most space possible for emergency vehicles.

> **ADH-YOU:** I'm sure I don't know what you mean. I don't just sit there in the middle of the road when an ambulance is right behind me.

Well defended, YOU. But I'm not only referring to those ADH-MALEVOLENTS who refuse to move *at all* for sirens. I'm speaking instead of a more subtle variety of emergency-response disrupters. See if you can recognize yourself in any of these examples:

(1) Some ADH-DRIVERS will hear sirens, but won't make any effort to ascertain the immediacy or proximity of the rescue vehicles until the noise is directly upon them; such drivers, most of the time, will turn out to have guessed rightly (that is, the emergency will usually not cross their road). And from their ADH-PERSPECTIVE, this result may be worth the occasional occurrence wherein an ambulance *does* arrive behind them, and cause them to scramble to get out of the way. Such Russian roulette ambulance awareness only occasionally impedes the progression of life-savers, so our ADH-DRIVERS have decided it's worth the risk.

(2) Other ADH-DRIVERS are happy to get partly out of the way, but they'd prefer not to move fully out of the emergency workers' line of travel because then it would be extra rough, after the fact, to get back into traffic. So they decide instead to leave the minimum space necessary for the emergency vehicles.

(3) My personal favourite ADH-DRIVERS are those who are already out of the way—perhaps because they have sidelined themselves, but more often because they're on a cross street of the rescue path—but are anxious to get moving and so are inching or signalling with the intent to join traffic the moment the path is clear of the emergency vehicle. It doesn't occur to these ADH-CLUELESS characters that emergency responders are not omniscient, and so they will not know the immediate intentions of twitchy cross-street dwellers. As such, the ambulance driver must take precautions by hesitating and perhaps slowing down when passing such eager drivers.

Now, if you are an ADH-MALEVOLENT, then, of course your justification for each of the above is clear:

> **ADH-MALEVOLENT-YOU:** Well, I'm not involved in the emergency, so how would it benefit ME to get out of the way of the emergency responders?

Hear, hear, MALEVOLENT-YOU! And since you don't care about others for their own sake, my only remaining argument for you is once again that people have a tendency to follow the conventions of the majority. So, when you adhere to the most helpful practices during someone else's emergency, you have the opportunity to gradually incline others (who, understandably, want to be just like you) to do the same.

> **ADH-MALEVOLENT-YOU:** Intriguing.

Yes, and eventually this could improve response time ever so slightly when it is you who needs the emergency aid. Such tiny morsels of time can seem enormous when you're gasping for air.

On the other side of your ego, if you are not ADH-MALEVOLENT, your crime is usually not so vicious.

> **ADH-YOU:** Thank you. It's nice to be appreciated.

Yes, well done, YOU. You are not necessarily malicious towards emergencies; however, you do seem to be so caught up in your own needs that you don't always consider how you might adversely impact crisis situations. So my request to you is this: when there is an emergency in your vicinity, please consider everyone on the roadway to be a member of the response team. Your job is to get out of the way as immediately, clearly, and completely as possible.

> **ADH-YOU:** I guess that could be fun. All right, I'll try it.

Way to go, YOU!

Patience is a Life-Saver

Now, in order to decrease the number of incidents that provoke emergency vehicles to become involved in our daily interactions, you might consider providing something closer to the safe driving that you promised you would when you acquired your licence.

> **ADH-YOU:** I know how to drive, thanks.

Yes, even though you may not always practise what you signed on for, I think you have a pretty good idea of what safe driving officially entails. Nevertheless, I think sometimes maybe you ignore certain safety expectations for the sake of getting more quickly to where you're going. To illustrate this concept, I would like to focus on one situation in particular that encapsulates your general lack of driving caution.

Let's say you're happily driving along, minding your own world domination plans, and you notice a car stopping in the middle of the road just ahead of you, and you don't know why. What do you do?

> **ADH-YOU:** That's easy, I switch lanes and zip on past them, perhaps flipping them a bird on my way by.

Right, thank you for your honest assessment. Unfortunately, I'm going to ask you to stop doing that. You see, despite your impressive reasoning to the contrary, there might in fact be a rational explanation for the other driver's stoppage.

> **ADH-YOU:** Like what?

Well, very possibly there is a pedestrian crossing the road at the crosswalk—a pedestrian you couldn't see because the car in front of you was blocking your view. So, instead of risking that possible pedestrian's life, please halt your vehicle for just a moment so you can figure out the situation before you drive over it.

SIGNALER MINGLER

Do you see any benefit in signalling while driving (or riding)?

> **ADH-YOU:** Sure, if I'm trying to change lanes, it's a good way to alert people that I want into a spot.

That's what I figured. For you, signalling other drivers is solely a service to you, because it helps you to get where you're going.

> **ADH-YOU:** Obviously! Is that supposed to be a revelation? Ha, ha, who did you think it was for? Guess what: when I'm having dinner and that's also for my own benefit.

Hee, hee, delightful comedy, indeed, YOU. But actually, signalling while driving can benefit the drivers receiving the blinking communication, as well.

> **ADH-YOU:** How?

Well, have you ever had someone *else's* signal save you time even if there was no benefit to them?

> **ADH-YOU:** Nope, never happened, bud. Their signal may sometimes be useful to me, but it's always of use to them at the same time.

Okay, well how about when a driver is opposite you in an intersection and they're signalling that they're going right: doesn't that make it easier for you to determine when it's safe to make a left turn?

> **ADH-YOU:** Sure, I guess.

And, in such a case, since *they* always could turn right regardless of your plans, is it not possible that they applied their signaller without any tangible driving benefit to themselves, while still benefitting other drivers?

> **ADH-YOU:** Nice try, Matlock. They were probably just doing it out of habit.

Well postulated, YOU. Nevertheless, my point is that it's *possible* to signal for the benefit of those travellers around you without, in each case, gaining anything in particular for yourself. And the more we all signal, the smoother we'll make the journey for each other. Plus, as the circle of signalling goes, the more considerate you are, the more considerate others may be of ADH-YOU.

> **ADH-YOU:** Fine. They'd better be.

Thanks, YOU!

Meanwhile, you may think that using your signaler is for the benefit only of your four-wheeled friends.

> **ADH-YOU:** Obviously. Who else would I signal for? The trees?

Hee, hee, good one, YOU. No, it turns out that pedestrians also benefit from accurate signaling by drivers.

> **ADH-YOU:** I'm not sure if that's a revelation or not. But I know I don't care.

Well put. Nevertheless, even when only pedestrians are around, I submit that the benefits of goodwill between you and those strange bi-pedal travellers will easily make up for the energy required for consistent signalling.

YOUR ALARM MAKING

This one's just for ADH-CAR-DESIGNERS. I understand that you need a noise-based way for car-owners to verify that their alarms are set when they've clicked them on with their key. But your frequent use of the common honk for this purpose is, I suspect, watering down the potency of its original meaning. Every thousand times a honk is used for the non-emergency purpose of confirming one's alarm, there will surely be a greater number of people who feel less urgency to check for possible danger when they hear a car honk on the road.

> **ADH-YOU-CAR-MAKER:** C'mon, I'm just trying to save a buck here. I see no reason to set up a special alarm noise feature when I can use the horn already built into the car.

Excellent point. But consider this: each time one of your customers has a delayed reaction when hearing a honk and consequently gets into a crash, and suffers an injury such that they can't drive anymore, they're less likely to buy more of your cars.

Chapter 15

Commuter You vs. Commuter You vs. Commuter You

I suspect that the battle for road space between pedestrians, cyclists, and horse-powered vehicles has been warring on for centuries. Well, finally, today, I am ready to declare that the real troublemaker is . . . drumroll . . . those suffering from ADH-ME!

> **ADH-YOU:** Gee, I didn't see that coming.

Hee, hee, can't blame an author for trying. In any case, with a wee bit more consideration from ADH-YOU towards your fellow travelers, life doesn't have to be so adversarial.

> **ADH-YOU:** I doubt it.

Fair enough. But consider this: while sometimes we are drivers (who don't like pedestrians), other times we are those very pedestrians (who don't like drivers). So when you are in Transit Mode A, I want you to remember how you felt when you were in Transit Mode B, and try to treat the B people as you wanted to be treated when *you* were a B person. This is similar to the fancy rapport-building skill known as "empathy." If you use it, you should find it easier to get along with your fellow travelers. Indeed, with that in mind, let us look at the greatest transportation rivalries.

DRIVER YOU VS. PEDESTRIANS

First, to DRIVER-YOU: most motorized worlds have crosswalks, where it's mandatory for drivers to stop when a pedestrian is either walking in them or attempting to do so.

> **ADH-YOU:** Seriously? I already have to stop for red lights, emergency vehicles, and idiots slamming on their brakes. Why should I have to make way for someone who doesn't even have the smarts to be driving a car?

I understand your irritation with pedestrians getting in your way, but sadly, those are the rules. Maybe you could consider this a matter of public safety. That is, the longer a pedestrian waits for cars to stop zipping through a legal crossing point, the more the would-be walker may become impatient and edge their way onto the road in the hopes of giving fly-by drivers a more obvious impetus to brake. Sometimes these informal games of chicken can cause accidents.

> **ADH-YOU:** Nah, that's their fault if they're going to put themselves at risk.

Okay, well, maybe once again you'd consider an argument from reciprocity. It turns out that many pedestrians are drivers, themselves, and so may remember your gesture when your roles are reversed (and *you're* the person stuck at a crosswalk).

> **ADH-YOU:** Nah, I don't need reciprocity. Cars'll stop when I tell 'em to.

Okay, I have only one arrow left in my quiver. It may be worth remembering that going to jail for accidentally wounding a pedestrian would be less fun than *not* going to jail.

> **ADH-YOU:** Fine. If you're going to play the jail card, I guess there's not much I can do.

Thanks, YOU!

Chapter 15: *Commuter You vs. Commuter You vs. Commuter You*

PEDESTRIAN YOU VS. DRIVERS

When you're wearing your pedestrian hat, you probably don't usually remember this, so let me remind you now: it turns out that driving can require concentration to make sure one doesn't collide with other commuters. As such, even though I know you are more important than drivers when you're walking, let's help them to avoid running you over.

> **ADH-YOU:** Of course I don't *plan* to get run over.

That's a good start, YOU. Next, I suggest that—even in cases where you have the right to cross a driver's path—you ensure that you have acquired some sort of a signal of acquiescence before you boldly go into the street. Once you receive this agreement from a driver, it doesn't hurt to give them a quick "thank you" wave.

> **ADH-YOU:** Why? They're legally obligated to stop.

You're totally right. But, given that many people don't follow that rule, why not offer those who *do* some appreciation for going against their driverly instincts? Moreover, just as you might thank a restaurant server for bringing you your meal even though you expected them to do so, it never hurts to thank someone when they do something for you. And—as I told the drivers above when I asked them to stop for you—such good manners may help provoke goodwill and increased compliance of this rule.

> **ADH-YOU:** Fine. Are we done here?

One last point—and this one may be the most controversial—when you come to a crossing point, and a driver politely complies with their legal obligation and stops for you, no one would complain if you were to walk across the street at a clip faster than a sloth's. If you have a medical reason to move gradually, then please go about your slowness, but, if not, why not let the driver know that—while you expected them to stop—you still think their time is worth something, too, and so are willing to make reasonably quick work of the delay?

> **ADH-YOU:** But I *don't* respect their time.

Okay, well, as ever, if you're not willing to do this out of politeness to the enemy, then consider doing it for your own sake, because such generosity will surely help to limit driver resentment towards pedestrians, which in turn may occasionally cause the four-wheelers to treat you better.

CYCLIST YOU VS. DRIVERS

In my experience, drivers don't notice us cyclists as consistently as they do other drivers. I suspect that this is largely because drivers' eyes have been trained through experience to look for other four-wheel creatures; as a result, two-wheelers are less conspicuous in their windshield of vision.

> **ADH-YOU:** Idiots!

I don't know about that. But whatever the cause of the driver blindness to cyclists, it does mean that you and I have a duty to our self-preservation to cycle defensively. For instance, whenever I'm on my bike, I assume—until proven otherwise—that each new driver I meet doesn't see me. So, even in cases where legally I have a right to manoeuvre into a particular space on the road, I sometimes won't if I haven't yet received a signal from the driver that they see me.

> **ADH-YOU:** I'm pretty noticeable, bud.

No doubt about it, attractive YOU! Nevertheless, there's a lot on the road for drivers to watch out for, so I suggest making sure they see your beautiful self before you cross their line of travel.

> **ADH-YOU:** Nah, I'm good. I haven't been run over so far.

Okay, well, if you're not willing to ride defensively, I suggest that you at least don't cycle *offensively*.

> **ADH-YOU:** What are you talking about?

Well, I'm ever amazed by cyclists who weave through traffic and force their way into driver-dominated lanes, again without any assurance that the nearest driver has noticed them and is allowing space for them.

> **ADH-YOU:** Why shouldn't I burrow in there? I should be treated no differently than a car.

Yes, in a perfect world, I would support your initiative, but, sadly, you haven't yet created a perfect world for us to live in. I don't dispute that you're always in the moral right when making cycling decisions, but sadly car handlers don't always see our moral right of way until they've run us over. Thus your insistence on claiming your rightful spot on the road on every occasion surely provokes drivers to dislike and fear cyclists and to either drive more aggressively around us, or far too passively (which can cause problems, too, as it's tricky to read such uncertain traffic).

> **ADH-YOU:** Okay, I'll think about being a cowardly cyclist. Next, please.

Okay, I also have a concern with your belief that it's okay to zip through red lights and stop signs without stopping. I once heard a cyclist rights' activist explain that the reason he felt justified in doing this was because it's inconvenient to have to stop one's bike for every red light.

> **ADH-CYCLIST-ADVOCATE:** Imagine if—while driving—at every red light you had to stop your car, unbuckle your seat belt, and then get out of the car.

I call misdirection! First of all, it is only a subset of cyclists who have speed-enhancing pedal-attached-shoes that can take part in the "unbuckle" part of the analogy. The rest of that argument, meanwhile, is overstated. Yes, it's annoying to stop when you've built up some hard-earned momentum, but it's also annoying to stop one's car. Regardless, I submit that traffic signals are not about convenience: they're about traffic safety. So, even if it's psychologically irritating to stop, so are serious injuries, and I don't see how we cyclists should be allowed special exemption from following stopping rules that are in place for the safety of everyone. Please desist.

DRIVER YOU VS. CYCLISTS

This section has been sponsored by our friends, the ADH-MA-LEVOLENTS, who, while driving near cyclists, often like to pound on their horn and/or yell at the vulnerable two-wheelers.

> **ADH-MALEVOLENT-YOU:** Heh, heh, yeah it's pretty funny.

Yes, I know this is a funny gag that amuses the entire population of your car when you do it. I wonder, though, if you might consider the perspective of the cyclist and the possibility that—

> **ADH-MALEVOLENT-YOU:** Let me guess. My honking reminds them that they're a loser who doesn't have a car.

Close, I was thinking that being startled from behind like that could provoke a dangerous mishap.

> **ADH-MALEVOLENT-YOU:** Nah, I haven't taken out any cyclists so far.

Yes, well, even if you don't cause a bike crash with your sudden honks (or shouts), please consider for a moment that being suddenly yelled at while riding is a stressful experience for the receiver. So I propose that you not scare innocent cyclists in your path unless you have proof that they have recently murdered someone.

> **ADH-MALEVOLENT-YOU:** Well, that's not much fun.

Yes, fair enough. So how about, instead, you just startle your hilarious friends by suddenly yelling at *them* while you're driving? That way, you'll know for certain you've got a victim who enjoys that type of humour.

> **ADH-MALEVOLENT-YOU:** But I'd rather laugh *with* my friends at someone else.

Brilliantly noted, YOU! I suppose directing your delightful shouts towards your buddies wouldn't be as satisfying, because it's more fun to bond with them over a victim who can't reply. I can appreciate that. So, I know it's a big ask, but do you think it would be possible to give up the sudden-honking/shouting humour altogether?

> **ADH-MALEVOLENT-YOU:** Sorry, bud, can't help you. I'm gonna need something from you in order to give it up.

Hmm, how about this: in exchange for curbing your participation in this behaviour, I offer you a story of ultimate victory for your side in the "barking driver vs. cyclist" wars? If you accept this deal, you may read the story, *Revenge of the Heckled*, below. If not, please skip ahead; maybe go yell at a baby in a stroller while I share the following juicy tale with other readers.

Revenge of the Heckled (Exclusive Reading)

I am often baffled by the drive-by hecklers I encounter during my bike travel. You see, even though I am sure they are hollering wonderfully witty remarks, the speed of their travel almost always makes the cleverness unintelligible from the perspective of a comparatively slow bike rider who has wind in his ears. In fact, the exhortations of drive-by shouters usually sound a little something like, "Mouoooble Doouuble!"

I have frequently wanted to inform such passing poets of the fogginess of their communication, but they usually drive past too quickly for me to reply. One evening, though, I was pleased to be offered an opportunity to respond.

As I travelled down a hill in my neighbourhood, a group of comedic geniuses spotted my flashing bike light and abruptly interrupted my train of thought.

COMEDIC GENIUSES: Mouoooble Doouuble!

I was startled into nearly losing my balance. Once I caught myself, I looked up at the fleeing verbal assaulters and I lamented their ignorance. They would never know that their noise sounded merely like a yawn fighting a groan, and that I could not hear any of their impeccable wit. But just then the scurrying hecklers stopped: they had been blocked by a red light. I quickened my pedalling and sprinted towards them. It was my turn to heckle.

COMEDIC GENUIS: That was harsh-awesome, man. I was like, "Mouoooble!"

COMEDIC GENIUS FRIEND: And I was like "Dooouuble!"

Chapter 15: *Commuter You vs. Commuter You vs. Commuter You*

COMEDIC GENIUS: Hey, do you wanna punk that girl on the tricycle up there?

SETH (*suddenly yelling into comedic geniuses' car window*): Mouoooble Doouuble!

Yes! I'd given them a taste of their own shout-mumbling! As I subsequently peered into their vehicle while I continued riding past, I was delighted to spot four startled teen-entertainers, who, for a moment, seemed to be without retort. This caused me great grinning until I looked forward again to discover I was aimed, with my reasonable clip, directly at the same red light that had stopped the acerbic commentators. There wasn't time for me to brake safely, so the best thing to do was to make a right turn, but it was too tight an angle at my speed, so my manoeuvre turned into an out-of-control swerve. I just barely kept my balance as I completed the operation, but not without looking as though I could have fallen at any moment.

Cruelly, this awkward result was not lost on my former hecklers who immediately opened their windows to broadcast their laughter for my blushing ears.

MOTOR-PSYCHO YOU

I've left you motorcyclists till the end of this discussion because I find you to be a difficult group to categorize. You are as vulnerable as bicyclists—perhaps even more so—and so your existence is another good reason for drivers to earnestly scan for two-wheeled travellers.

Moreover, travel by motorcycle is, I understand, more considerate to Mother Nature than other forms of travel, so—even if going green is not your official motor-vation—your mode of transit deserves some respect.

> **ADH-YOU:** Accepted. What's the catch?

Well anticipated, YOU. I wonder what we should do about the fact that some of you motorcyclists set your machines to be so loud (beyond what's legally allowed in many places) that you disrupt the well-being of those you pass. (Loud and aggressive sounds such as those coming from your exhaust pipe are stressful to human beings and so can provoke and exacerbate health problems.) On first glance, the answer is that we should strictly enforce the noise laws.

> **ADH-YOU:** No way, man. Loud pipes save lives.

Yes, I've heard your contention that possessing such angry-sounding vehicles helps you ride safer because you are more conspicuous to drivers and so are less likely to be run over. As someone who knows what it's like be invisible to the 4-wheeled, I can't deny that there could be merit to this notion. Indeed, when I put aside my bias against such ear-scarring motorcycles, I can't conclusively say that you're wrong that you remain safer by revving your engine. I searched the internet for such proof, but painfully I could not find it.

And yet, oddly, I am also not able to find evidence that you are in fewer accidents than the motorcyclists who don't rejig their engine to screech at those nearby. In fact, given that those riding quieter motorcycles can better hear danger coming towards them, they may, in fact, be the safer ones. So I can't help wondering if you loud riders have invented this excuse retroactively to justify your already preferred behaviour—that of acquiring attention via your loud bikes.

> **ADH-YOU:** Nope. That's just a bonus.

Before you lock in that answer, I request that you look deep into your ego and consider whether you *really* set your motorbike's voice so harshly because you think it's safer. Or is it possible that your motivation is actually based on your desire to build your tough image? If the latter, then maybe you could construct your reputation via different means—perhaps something that isn't disruptive to other people's enjoyment of life? For instance, it is clear that wearing bright colours *does* make motorcyclists more conspicuous. I know a rainbow jacket might not be as cool as ear-drum-popping pipes, but since you claim safety is your *first* concern, I can't see how you can argue against it. Just remember, "Loud clothing saves lives."

Chapter 16

Customer You

Chapter 16: *Customer You*

You may be surprised to discover that, as a customer, you have some responsibilities as well as—

> **ADH-YOU:** Wait a minute. Isn't the customer is always right?

That's the cliché, certainly, but—

> **ADH-YOU:** *Always* right?

Yes, that's what the phrase says, but—

> **ADH-YOU:** Thank you. Then why do we need this chapter?

Well, I have just a few tiny tips to make you feel not only right, but morally righteous while you're fighting for your customer dreams.

> **ADH-YOU:** Fine, but if you try to make me feel wrong in any way, I'm skipping this chapter.

Understood. Thank you for the warning.

BEFORE YOU RANT

You work hard for your money, or maybe you don't, but in either case, it's yours and you expect value for it.

> **ADH-YOU:** Obviously.

So, when you go into a store, you have a certain expectation of service and quality; if you don't receive one or both, then—correct me if I'm wrong—you feel it's your job to make it clear that you are unhappy.

> **ADH-YOU:** You are not wrong, but why do I get the feeling you're going to try to make me *feel* wrong?

No, no, I have no disagreement with your frustration. But there are three obligations I'd like you to consider before you commence your rant at the customer service person in front of you.

(1) JUSTIFY YOUR CONTEMPT:

Is the circumstance about which you are poised to unleash your righteous anger based on genuine unfairness towards yourself, or might it be more of a pet frustration?

> **ADH-YOU:** We already agreed that I'm always justified.

Oh, yes, of course. I just mean: is it unequivocal mistreatment of you, or might it be just something that irked you? Before you answer, consider the following incident, which occurred while I was working alone at a bread store:

> **CUSTOMER:** Hi, where's the nearest gas station?
> **SETH:** Oh, sorry, I don't know—
> **CUSTOMER:** You don't know where a gas station is?
> **SETH:** Sorry, yeah, I'm new to the area.
> **CUSTOMER:** Well, where do you get *your* gas?
> **SETH:** Sorry, I don't drive.

The customer rolled his eyes over into the back of his head and stomped out of the store. I could empathize with his irritation, and I probably asked my co-worker for the information during our next shift change, so that I'd know just in case another customer asked me for gas station directions in the future. But the fact was, as a bread-store clerk, I hadn't been trained on local business locations; my ignorance was innocent and in no way contradicted the store's advertised purpose to provide bread to the public. And, yet, by the disdain with which I was treated, I felt as though I'd betrayed a sacred bread provider oath.

I'm not suggesting that the ADH-CUSTOMER shouldn't have been annoyed—he was now going to have to walk all the way next door to Subway to acquire the answer to his inquiry—but I wonder if he needed to aim his displeasure so aggressively at me?

> **ADH-YOU**: Well, if I were the one snapping at you, I'm sure I would have had a good reason.

Of course! You always have a good reason to be annoyed. That is never in dispute. But the question is: *has the person or business at whom you're sending your wrath done something clearly wrong?* If you're not sure, try asking yourself this:

> **ADH-YOU**: If I had been the cause of this problem, would I have forgiven myself?

While you ponder that, let's move on to my second request.

(2) JUSTIFY YOUR VICTIM:

In situations where you *do* have a legitimate beef with a business: would you mind asking yourself if you're talking to the right person?

> **ADH-YOU**: What are you babbling about now?

Well, in many cases, the person to whom you're directing your ire is, in fact, simply enforcing a policy as instructed by their employer; they likely have little to no discretion around its implementation (unless they don't mind losing their job on a moment's notice). For instance:

CUSTOMER: How come this Heidelberg rye bread is ten cents more that it was yesterday?

SETH: Apparently, the price of rye has gone up, so—

CUSTOMER: That's B.S.. That's just the company line.

SETH: Um, well, that's what I was told.

CUSTOMER: Come on. You can do better than that. You don't have to be such a corporate stooge.

SETH: Well, that's what I was told. But if you'd like to make a complaint—

CUSTOMER: Yeah, a lot of good that'll do me.

Please don't misunderstand me. I do think there's room to let the frontline representative know about your displeasure so that they can pass you and/or the complaint upwards, but I wonder if you need to ruin the employee's day in the process.

> **ADH-YOU:** Hey, you're the customer service person standing right in front of me. You wouldn't want me to be rude by *ignoring* you, now would you?

Well played, YOU! That segues nicely to my final question for you to consider.

(3) JUSTIFY YOUR TONE:

If you are justified in your anger, and you are speaking to the right person, is there a polite means available to resolve the dispute?

> **ADH-YOU:** Yeah, if you'd like to politely give me what I'm asking for, I'll politely accept it.

Nicely done. Nevertheless, I'd just like to point out that, regardless of whether the person you're dealing with is in the wrong—

> **ADH-YOU:** They are.

Regardless, civil assertiveness can sometimes be a meaningful middle ground between hostility and taking on the role of a doormat. Not only is such graciousness good practice for the sake of general civility in our society, it's also handy in those rare cases when you eventually discover that, oops, you were wrong.

> **ADH-YOU:** We agreed we weren't going to consider that option.

Right you are ... but ... um ... maybe a family member gave you some wrong information, which you—quite rightly—had every reason to believe was correct. Is that possible?

> **ADH-YOU:** I guess it's possible. I'm the only one in my family who's not an idiot.

Right, so in such an unfortunate circumstance, the moment you realize you received inaccurate information from your lesser relative, you will be grateful if you conducted the conversation with the customer service person with civil language and intonation.

> **ADH-YOU:** Why?

Well, because then you'll have no reason to be embarrassed. Even though you turned out to be "wrong," you weren't rude to the clerk during your time of being incorrect, and therefore you won't have to take the walk of shame on your exit.

> **ADH-YOU:** I've never been in a position to take such a walk. However, I do not foresee that I would enjoy it.

Exactly! So, to avoid that cruel result, I suggest that, when you're shopping, you act as though you're a guest in someone else's entrepreneurial operation. Yes, you're there to negotiate a deal with them, but it is still *their* place of business. If you don't like the way they cook their fries, you can point it out if you think it'll make your experience better now or in the future, but it also may just be that they have settled on different cooking priorities than you, so maybe you can simply choose a different vendor next time.

DISCRIMINATING MANNERS

Another tiny thing I'd like to point out is that, when you're buying items from shops, or fast food restaurants, or newspaper stands, you are welcome—if you like—to look the servants in the eyes and even smile. I promise it won't hurt, and you may find that they will smile back as though they are surprised to be treated for a moment like a fellow human being. Consider the story, *Bub*, below.

Bub

One day, while he was working at a coffee shop, my brother witnessed the following exchange between a father (whom we'll call "Bub"), his son ("Bub Junior"), and a smiley barista:

> **BARISTA (smiling to Bub Senior):** Hi there.
>
> **BUB SENIOR (looking up at the menu board):** I need a tall coffee and a short hot chocolate.
>
> **BARISTA:** Would you like that for here or to go?
>
> **BUB SENIOR:** What?
>
> **BARISTA:** Would you like your drinks in for-here cups or to-go cups?
>
> **BUB SENIOR:** Oh, whatever . . . um . . . just regular cups.
>
> **BUB JUNIOR:** Daddy, I want one of those candies!
>
> **BUB SENIOR (with a firm, but fair voice):** Now, Bubby, is that the way we ask for something? What have you forgotten to say?

BUB JUNIOR (*annoyed*): Please.

Meanwhile, my observing brother couldn't help thinking how ironic it was that Bub Senior—a definitively manners-free customer—was lecturing his son on the importance of manners. It seemed that, for Bub, there was a scarcity of polite manners available to him, and so he was only able to spend them on the elite people in his life.

FROM RED TAPE TO RED FACE

You know how you hate red tape and bureaucrats?

ADH-YOU: Bureaucrats? More like moron-crats.

Good one! Yeah, I'm with you: it's so—

ADH-YOU: Wait! I've got a better one. Set me up again.

Okay, you know how you hate bureaucrats?

ADH-YOU: Bureaucrats? More like bore-o-crats.

Nice! That *was* better. So, like I was saying, I agree with you: it's so annoying when you have to jump through bureaucratic hoops to do something simple. Nevertheless, red tape is generally derived from experience. Infrastructure-creators have learned over the centuries that if they set up a system with malleable, common-sense rules, the general ADH-PUBLIC will exploit their lack of rigid definition. Thus, we have red tape—often with silly-seeming results. I'm sure you're right that over-zealous bureaucrats can go too far and protect against farfetched risks, but try to remember that red-tape purveyors have gotten in trouble before because of your imaginative interpretation of their guidelines, and so they must safeguard against *all* possible "confusions."

> **ADH-YOU:** Nice try, bud. You're not gonna convince me on this one.

Fair enough. If red tape still seems ridiculous to you, feel free to mock it on your own time. However, it would be nice if you could remember that the person who is implementing the rules on behalf of an organization is often doing so at the behest of someone with powers greater than their own. Would you be willing, then, to not take your aggressive irritation out on the person who's following the bureaucracy set by someone with more power than them?

> **ADH-YOU:** I have to be honest with you. I can't promise that. Also, I'm not even sure I know what you're talking about.

Okay, consider how you would behave in the following scenario:

> **AIRPORT ATTENDANT:** Do you have any liquids in your carry-on?
>
> **ADH-YOU:** Yeah, I always bring an orange juice with me—low blood sugar.
>
> **AIRPORT ATTENDANT:** Well, unfortunately, for security purposes, we don't allow outside beverages on the plane. There will be juice available on board.
>
> **ADH-YOU:** But where am I gonna put the juice I brought?
>
> **AIRPORT ATTENDANT:** You're welcome to drink it and then come back.
>
> **ADH-YOU:** But I'm not thirsty now!

> **AIRPORT ATTENDANT:** Well, I'm sorry. You can't bring it on the plane.
>
> **ADH-YOU:** Oh, c'mon! Do you really think I'm planning to do something sinister with a bottle of juice?
>
> **AIRPORT ATTENDANT:** No, I don't. But airport security dictates that I can't let you take it on board.
>
> **ADH-YOU:** I've been a law-abiding citizen all my life. I think you can make an exception in my case.

Now, I wonder if you might consider the possibility that, even if the airport attendant *did* have the authority to override their bosses' orders, they don't actually *know* you: so what basis do you think they have for giving you exceptional status?

> **ADH-YOU:** I've never committed a crime in my life. They can look me up if they want. I've got nothing to hide.

Okay, let's try this from another angle. Watch how you behaved towards my sister years ago when she was working at a post office:

> **ADH-YOU:** You have a letter here for me.
>
> **SETH'S POSTAL SISTER:** Your name, please?
>
> **ADH-YOU:** Mr. ADH-ME.
>
> **SETH'S POSTAL SISTER:** Okay, here it is. I'll just need some I.D.
>
> **ADH-YOU:** I don't have it on me. I biked here.
>
> **SETH'S POSTAL SISTER:** Okay, then, sorry, I can't give this to you now—it's registered mail, which means that I need proof of who you are.
>
> **ADH-YOU:** Trust me, I'm ME. Why would anyone impersonate me?
>
> **SETH'S POSTAL SISTER:** I have no idea. But the person who sent the letter registered it, which means

they paid for me to verify the receiver's identity as matching the name on the package.

ADH-YOU: But she sent it to *me*, which means she's obviously okay with *me* getting it!

SETH'S POSTAL SISTER: Yes, but she paid for me to verify your identity, so I'm in no position to argue with her.

ADH-YOU: So you're calling me a liar?

Here's a good way to think about this one: if, let's say, someone came along, impersonated you, and took your letter for themselves, would you be angry?

> **ADH-YOU:** You're damn right I would! It's *my* mail.

That's a good point, YOU! Indeed, in such a hypothetical case, how could my postal worker sister be so negligent as to take a stranger's word that they were you, when of course you are the one and only you? And, unfortunately, by the same evidence standard, without *your* identification, my sister had no way of knowing whether you were you or that stranger impersonating you.

> **ADH-YOU:** Why?

Well, you see, an important lesson of this book is that—as wonderful as you are—strangers are incorrigibly ignorant of you. So they may require more than just your own intuitive understanding of your YOU-NESS before they'll give you your due.

Chapter 16: *Customer You*

THE "HOW ARE YOU?" PARADOX

Please consider the following phone conversation between you and an employee at a company with which you'd like to do business.

> **EMPLOYEE:** Hello, Photography Solutions, how may I may help you?
>
> **ADH-YOU:** How are you?
>
> **EMPLOYEE:** Um, good thanks, how are you?
>
> **ADH-YOU:** Good. I need a favour.

Does that sound familiar?

> **ADH-YOU:** Yes! Finally, you're not trying to make me look bad. That's my trick for when I need something from someone. I ask them how they are. Then they feel all warm and fuzzy, and are more likely to give me what I want. Awesome, eh?

I see your point, but I'm afraid there's a small issue with this technique.

> **ADH-YOU:** What's the problem this time?

Well, it's actually awkward for the receiver of the call to be asked how they are before they know who you are.

> **ADH-YOU:** I don't follow.

Well, imagine a stranger came up to you and asked you how you were.

> **ADH-YOU:** Sounds like a very nice stranger!

And maybe they are. But unfortunately when someone who hasn't introduced themselves to you asks how you are, it can feel like they're jumping ahead in the basic order of social operations. So I think you'll find that when people receive your "How are you?" they're not so much feeling warm and fuzzy, but instead confused as to *why* you're skipping a social step.

> **ADH-YOU:** Seriously? Asking a friendly question is causing them to panic?

I know; it's weird. But here's the thing: many of your ADH-BRETHREN have long been using the "How are you?" technique in the same way that you have, i.e. as an attempt to manoeuvre your way into the receiver's goodwill. Consequently, most people who have ever answered phones for a business will quickly sense from your faux "How are you?" that you are probably about to try to manipulate them.

> **ADH-YOU:** Are you serious? They know my intentions even when I'm being friendly? Are they psychic?

Well guessed. But there's actually a more logical explanation. As mentioned, the "How are you?" precursor to asking for a favour is so common in the customer service world that it's hard not to notice the pattern.

> **ADH-YOU:** Well, this is a twist. So I don't have to be nice anymore when I'm talking to businesses on the phone?!

Not quite. Being friendly with people you want to do business with is still a welcome policy. However, when your supposed friendliness comes across as manipulative, it won't *feel* friendly to the receiver. So, instead of rushing in with a "How are you?" at the start of your phone conversations with customer service employees, I invite you to begin by introducing yourself or your request, while maintaining a friendly tone of voice throughout your interaction. Then, if the discussion develops, you're welcome to throw in some friendly questions at a more natural point in the interaction.

Chapter 17

Presenting You

> **NOTE:** I will be focussing my presentation examples on adult scenarios (including university lectures and public workshops), but if you're a child reader you can certainly apply some of these ideas to your wee ADH-EXISTENCE.

The classroom is one of those arenas where your ADH-PERSONALITY shines through, am I right?

> **ADH-YOU:** Nailed it.

Yes, as an elementary (and perhaps high school?) student, you saw school as a place where you were celebrated for your every opinion and creative offering. So now, as an adult student, you associate any classroom with those fond memories, and so, when you attend, you're itching to get your ideas out there to be cheered on again. But there's just one small problem: now that you're an adult, the teacher will be most proud of you if you're able to holster your feedback in certain situations.

> **ADH-YOU:** Awe, man.

I know. Life's strange.

STUDENT YOU

Question Questions (That Are Not Too Bright)

Let me clear something up: there *is* such a thing as a stupid question.

> **ADH-YOU:** Of course there is! It's simple logic: there are stupid people, and some of them must sometimes ask questions, and so, voilà, stupid questions.

Hee, hee, good one, YOU! Although, that's probably not what the cliché-framers mean when they say there are no stupid questions; instead, they intend to say that there are no questions that are stupid to ask because the answers to them may help you learn.

And I see the cliché-makers' point: even stupid misunderstandings can provoke useful questions. My objection, though, is to questions that are formed without consideration of their circumstance. For instance, if a question has just been answered, then instead of posing your replica query anyway (on the basis that you had it queued up, and/or you think it makes you look good to ask it), go ahead and let the just-given answer waft its way into your brain to meet your curiosity. If the answer offered doesn't solve your confusion, *then* feel free to offer a follow-up question.

Similarly, sometimes someone will say something that intrigues you, and so you'll put your hand up to comment. But, then tragically, the topic will change before you're called upon by the moderator. Nevertheless, you will feel so attached to the comment that you wanted to make that you will force it into the conversation anyway.

> **ADH-YOU:** No, I wouldn't do that.

Well, let's have a look at a clip (from a philosophical workshop on ethics):

> **MODERATOR:** So who thinks lying is *always* bad?
>
> **ADH-YOU (*in your head*):** I lied to my mom once and I felt really bad about it. So I realized forever-more that lying is bad.
>
> **AUDIENCE MEMBER:** I think lying is bad because if we can't trust each other, society will devolve into chaos.
>
> **MODERATOR:** Okay, so that's an interesting argument for why, in general, we should aim to tell the truth. But what if a convicted murderer asked you where your house is, would you tell them?

Chapter 17: *Presenting You*

AUDIENCE MEMBER: Well, have they paid their debt to society?

MODERATOR: Maybe. But let's say, for whatever reason, someone who you think is dangerous demands to know the location of your child. Do you tell the truth?

ADH-YOU (*importantly, to the group*): I'd like to point out that I lied to my mom once and I felt really bad about it. So I realized then that lying is bad!

Do you remember saying something like that during a philosophical workshop?

> **ADH-YOU:** Maybe.

And do you see how your comment—while a wonderful and relevant answer to the moderator's initial question—has become antiquated in the unfolding conversation, which is now much more precise?

> **ADH-YOU:** But it was a brilliant point, don't you think?

It certainly was! Nevertheless, your timing of it, sadly, didn't measure up.

Question Questions (That Are Too Bright)

There is also such a thing as a question that is too smart.

> **ADH-YOU:** Well, then I guess I'm going to be guilty of this one.

Well admitted, YOU! So—

> **ADH-YOU:** I'm looking forward to the example on this one.

Right, so sometimes you will be particularly proud of yourself for knowing something about the topic that is presented and so you will feel an urge to let the others in attendance know about your expertise. If you're feeling passive you'll convey your expertise by nodding vehemently during the lecture. However, if you're in a more assertive mood, you will "ask" a question that directly highlights your brilliance:

> **PRESENTER:** Welcome to "Modern Hockey Trends." I'm Dr. Hockey Stick. Scoring in the NHL is down from what it was in the '80s and early '90s. Experts believe that—Yes?
>
> **ADH-YOU:** Well, of course Wayne Gretzky is the only player ever to break the 200 points barrier, which he did four times in the '80s. Mario Lemieux came close with 199 points in 1989, so do you think anyone will ever cross 200 points again?

As a hockey fan, I find this to be an interesting query, but unfortunately it seems to have accidentally disrupted the flow of the presentation, which wasn't dealing with specifics such as yours just yet. My request is for you to let your speaker lead the conversation, and for you to wait for your impressive question to become relevant before you ask it.

> **ADH-YOU:** Sounds boring.

Yes, I admit there are disadvantages to waiting. For instances:

(1) The speaker might steer the discussion away from your showpiece material, thus muting your contribution altogether, or, worse,

(2) The speaker might answer the question before you have an opportunity to ask it, thus destroying any chance you had of impressing with it.

> **ADH-YOU:** Well then I'm just going to ask my question before they can ruin it.

I see your point. But there is a teensy problem with that strategy. It turns out that—when you ask a question solely for the purpose of demonstrating your brilliance—most in attendance will internally smirk at your ego-driven query. So, despite your best intentions, such inquiries actually harm your reputation more than they enhance it. So, counterintuitively, your best bet for improving your reputation is to discontinue these sorts of self-promoting questions.

The Smartest Person In The Room

If you have an especially enthusiastic ego, you may go beyond performance-questioning to performance-commenting—and even "correcting" the speaker—to let everyone in attendance know you have the brightest intellect in the room.

> **ADH-YOU:** What's wrong with that? I *am* the smartest.

Yes, you know that, and I know that, but the problem is when you try extra hard to get this point across, you may prove irritating to your fellow humans.

> **ADH-YOU:** Why? I'm just making them aware that I'm there, and available to help improve their learning.

Yes, it's baffling that anyone wouldn't appreciate your magnanimity, but I have a theory that might help to explain their reticence. Even though you are the smartest, the audience may have specifically attended the lecture to learn what the alleged expert thinks, and so they may feel that your contributions are getting in the way of that discovery.

> **ADH-YOU:** Seriously?

I'm afraid so. Consequently, it may be worth letting the so-called expert finish their thoughts before you correct them. In fact, allowing yourself to "learn" from the speaker may enable you to supplement your genius with further knowledge to destroy your future competitors.

> **ADH-YOU:** Fine. But I'm not the only one who talks back to the speaker, you know?

Good point, YOU. In fact, the story, *Problem Solved*, below is an example of one your ADH-RIVALS stretching her self-confidence so far to outsmart her presenter that she nearly broke her own ego in the process.

Problem Solved

One of my all-time favourite episodes of audience superiority comes from an alternative high school where it was up to the students to determine what they were interested in, and then to ask their instructors to teach them about those subjects. One day, the students decided they wanted to learn about philosophy, and since my aunt had been a grad student in the subject, they asked her to teach them about it. (And, because I was a philosophy student in university at the time, I attended the lecture as a guest viewer.)

My aunt began the presentation by explaining that philosophy wasn't easy, because every notion can be challenged, so one constantly has to examine and justify every belief. She went on to say that perhaps the most difficult problem in all of philosophy is the "mind–body" problem, which—after thousands of years of study amongst many great philosophers—had not yet been answered to the satisfaction of many. She then began to give a brief description of the problem, but her exposition was interrupted by a student, who had already spotted the answer to the great question.

> **ADH-STUDENT:** Well it's just X, right?

Wow. Thousands of supreme minds had failed to see what this young brain had instantly recognized! It was perhaps the single greatest epiphany in history. Although, I suppose there was one other possibility: maybe the student had accidentally over-simplified the problem such that her apparent solution didn't take into account every nuance of the argument. I doubt that's the case because she seemed pretty confident she'd solved the issue. Nevertheless, on the tiny chance her grand solution were to be proven insufficient, the damage to her ego would have been significant.

Similarly, it would be tough to admit, after claiming to have cured cancer, "Oops, sorry, I actually only cured how to spell it."

The Windiest Person in the Room

Meanwhile, when—during a presentation—you announce loudly and conspicuously to your neighbour every brilliant thought that comes to your brain, please be advised that such showmanship can inadvertently be disruptive to your fellow audience members, and disconcerting to the presenter.

Consider the below story, *Windbag*, for an example of an ADH-EGO going wild during others' presentations.

Windbag

A few years ago, I attended an academic conference at which a fellow possessing a grand ego sat close to the podium during others' presentations and attempted to entertain anyone near him by providing commentary about the commentary. It was one of the most impressive displays of ADH-ME I have ever witnessed. In fact, he even inspired me to send the following Twitter comment:

> **SETH TWEET:** Dear Windbag: I know you want to impress with your every sweet digress, but if you talk over those you address, sometimes more is less.

I hope you get from that message that, although your and Mr. Windbag's ADH-DIGRESSIONS are indeed impressive, if you unleash them when someone else has been given run of the microphone, you may create the impression that you think your random thoughts are more significant than the prepared work of the speaker.

> **ADH-YOU:** And they are.

Right, sorry. But, even though that's true, your best bet is not to advertise it, because ANTI-ADH-YOU bigots will not be able to accept that you're that much smarter than everyone else (and so they may rudely call you a "windbag" in their jealousy-fuelled Twitter accounts).

Your Washroom Break

I am often surprised that at significant training sessions, some adults will take washroom breaks in the middle of important moments of the information session. Most training events include scheduled intermissions, so as adults, I'm not sure why we can't plan our physical needs around them.

> **ADH-YOU:** What if it's an emergency?

Yes, I'm sure "emergencies" happen, but I suspect they happen much less frequently than the occurrence of people leaving the room merely to quench their immediate preferences. In fact, I suspect that participants of this mid-presentation washroom-seeking behaviour simply do not like feeling in any way uncomfortable and so they've decided that their preference trumps the need to stay with the lecture.

> **ADH-YOU:** Would someone get this man a gold star? Of course that's why I do it. You really expect me to be uncomfortable?

No, of course not. I would never ask that of you, but I will point out that such breaks are more disruptive than you may think. Along with the physical diversion, your coming and going may be pedagogically disruptive to the presenter on duty, who may be about to say something crucial and so, upon noticing your absence, feel obligated to hold it.

> **ADH-YOU:** Ironically enough.

Yes, good one, YOU! So, if at all feasible, perhaps you could consider planning ahead to avoid mid-presentation washroom breaks.

In fact, you might notice that presenters, who have the same design of bladders as the rest of us, almost never excuse themselves mid-presentation. Are they super human? Or, even more impressive, are they better than you?

> **ADH-YOU:** Obviously not!

I believe you. But, if you want to prove so to everyone else, you could try leaving the room to visit the water closet no more often than your presenters do.

QUESTION & ANSWER YOU

Question & Dancer

At every speaking event or panel discussion that I have ever attended, the Q&A portion of proceedings is a cringe-collecting ordeal as otherwise nice-seeming people step up to the coveted microphone and confidently babble out untamed swarms of opinions, pet speculations, lengthy anecdotes, and general verbal meanderings while the esteemed speakers whom the rest of us came to hear nod politely. We're all used to such hearty-winded folks in our daily lives, but it is baffling to comprehend when there is a time-limited lineup of people behind the pontificator awaiting their turn to ask a question of the elite people on the other side of the podium.

My judgmental coding has always told me to dismiss such babbling questioners as self-absorbed social simpletons who deserve only an eye roll of analysis.

> **ADH-YOU:** Wow, harsh.

It's true. However, I have recently acquired a tentative epiphany. Maybe the circuitous orators know not what they do. Perhaps they have a genuine hope to add something useful to the public conversation, but in the moment of offering, the anxiety of suddenly residing in front of a crowd provokes their thinking to become obstructed by fireworks of nerves. In such a state of anxiety, it is understandable that many of us might lose track of our noble plans for our question. Whether I am right or wrong in this generous assessment of the baffling babbling of eager questioners, I am nearly certain that they are not intending to be as annoying as their results. Instead, something in their psychology is blocking them from seeing their impact on everyone else in the room.

> **ADH-YOU:** Nope, I'm never nervous. So whatever you're insulting me for here has nothing to do with that.

Fair enough. In that case, it's your ADH-ME that's causing the issue. So, if you don't mind, I'd like to give you a little workshop on how to ask questions in Q&A that won't annoy the rest of the audience into suicidal thoughts.

> **ADH-YOU:** What do I have to do?

Okay, I imagine you're at public presentation on a topic you're interested in.

> **ADH-YOU:** Okay, how about presentation on ME?

Great idea, YOU. But let's get a little more specific. How about we focus on your trouble with being a bit of a braggart? Let's say you go to a talk by an expert on the risks of bragging too much.

> **ADH-YOU:** I like it! I've got a question for that jackass.

Okay, great, so imagine the jackass, whom I'll refer to as Dr. Anti-Brag, has just finished his presentation in which he argues that when we brag a lot we actually end up reducing people's appreciation of us. You're first up to ask a question. Let's see how you do:

> **MODERATOR:** Thank you, Dr. Anti-Brag, for that lovely presentation. It's now time for Q&A, and I see we have a lot of people in line to ask a question and we only have 15 minutes, so could everyone please not give a sermon. We're looking for nice and concise questions so that we can get in as many as possible.
>
> **ADH-YOU:** Right, thanks. Hi There, Dr. Anti-Brag. That was an interesting talk, I guess. I liked some of your jokes. But there was a lot of stuff I didn't agree with—like, I don't really see why someone would mock me for being honest about how awesome I am. I mean, are people against telling the truth now? Do you really want people to be all fake humble and pretend like they don't realize they're awesome? No. We'd all rather an honest person. Anyway, the other thing I've noticed is—

Okay, sorry, can I stop you there?

> **ADH-YOU:** Um, okay, but I was just getting warmed up.

I see that, yes. But I'm just noticing that you've already put in 20 seconds of introduction, and we haven't even gotten to the content of your question yet.

> **ADH-YOU:** Right, so?

Well, it's just that, there are probably a lot of people in line to speak to the presenter, and at the rate you're going, your question is going to take up half of the Q&A session. Ideally, it's best to keep your question to no more than thirty seconds.

> **ADH-YOU:** Thirty seconds? How?

Well, maybe you could trim your general thoughts on Dr. Anti-Brag's presentation and cut straight to your question.

> **ADH-YOU [Long sigh]:** I was just being polite, but, fine, I'll cut the intro.

Awesome, thanks. So can you try again?

> **ADH-YOU:** So, as I was saying, thank you for taking my question, Dr. Anti-Brag. I have three comments and a question for you—

Right, sorry to interrupt again, but—and maybe you didn't hear?—but just a minute ago in her introduction to the Q&A, the moderator requested that everyone just ask questions and not provide sermons.

> **ADH-YOU:** Yeah, I'm *asking* a question.

Yes, but you're also prognosticating three comments. That sounds suspiciously like a serm—

> **ADH-YOU:** What are you talking about? Three comments aren't the same as a sermon.

Right, of course, but I think the moderator was being playful with the term "sermon," and just meant to request that everyone try to hone their commentary down to a single interrogative statement.

> **ADH-YOU:** But my comments are a vital set up for my question.

I'm sure they are. And, if this were any other sort of conversation, I wouldn't pester you about it, but unfortunately there are a lot of people who want to ask a question, and even more who want to hear Dr. Anti-Brag speak, so if you talk for a long time, we'll have fewer questions, and less time for Dr. Anti-Brag to reply.

> **ADH-YOU:** Okay, fine, I'll be quick.

Great, go ahead.

> **ADH-YOU:** So it seems to me that people confuse self-awareness for bragging. Like, I've won several tennis awards, and so, when people talk about tennis, I always make sure they know that I'm an elite tennis player. Actually, I was talking to my friend, Jane, about this yesterday. She had this funny idea that people criticize us for bragging because they're jealous, which makes me realize that there's a lot more jealousy in the world than I thought, and—

Okay, can you hang on again?

> **ADH-YOU:** What? What's happening?

Ah, yes, just as I thought. I believe you were in a bit of trance there while you were asking your question.

> **ADH-YOU:** How do you mean?

Well, you were just kind of following your words obediently wherever they went without really checking to see if they were helping you get to the heart of your question.

> **ADH-YOU:** Yeah, I was really on a roll, wasn't I? I felt like I was all by myself, just riffing, without anyone else around. It was pretty freeing actually.

I can imagine. And, if this were a therapy session or a poetry slam, I'd be cheering you on. But, since we're in this limited-time Q&A set up, I think it would be best if you tried to plan out your question to avoid unnecessary tangents.

> **ADH-YOU:** Unnecessary tangents? I was telling a funny story.

Fair enough. If that story was vital to your introduction, please ignore my suggestion. But I suspect the story was more of a spontaneous aside than a planned expedition.

> **ADH-YOU:** Yeah, it just popped into my brain in the moment. So what?

Well, it's just that, if you indulge every passing sidetrack that visits your brain while you're at the microphone, it will be very difficult to find your way back to the point of your inquiry.

> **ADH-YOU:** That reminds me of the time my sister got lost on her way to work because she decided to take a shortcut around some construction, and she got mixed up which way the water was.

Yeah, that's funny. To avoid your sister's fate, I suggest you create a quick verbal map for yourself of the key points you'll need in order to establish your question.

> **ADH-YOU:** I had that before! But you said I couldn't make all three of my comments before my question!

Right, I see how that's confusing. Yet—correct me if I'm wrong—but I believe those three comments were going to be three self-contained presentations with their own beginnings, middles, and ends.

> **ADH-YOU:** So?

Well, each of those comments is a separate entity worthy of a question of its own. Whereas, I'm looking for just the key trimmed-down elements that will give your lone, specific question its best chance of being understood. Does that make sense?

> **ADH-YOU:** I guess, but I'm pretty easy on the ears. I think I'll be fine.

I can't argue with that. But you know how sometimes—when you ask a question at a Q&A—the expert misunderstands what you're talking about, and so answers a *different* question.

> **ADH-YOU:** Yeah, it's pretty embarrassing for them.

Possibly, but also I submit that—if you don't have a clear structure that leads ever-so-definitively to your final query—it can be hard for someone who doesn't know you to realize exactly what you're getting at.

> **ADH-YOU:** Fine, so what goes into this verbal map?

Well, that depends. Let me ask you this: which one of these would be the best supporting material for your question: a joke, an anecdote, or a quick summary of your position?

ADH-YOU: Yeah, all of those sounds good.

Right, but for the purpose of this exercise, please pick just one option.

ADH-YOU: Um, okay, well, I'm pretty funny, so I'll go with a joke. There's this one about an insomniac dog that I think'll illustrate my question perfectly.

That's great. But, before you unleash your humour, there are two things to remember about jokes during the Q&A. First, since we're not at a dinner party, you again want to be as succinct as possible.

ADH-YOU: Check.

And also, be aware that, after you finish the joke, Dr. Anti-Brag—who's pretty funny, himself—might want to retort.

ADH-YOU: That's fine.

Right, but I bring it up because if the speaker does attempt to joke back, you may be tempted to ignore their retaliatory humour because you weren't anticipating it. And that can make you look like you were in possession of a good joke, but not a sense of humour.

ADH-YOU: I don't like that. Hmm, okay, I'll just outwit them right back.

Fair enough. If a brilliant retort to their retort lands beautifully in your mind, please share it with everyone in the room. However, if nothing delightful arrives in your moment of need, there's no need to panic and try too hard to come up with a scintillating reply. In fact, you can actually build rapport with both the speaker and the speaker-aligned audience if you let the speaker win the funny.

> **ADH-YOU:** But you said I wasn't supposed to ignore their joke! Make up your mind, Captain Contradiction.

Again, I apologize for the confusion. But there's actually a third option between ignoring and winning, and that's to simply laugh at the speaker's joke, perhaps adding in a "Yeah, exactly." You can then smile and continue on with your question.

> **ADH-YOU:** This is getting too complicated. Maybe I'll do an anecdote instead.

Great, that can be nice groundwork for your question. But just remember: in order to be brief, you want to avoid chasing tangents during your story. Try to stick to the essential beats of—

> **ADH-YOU:** I never chase tangents. Well, except maybe this one time when I was in a job interview, and the man interviewing me was so tall that he made me nervous. I don't usually get nervous . . . well, except this other time when I was playing basketball, and—

Yeah, that's good to hear that you don't usually chase tangents, but when you're in front of an audience, it can be easy to lose track of what you're saying, so again I suggest investing in some serious planning of precisely what story parts will make it into your final draft. That should help you to avoid Sudden Tangent Syndrome.

> **ADH-YOU:** Yeesh. That sounds complicated, too. What's my other option? The summary thing?

Right, you could provide a quick backgrounder of where your curiosity it lies, and then segue straight into your question.

> **ADH-YOU:** Actually, that's not bad, because I have a lot of expertise as well as some pretty heroic accomplishments in the area I want to ask about, so I'd be happy to provide a good chunk of my background.

Oh, sorry, that's not quite what I meant by backgrounder. Poor word choice on my part.

> **ADH-YOU:** But I like the idea!

I understand. But the thing is: introducing yourself in such self-flattering detail can be risky. Unfortunately—unless those points of accomplishment or heroism are vital to establishing the legitimacy of the content of your question—they may sound suspiciously like resume and/or virtue signalling if they aren't phrased just right.

> **ADH-YOU:** Okay, so how do you want me to map the background of my question?

Well, let me ask you this: what provoked the question you want to ask?

> **ADH-YOU:** Well, I was confused when Dr. Anti-Brag said that we should avoid "bragging," on the grounds that people are suspicious of us when we self-celebrate. But I was thinking maybe that's because a lot of braggers are lying. But I'm not lying. So I'm wondering whether he studied whether people are equally as suspicious of honest self-aggrandizers as they are of lying ones.

Fair enough—that's an interesting point. And, if you put a question mark on the end there, you've actually got a pretty clear and concise question all set to go already.

> **ADH-YOU:** Really? Wow, I'm awesome. How'd I do that?

Well, you first summarized the content that led to your curiosity, and then you segued quickly into your actual curiosity. Beautifully done.

> **ADH-YOU:** Awesome, so I'm all set then?

Nearly. I just have one more concern. How will you know when your question is finished?

> **ADH-YOU:** Um, I dunno—I'll know when I get there, I guess.

Yeah, see, that's an issue. A common problem amongst those suffering from MQS—

> **ADH-YOU:** MQS?

Oh, yeah, sorry, Meandering Question Syndrome.

> **ADH-YOU:** Okay, go on.

Well a common symptom is that—after all the work of getting into the line for the Q&A, and then listening to others pontificate—many MQSers will feel delighted to finally have their place at the microphone, and so won't want to give it up. Consequently, even when the heart of their question has been clearly understood by everyone present, our noble MQSer will continue throwing words on a fire that is already blazing. They'll just keep on meandering about the same point, and they won't stop—

> **ADH-YOU:** Aren't you kinda doing that right now?

Oh, right you are. Thank you.

> **ADH-YOU:** Yeah, you're welcome, Captain Hypocrite. So how do I avoid that?

Well, the most effective system is to pay attention to your words as you're saying them. When you hear yourself complete the goal of your question, get out of there. But, if you have trouble listening to yourself while you're talking, watch the mouth of the person to whom you're directing your query. If they stop their nodding and start taking a breath, that means they're about ready to respond, which means they believe they understand the Q in your query, and it's okay for you to STOP.

> **ADH-YOU:** Okay, I'll do that. Can I ask my question now?

Unfortunately, they've run out of time for questions in our hypothetical scenario, but you'll get 'em next time, YOU.

> **ADH-YOU:** Yeah, I will!

Late Has To Wait

If you're late for a class or a public presentation, then unfortunately it's up to you to determine what you've missed.

> **ADH-YOU:** I don't follow you.

Well, there's no need to slow down the production by asking questions of the presenter about what happened before you got there.

> **ADH-YOU:** Sorry, I still don't see what you're on about.

Okay, well, try to avoid a scenario like this:

PRESENTER: So, in conclusion, I think it is clear that eugenics is a dangerous practice that can contribute to fascism.

ADH-YOU (*just arriving*): What's "eugenics"?

I've exaggerated your silliness here. I hope that you would, in fact, recognize that in order for the word to play so prominently in the presenter's conclusion, it was probably defined earlier in the lecture. Nevertheless—

> **ADH-YOU:** Well, if it was defined before I got there, then I wasn't there for that part, so why shouldn't I ask for the definition now?

Well, your fellow audience members—who *did* manage to get to the presentation on time—have already been given that information, so why should they be punished for your lateness and have to hear it again, at the expense of learning something new?

> **ADH-YOU:** Because I want to be able to follow along!

Yes, it is tricky to keep up when you come in late, isn't it? But it turns out there are other ways for you to catch up:

(1) Pay attention and see if you can figure out what's going on by listening for context clues provided by the instructor/presenter.

> **ADH-YOU:** How do I do that?

Well, you know how when you turn on *Seinfeld*, you can—

> **ADH-YOU:** I never found *Seinfeld* very funny. Seemed like he was making fun of people for doing normal things. Like, what's wrong with "close talking"? To me, that show was more of a drama than a comedy.

Sorry, I wasn't meaning *Seinfeld*, in particular. Pick any show that you like to watch.

> **ADH-YOU:** Okay. Let me think . . . got it!

Great, and do you ever notice how, when you turn on the TV and start watching in the middle of an episode, you can figure out most of what's happened based on the things the characters say and do?

> **ADH-YOU:** Yeah, it's not rocket science, man. It's just a TV show.

Right, okay, so please take those tools of inference that you use when you tune into an in-progress TV show, and apply them to cases where you join a lecture already underway. You may be surprised by how much you can figure out on your own.

> **ADH-YOU:** I'm never surprised by how much I can figure out.

Great! But, if that doesn't work, you can also try the next options on this list:

(2) When there's a pause in the lecture, try whispering a quick clarifying question to your neighbour.

> **HINT:** Avoid open-ended questions such as:
>
> > **ADH-YOU:** What's been said so far?
>
> That'll take too much time to answer; instead, aim for a query which will help you confirm or collect context in only a few words. Try this:
>
> > **ALTERNATE-YOU:** So do I have it right that the earth revolves around the sun, not the other way around?
>
> Perfect!

(3) Take notes that you can use to help you research the missing lecture links after the lecture, and/or ...

(4) If you're living in modern times, then as inconspicuously as you can, use the internet on your smart phone (or robot) to investigate the confusing parts of the lecture.

PRESENTER YOU

Your Perfect Perspective

At some point, now or later, you may be the person at the head of the class or presentation.

> **ADH-YOU:** Finally!

Yes, and on the apple-receiving side of the teacher-student relationship, you will get to enjoy the position of being the one with the answers.

> **ADH-YOU:** Finally, people will acknowledge my omnipotent understanding of the world!

Are you sure you don't mean "*omniscient* understanding"?

> **ADH-YOU:** What's the difference?

Well, I believe omnipotent means all-powerful, and omniscient means all-knowing.

> **ADH-YOU:** Fine. It's the second one, then. I'm omniscient. And I look forward to people finally realizing that.

Excellent. Now, one thing I'd like you to keep in mind when operating from your omniscient perspective is that, when you ask questions of your not-so-knowledgeable students, they can't necessarily read your brilliant mind.

> **ADH-YOU:** Of course they can't. What are you on about?

Well, it's just that sometimes, when you ask a scenario-based question of your students, you seem to assume they automatically recognize from what angle you're imagining it. Consider this hypothetical case:

> **ADH-YOU-PRESENTER:** Today, we're going to learn about driving. So let me ask you this, everyone: what do you think makes a car move?
>
> **STUDENT:** Gasoline?
>
> **ADH-YOU-PRESENTER:** No, it's the driver that makes the car move, of course.

Okay, so do you see how technically your student's answer was right from a certain point of view?

> **ADH-YOU:** But it wasn't the point of view I was looking for!

Exactly, so you've actually corrected your student for not reading your mind about which perspective you wanted them to take. Maybe in the future you could design your question to be less ambiguous. And if your students provide an answer that is technically correct but not the answer you were seeking, I request that you resist telling them they're wrong.

> **ADH-YOU:** What else can I do when they're so off base?

Brilliant question! I suggest you accept their answer, and politely transition from it to yours.

> **ADH-YOU:** I don't see how.

Okay, watch this.

> **ALTERNATE-YOU:** So, students, what do you think makes the car move?
> **STUDENT:** Gasoline.
> **ALTERNATE-YOU:** Exactly, and who activates the gas?
> **STUDENT:** The driver?

See how with a simple sleight of segue you got the answer you were looking for without accusing the student of being wrong for not guessing your perspective?

> **ADH-YOU:** I guess. If that's makes a difference to you.

Perfect.

The Substitution Game

Next, I would like you to avoid trading in the questions that you're asked for easier ones. For instance:

ADH-PRESENTER: Graffiti is a legitimate form of art, and therefore it is my contention that it's unethical to paint over it.

AUDIENCE MEMBER: If it's unethical to paint over art, then wasn't it also unethical for the graffiti artist to paint over the architecture, which is a legitimate art form as well?

ADH-PRESENTER: I'm glad you brought that up. It's a common misconception that graffiti is not a legitimate form of art. But, if you think about it, a graffiti artist is no different from any other artist; they're just using a different canvass.

Do you see how you took the architecture fan's complaint that your lionized graffiti artist was painting over legitimate art, themselves, and pretended you were responding to an imagined, easier-to-handle query about whether graffiti was, in fact, art?

ADH-YOU: I guess. But, in my defence, so what?

Well, while answering a different question than the one you're asked may help you to escape answering it, your faux response will likely in turn alienate your questioner to the point that they will be none-too-friendly when filling out their comment cards.

ADH-YOU: Fine, what do I have to do to "cure" the problem this time?

Well that depends on why you chose to spin out of the question in the first place. I see three major possibilities:

(1) POLITICAL SPIN:

If you're in a political role, you've probably been taught to avoid giving answers that could offend any members of your audience (even if your answer is well reasoned). It's hard to argue with that, except to say that playing cat and mouse with a genuine answer will alienate those in your audience who are paying attention to your actual words. So you may want to talk to your campaign manager to see if they can give you a wee bit more freedom to answer questions sincerely.

(2) INCOMPLETE SPEAKER KNOWLEDGE:

Sometimes you as a speaker may feel unwilling to respond to a difficult question because you're not sure you know the answer to it. So you might pretend to have misheard the question. For instance:

> **STUDENT:** Professor, is the artistic movement that you're talking about related in any way to the similar movement that occurred a century before?
>
> **PROFESSOR:** Well, that's an interesting question, but your chronology's off a little because the two movements actually happened about one hundred years apart from each other. Any other questions?

I understand that sometimes people may ask a question you haven't prepared for, and so it can be scary to let your thoughts go blindly into your mind to seek out a response, but I think you may find the endeavour worthwhile nonetheless. I recall attending a workshop presentation by a future friend of mine. I asked him a question he hadn't been asked before, but instead of sidestepping it, he said, "That's an interesting question. I hadn't thought of that. I suppose I would say . . ." and he went on to invent an interesting possible resolution to my curiosity. Consequently, I found myself admiring him so much more than I would have if he had dodged the question with a pretend answer.

This isn't to say that you always need to land on an answer when encountering an unfamiliar query. If you don't immediately see a worthy solution, it's okay to acknowledge that you hadn't previously considered the question and so don't want to rush in a guess. You can then promise to give it some thought in future and get back to the question-asker later.

(3) **SPEAKER LAZINESS:**

Sometimes you as a speaker will be feeling too lazy to listen carefully to a question; instead, you will assume that it matches an answer you already have set to go in your head.

> **ADH-YOU:** Lucky audience!

Well the tricky thing is the audience may feel frustrated by this non-answering technique especially since it's so easy for speakers to avoid.

> **ADH-YOU:** I don't follow. Let's get to the example.

Fair enough, I recall attending a professional workshop with some of my colleagues, and I was having a good time learning new tricks from an articulate speaker who clearly knew her stuff. She eventually provoked a curiosity in my brain about her methodology, so I asked a question that went a little something like this:

> **SETH:** So, in your system, how do you identify when the risk is imminent versus—

And her reply was a little something like:

> **SIMPLIFYING EXPERT:** Well, imminence means the risk is likely to happen at any moment, as in immediately.

So the expert had confused my curiosity about how and when she, specifically, identified "imminence" with a question about what the word meant. This would be akin to a celebrity responding to a paparazzi's query about whether they were getting married by defining the word "marriage" for the reporter.

> **ADH-YOU:** Hee, hee, that would be dumb for a reporter to ask what marriage means!

Exactly! And I could have forgiven the expert's confusion about my question if the workshop weren't a professional supplement given to people already in her field. That is, "imminence" is a common word in our world, so for me not to know what it meant would mean I was incompetent. Before leaping to *that* conclusion, it would have been kind of the presenter to take a moment to consider whether I might have meant something slightly less embarrassing.

> **ADH-YOU:** But people *do* ask a lot of stupid questions. How do I know which is which?

Fair point, YOU. In general, my suggestion is this: if a question seems too easy to be true, double check with the questioner to make sure you have it right. Thus, if you did have it right, no harm done, but, if you had the question wrong, your clarification will save your questioner much frustration, as they won't have to suffer through an answer that simplifies them to the lowest common interrogator.

Chapter 18

Work You

Unfortunately, for many of us, our jobs involve a lot of work and little play, so you're probably hoping for a reprieve from ADH-ME reduction strategies during those tedious hours.

> **ADH-YOU:** And yet something tells me you won't be giving me a break.

Well caught, YOU! Sadly, you are right: I cannot offer you such freedom. You see, work is one of the leading arenas in which one's identity is formed—

> **ADH-YOU:** So?

Well, I suspect that if you don't do your ANTI-ADH-ME exercises during such a significant portion of your existence, the ADH-BEAST will re-take you.

EMPLOYEE YOU

You've probably learned from your cliché book that everyone makes mistakes. As I'm sure you were delighted to learn in Chapter 10, the victim of your innocent blunder is not necessarily entitled to an unlimited apology from you.

> **ADH-YOU:** I don't make mistakes, but that's nice to know in theory.

Good point, YOU! But, in case it ever comes up, I can console you with the news that, if your error was committed without malice or negligence, and you have apologized, then a reasonable colleague or employer probably won't be too hard on you for it.

Nevertheless, have you noticed that your boss—who usually seems like a fair person—sometimes continues to question you about a negative result of your actions that you've already stated was unintentional?

> **ADH-YOU:** Yeah, why are they hounding me about it? There's nothing I can do about it now.

Well put. Can you think of any reason your boss is irrationally pestering you about something that's too late to change?

> **ADH-YOU:** Obviously it's because they're a jerk who likes to rub their employees' noses in their so-called errors.

Yes, that is possible. But I submit that there's also a tiny chance that your boss is not actually looking for your guilt-soaked cranium on a platter, but instead is searching for a simple assurance that you will avoid committing the same foul again in the future.

> **ADH-YOU:** What for? I didn't do it on purpose.

Yes, but your boss may be hoping for proof of understanding, some sort of evidence that you comprehend precisely what it will take to remove the bungling behaviour from your repertoire. Consider the following hypothetical circumstance:

> **PRISON WARDEN:** I was looking at the visitor log, and I don't see that Mr. Hendricks visited Mr. Dawson. Wasn't he here?
>
> **ADH-YOU-PRISON GUARD:** Yeah, he was here.
>
> **WARDEN:** So why isn't he in the log?
>
> **ADH-YOU-GUARD:** Oh, sorry, we were really busy that day so I wasn't able to mark everybody down.
>
> **WARDEN:** Oh. That really can't happen: legally, we must log every visitor.
>
> **ADH-YOU-GUARD:** Yeah, I know, but he was in a rush.

WARDEN: I understand, but we have to mark him down anyway. No matter how busy we are, we still need every visitor in the log. If people have to wait, they have to wait.

ADH-YOU-GUARD: Right, yeah, I know. So are you looking forward to the weekend?

WARDEN: Um, sure. Sorry, I don't mean to keep harping on this, but you understand that we're legally obligated to log every visitor in case the police need the information in future?

ADH-YOU-GUARD: For sure, yeah, it's really important.

WARDEN: So there can be no exceptions. No matter what, make sure you log every visitor.

ADH-YOU-GUARD: Oh, yeah, I got it covered.

You may not be able to see it from where you are, but our hypothetical prison warden is currently wearing his skeptical eyebrows. He's not confident that you understand the seriousness of the problem here.

> **ADH-YOU:** I just *told* him I got it covered.

Yes, but he thought you already had it covered before this incident came up, so he's looking for evidence that you understand what went wrong, and that you have a reasonable plan to avoid the same in future.

> **ADH-YOU:** But I already explained that the reason it happened was because we were busy.

Yes, and that explanation would have been fine if you had used it merely as insight as to *why* you blundered. But instead, by your dismissive, I-got-it-covered reply, you seem to be indicating that your busyness justified your error such that it was no longer a true mistake. So, if you want to avoid a lecture from your boss, then consider saying something like this instead:

> **ALTERNATE-YOU-GUARD:** I can't believe I did that. We were so busy, I think I lost track of who we'd logged in, so I must have missed that guy. I know it's critical that we always log in everyone, so I will make sure, if we're busy in future, that I slow things down to make sure I get everyone.

See how, even though ALTERNATE-YOU didn't even use the incriminating word "Sorry," your hypothetical warden boss is nodding appreciatively and seems ready to talk about the weekend now?

CO-WORKER YOU

Helping Out

I suspect you'll be surprised to learn that sometimes it's okay to help out with tasks that aren't officially your responsibility, especially if you see that such aid would benefit the running of the ship.

> **ADH-YOU:** Yeah, I'm not only surprised, I'm not willing. I'll do what I'm paid to do, and that's all, bud.

That's understandable, and you're not obligated to sign on for this one. But, before you officially decline, consider this example. My spouse once worked at the front counter of a fast food restaurant. The drive-thru staff were considered the top employees because they had the most urgent business to tend to. Thus, my pre-spouse and other front counter staff would assist them when necessary. Occasionally, though, the busyness was reversed: nobody would be driving through, but a large pilgrimage of customers would walk through the front door and swamp the front till employees. Every available set of hands would have been helpful, but instead those elite drive-thru co-workers relaxed, relishing in the joy of not officially being responsible for the customers up front.

> **ADH-YOU:** Sounds about right. What else were they supposed to do?

Well, they might have considered helping out their co-workers; in doing so, they would have made a temporary, but profound difference in their inferiors' lives.

> **ADH-YOU:** Sorry, Pollyanna, but since when does one go to work to make friends?

Yes, I know, when you go to work, you're just there for the paycheque—

> **ADH-YOU:** Exactly, what do I care about my co-workers?

Well, first of all, going beyond expectations can do a reputation good when promotions or reference checks come around. Moreover, even if you're not concerned with that, please keep in mind that you're still working with other humans. When the lineup gets big, your fellow employees' stress goes up, so it would be lovely if you would assist in alleviating the situation (just as they've been doing for you when the circumstance is reversed). Such teamwork is not only good for them, but can also be fun for you as you can imagine yourself on an adventure as you slay the customer lineup.

> **ADH-YOU:** Fine. But this is the last time you get to use the adventure metaphor against me. I will not have my thrill-seeking addiction used against me again.

Fair enough. So the moral of this vignette is that, if you truly want to cure your ADH-ME, then acts of helpfulness for their own sake are a great step in that unselfish direction (and, hey, you might even acquire some friendships along the way from people who appreciate your unusual consideration).

Sharing Out

Now, I'd like you to consider that unusual creature found in most communal offices, "The task that needs to be done by someone, but isn't officially assigned to anyone." You tend to avoid ever taking on such chores, am I right?

> **ADH-YOU:** First of all, I don't know what you're talking about. Second, I already agreed to help out in the previous section even in cases where I shouldn't have to. What more do you want from me?

Good question, YOU. Let's say you work at a small office where no one in particular has been assigned the work of garbage removal, communal phone answering, or cake-acquiring on people's birthdays.

> **ADH-YOU:** Honestly, I have no idea who does that stuff. What's your point?

Right, and correct me if I'm wrong, but this isn't just about your lack of awareness. You are also blessed with an impressive level of willpower when it comes to, for instance, letting the communal phone ring without being answered.

> **ADH-YOU:** Not gonna argue with you there. I'd rather lose a customer than play secretary.

Well put. But here's the thing: it may be that your co-workers don't like picking up the phone either. Nevertheless, in order to do business, somebody has to respond, and so when some NOT-YOU takes on the task, you are enjoying the fruits of another's conscientiousness.

> **ADH-YOU**: I can live with that.

I know, but what you may not realize, in these scenarios, is that every successive time that one or two people do a communal task without receiving any offer from you of taking a turn, their resentment will grow. It will fester. It may never explode, but I promise it will cost you collegial assistance in ways that neither you, nor they, ever imagined. You may one day be in a rush, but have lost your car keys, and yet no one will be making any effort towards helping you find them. This likely won't be a coincidence.

> **ADH-YOU**: Well that's not fair!

I know. So, to avoid such a sudden, unexpected turn of karma, your best bet is to take on as close to an equal portion of the communal tasks as you can muster.

> **ADH-YOU**: I don't have time for that.

That is a tricky one. Well, another option would be to complete a higher than average portion of the communal chores that people in your office especially dislike. It takes less time, but maximizes your level of communal consideration.

> **ADH-YOU**: I don't know. I'm really having trouble getting my head around the idea of doing something that one of my co-workers will eventually do anyway.

Yes, that's challenging. So, if you really don't feel up to taking on an equal share, here are a couple of simple things you could do instead to mitigate your colleagues' resentment.

First, check to see if there is one person in the office who is always the one to get the cake for co-workers' birthdays: if you locate a solo cake-provider, your job is to make sure that his or her birthday doesn't get missed.

> **ADH-YOU:** Why? If they're this great cake fairy, can't they get their own?

Great question, YOU! Unfortunately, most people would find it awkward to be seek out their own birthday cake; it would be like sending yourself a congratulatory note. It can be done, but it's awkward.

Second, if one of your associates answers the communal phone and informs you that so-and-so is waiting on line 1 for you, please do not add to your helpful colleague's task-list by using them as your call-evasion device. For instance:

> **CO-WORKER:** Hey, YOU, Jim Friederman's on line 1 for you.
>
> **ADH-YOU:** What does he want?
>
> **CO-WORKER:** I don't know.
>
> **ADH-YOU:** Ask him what he wants.
>
> *You happily continue Facebooking while you wait.*
>
> **CO-WORKER:** He wants to know how he can get his Fidelity Drive working.
>
> **ADH-YOU:** Oh, it's easy, just tell him to restart the Excalibur system.
>
> *You send an excellent text to your BFF about last night's party while you wait.*
>
> **CO-WORKER:** He says it's still not working.
>
> **ADH-YOU:** Well, did you tell him to do manoeuvre X first?

No! None of that should have happened. It's your client, so you deal with him. If you really can't take the call right now, then ask that the customer be directed to your voice mail, but it's not your co-worker's job to play translator. You may be surprised to discover that your colleague has their own work to do, which means that your attempts to co-opt them as a shield is likely going to provoke bitterness that will in turn create actual venom in their mouths whenever they see you.

> **ADH-YOU:** Wow, sensitive much?

I know, but let me ask you this: if you accidentally picked up the communal phone when it rang, and the caller wanted to talk to one of your co-workers, would you be willing to play intermediary for your co-worker?

> **ADH-YOU:** No. I'm busy.

Good point, YOU. So, as you feel your ADH-ME start to recede, you should start to wonder why you would expect your co-worker to do a task that you would never consider doing for them.

The Credit

You're very observant, and I really like that about you.

> **ADH-YOU:** I wish I could return the compliment, but go on.

Well, you're also brilliant at learning new things. And that's neat, too. But when you *observe* a co-worker telling you about a clever solution they have for a common problem, then I recommend you don't present the remedy as *your own* to your shared boss.

> **ADH-YOU:** Why? It's a great way to impress the boss without much effort.

True that. But, unfortunately, while you may earn some temporary praise from your superior, if the co-worker with the original idea ever realizes that you gave yourself credit for it, you'll have earned a workplace nemesis. They may not tell you, or give you any hint of it, but trust me, they, along with their spouse and closest friends, will forever think you're a weasel.

> **ADH-YOU:** Well, that's a bit harsh, isn't it?

I know it's not fair. But that's the way the loathing crumbles. Similarly, when your colleague is flourishing on a project, I know how much fun it is to share in the collective glory when it's time to celebrate the results.

> **ADH-YOU:** I don't know what you're talking about.

Yes, I'm sure you don't realize you're doing it. Nevertheless, sometimes all you need is the fact that your co-worker asked you to contribute a moment's effort to a project, and you'll dominate the discussion when it's unveiling day. Sadly, though, if the lead contributor notices you taking more glory than you technically earned, your co-worker may once again acquire an irrepressible desire for revenge. So, as much as you can, please resist scavenging other people's achievements for your own exaltation.

Singing In The Power

To identify this favourite co-worker pastime of yours, consider a former colleague of mine who whistled (and sometimes sang) loudly through our workplace hallways.

> **ADH-YOU:** Lighten up. What's wrong with a little music in the office?

Well, you see, when you treat your workplace like your own personal shower, the resulting noise can be distracting to your co-workers. And so you may give the impression that you feel your quest for musical zest is more important than their efforts to complete their work.

Your assignment here is simple: before you start singing at work, or other places where people are trying to concentrate, ask yourself this: *Is your personal enjoyment of your musical abilities more important at that moment than what those nearby are working on?*

> **ADH-YOU:** How should I know? I don't know what they're working on. But I do know that . . . ♪ I am the very model of a modern Major-General. I've information vegetable, animal, and mineral! ♪

That's very nice. And very musical! But, if you're not sure whether your melodic fun is more important than the work of those nearby, imagine you were trying to focus on the most concentration-requiring task in your work day only to suddenly hear Karaoke Joe/Jane singing by your office. Would you like to turn their volume down? If so, I'm afraid you're going to have to turn yours down, too.

BOSS YOU

Pre-Criticism

Not unlike the organisms we met in Chapter 8, employees tend to be humans: such creatures are often sensitive when it comes to feedback, so it's worth being sure you're on point before offering it up.

> **ADH-YOU:** Hey, if I criticize my employee, it's because I don't have time for their mistakes.

Very good, I'm sure. But sometimes I've noticed that you will tell off an employee because you're assuming they're going to make the mistakes that others have.

> **ADH-YOU:** All the better. Now I've prevented them from annoying me in the first place.

Another excellent strategy. My only request is that, instead of reaming out your employee for the mistakes of others, perhaps just let them know about the common error you'd like them to avoid.

> **ADH-YOU:** I don't see a difference.

Well, it can be rather demoralizing to be criticized for something you haven't done. In some cases an employee may have even specifically avoided such an error, only to receive your remonstration anyway. Can you see how that might be frustrating?

> **ADH-YOU:** Fine. I'll wait till they screw up before I point it out.

Thanks, YOU! That's all I can ask for.

Helping Out

Similar to the "Helping Out" that we talked about in the Co-Worker section earlier in this chapter, the following is not a requirement of this ADH-REDUCTION-PROGRAM. Nevertheless, I think you will find that it will help you build a greater connection with your minions.

As a boss, you have earned the right not to do certain not-so-fun tasks. Congratulations! However, sometimes in your employees' world there will be occasions of extreme busyness or work-related crisis, and so—as with the co-workers in the earlier section of this chapter—your occasional assistance might build both morale and respect from your underlings.

> **ADH-YOU:** Why would they respect me for lowering myself?

Good point. Let me rephrase: if you dip below your usual rank to help out in a difficult situation, your inferiors may greater appreciate your magnanimous character. In fact, you may find that those you aid are more willing to help *you* out beyond their regular duties in future.

> **ADH-YOU:** If you say so.

I appreciate that, thank you! In contrast, consider the following story, *Ego & the Beast*, which depicts a former ADH-BOSS of mine who—in a situation where he could have assisted a subordinate without any cost to his own time—was sadly paralyzed by his ego.

Ego & the Beast

As previously mentioned, I used to work at a transit directions call-in centre. One day there was a transit crisis; several significant transit routes were delayed and so many of us call-takers had to seek alternate-directions advice from the "work leader" who resided in the centre of the room.

Meanwhile, Edmund Big Boss—who I happened to know from previous experience was overloaded with a biggie-sized ego—was monitoring the problem from his office. Soon, he came upon some pertinent crisis information and so—per his protocol—he left his power office and power-walked towards the work leader desk to inform him of the update. When Big Boss power-arrived, he power-waited for a moment for the work leader's in-progress conversation to finish (such waiting, I must admit, took some impressive Big Boss self-control).

Next to Big Boss, I stood in line awaiting my chance to ask the work leader a question. But, upon noticing that the unoccupied Big Boss was beside me, I figured I might save my customer some time:

SETH: Hi, I'm just wondering: do you know if the X-line is affected by the train stoppage?

BIG BOSS: You'll have to talk to your work leader about that.

I don't mind telling you that even I—a student of ADH-BE-HAVIOUR—was baffled. I did not expect that the ample star-of-the-show side of Big Boss's ego could be so easily overpowered by his snobby side, which preferred to maintain a separation between himself and the lowest common employee. But, given this was the case, Big Boss had no choice but to rebuff my question because—even though there was no official reason not to share the info (since he was planning on giving it to my work leader who would then have given it to me)—he could not fathom the possibility that for a tiny moment he would be doing the work of an inferior (the work leader) and talking to me.

MEETINGS & YOU

Staff meetings are a crucial place to keep your ADH-ME at bay.

ADH-YOU: That's silly! You can't spell "meetings" without "me."

Ha, ha, brilliantly point, YOU! But, the trouble is, during such group discussion, you have a high surface area of people to annoy. You don't need any more adversaries than you've already fostered in your everyday communication, so your best bet is to be extra careful in such fertile enemy-collecting territory.

This means, as we talked about earlier in this chapter, that you must resist collecting recognition for other people's ideas. It turns out that generally people won't remember exactly who came up with the good suggestions in the meeting, but they will remember which people stole theirs.

Moreover, meetings are a particularly good time to subdue your preference for interrupting others. For instance, when you come up with a good idea (well done!) at the same time that someone else is talking, stop! And then ask yourself this simple question:

> **ADH-YOU (*in your head*):** Is someone else speaking right now?

If someone *is* talking, hold that good idea for moment! Now, take your pen and quickly jot down your brilliant idea on your notepad—this won't bother the speaker, as it will appear to them that you're taking notes on what you're saying. Once you've written down your wonderful idea, it's safe and ready to be roused when there's an opportunity. But, again, don't rush it! Not only do you want to wait for the speaker to finish their point, but also you want to make sure your topic is relevant when you bring it up. For contrasting instance, watch how you would normally segue to your brilliance:

> **CO-WORKER:** I think we need to make sure we're not forgetting to change our passwords. We should formalize a system of changing passwords regularly.
>
> **CO-WORKER TOO:** I like that idea. So how could we set it up?
>
> **ADH-YOU:** Well I don't have any ideas for that, but I was thinking we should also update our logo.

No! Bad, ADH-YOU! Look at what you did. I'm proud of you for not interrupting your first co-worker, but you still intervened on a legitimate thread of conversation to start a different topic.

> **ADH-YOU:** But I waited until no one was talking. What more do you want from me?

I'm sorry, you're right: I was a little hard on you there. Staff meetings are challenging. For now, I just want you to consider whether the discussion in play has reached a conclusion or not. If not, please hold onto that notepad of ideas as tightly as you can and wait a little longer before you start your alternate thread.

> **HINT:** If you join a conversation with the phrase, "Well, I don't know anything about that, but..." and then proceed to a different topic, then more than likely you are causing great pain to the person who had strong hopes for the contention they'd put in play, only to have it discarded in favour of your unrelated notion.

THE BREAK ROOM & YOU

Their Food

I know sometimes it can be difficult to come up with good conversation topics when encountering your co-workers in the break room, so you may feel yourself reaching out and grabbing for any subject that is handy—even the food that your colleague is eating. For instance:

> **OBSERVANT YOU** (*spotting a co-worker in the lunchroom*)**:** I guess you like shrimp, eh?

Technically, this is a legitimate topic, but some people are sensitive about having their dietary habits examined, so you may want to be cautious.

> **ADH-YOU:** Wow, oversensitive, much?

Yes, I admit that those of us who recoil when our intended food becomes the flavour of the conversation are probably more sensitive than necessary. Nevertheless, in your efforts to reduce your ADH-ME, it's worth learning to avoid stepping on someone else's neuroses (even if they're silly) unless there's no other way around them.

Moreover (as talked about in Chapter 5), if you must comment on a co-worker's dietary selection, then—for the good of human-to-human relations—please stop yourself from pontificating on the portion size or health value of their food (unless your co-worker directly asks you for your wisdom on such matters).

> **ADH-YOU:** But Dr. Oz said—

Yes, I know you've got some great wisdom to offer, but I think you'll find that there is an almost universal dislike for *those* observations when they're unsolicited.

They're Reading

Unfortunately, when you assume that someone else's break time is yours, even though you have not made prior arrangements with them to share it, you may be stepping on their preferred choice of activity during their cherished free time.

> **ADH-YOU:** I have no idea what you're talking about.

Thanking you for speaking up, YOU. Maybe an example will help. As someone who likes to read on his lunch break at work, I have realized over the years that, if I am in the common lunch room, I have no defence against those who would prefer that I be talking to them. For instance:

> **ADH-CO-WORKER:** So, what are you reading?
>
> **SETH:** Oh, it's a biography of John Cleese. The writer of it is quite funny, himself—
>
> **ADH-CO-WORKER:** Oh, yeah? I saw a really funny movie over the weekend . . .

And we're off on a conversation that leaves me without a viable pathway back to my book. Very cleverly done, YOU! Indeed, let's agree that the question "What are you reading?" often means, "I see that you're reading, but I'd rather you spend your break listening to me, so—using your reading as a segue—I will now commence that conversation."

> **ADH-YOU:** You got it, Captain Obvious.

Glad to hear I'm on the right track, Admiral Snarky. And you may be pleased to read that I'm not going to try to talk you out of your "What are you reading?" question when you're in a common lunch room. As I see it, some people may be reading during their break because they're too shy to engage in conversation, so I think it's reasonable to invite them to participate in an alternative activity.

> **ADH-YOU:** Exactly!

However, your advanced task is this: pay attention to the non-verbal responses of such would-be common-area readers and see if you are able to detect whether they'd prefer to get back to their book. Say, for instance, your colleague keeps a finger in their book to mark their place while they're responding to you: that probably means they're yearning to return to their reading.

> **ADH-YOU:** That can't be right. That's what my previously reading co-workers *always* look like when I talk to them.

Hmm, that *is* strange.

> **ADH-YOU:** Yeah, so how about we look at it from the opposite angle. What's the symptom of them being *interested* in a gab-session with me?

Great question, YOU! An interested converser would probably put a bookmark in their reading, and turn to face you.

> **ADH-YOU:** That doesn't sound familiar.

Fair enough, maybe that one's too difficult to detect. You know, it's actually easier to spot the signs of non-interest. For instance, if they answer your questions with short-burst replies and then seem to inch their eyes back to their novel, once again they're probably hoping to find out what's about to happen to Harry Potter.

> **ADH-YOU:** But that also sounds like the people I delight with my conversation!

Is that so? Then I'm afraid it's time to start releasing some of your conversational catches back to their reading. And, if you can let those readers go, without even a sharp comment about their misplaced priorities, then you will have made significant progress in—

> **ADH-YOU:** Seems kind of impossible, bud.

Fair enough. It would require an advanced level of other-people-awareness to be so attuned to the needs of your nearby reading colleagues, so I don't expect you to develop those skills right away. In fact, I am willing to accept that I read at my own risk in the common lunch room at work. However, one day, when I found refuge outside on a park bench, hidden amongst some trees, I don't think I was unreasonable in my expectation that I would be free to read there without co-worker intervention. Two minutes in, though, I looked up from my book to see a co-worker standing over me:

ADH-CO-WORKER: What are you reading?

Diabolical! She took over my entire break telling me stories of her and her husband's reading preferences, despite the many times that I politely indicated that I was interested in returning to my own.

So, whereas I won't try to stop you if you feel you must interrupt your common-area co-workers with questions of what they're reading, I discourage you from disrupting the pastime of the person who has fled to a zone not officially shared by their colleagues.

> **ADH-YOU:** But what if I'm bored and in the mood to chat?

Yes, I see your point. In a perfect world, your preference for how your co-workers spend their break time would be paramount; tragically, though, in the NON-ADH-ME world, we must learn to let our colleagues choose for themselves how they spend their free time. The silver lining here is that, if you don't interrupt people just when they're about to learn whether Moby Dick will be defeated or not, they may feel less inclined to avoid your excellence next time.

Chapter 19

Attending You

As we learned in Chapter 12, please beware of the "Always be yourself" and "Just be yourself" fallacies, which insist that you can never go wrong by being YOU. These false promises are especially important to resist when you're attending events where there are plenty of strangers for you to annoy.

> **ADH-YOU:** No, that's backwards. Strangers have been missing out on me. So shouldn't I make up for that immediately?

Good thought, but no. Unfortunately, strangers lack your friends' special understanding of what makes you so wonderful; consequently, when you unleash your full YOU on them right away, they're much more likely to misinterpret you as inconsiderate. Instead, I once again ask you to consider the modified axiom, "Be as much of yourself as won't ruin the fun of others."

YOUR ADH-FAMILY

When you go to public places that are not designated for running and screaming, and your kids commence running and screaming, the fact that they are kids doesn't necessarily absolve you of a duty to intervene for the sake of others.

> **ADH-YOU:** Once again, I have no idea what you're talking about.

Right, well, for instance, when you're in a special location such as a restaurant, movie theatre, or classical music hall, and your little yeller starts up a big one, I wonder if you might consider taking your bundle of noisy joy out of earshot.

> **ADH-YOU:** Oh, c'mon, kids will be kids.

Well observed, YOU! It's true: kids will indeed be kids. And nobody expects them to behave as adults, nor to be as full of decorum as mature humans—but there are certain places that are not appropriate for your kids' maximum volume.

I refer you, for instance, to a wedding that I emceed. A few wee ones decided that a fun place to play would be directly in front of the podium where various honoured guests of the bride and groom were to be saying touching things about the new couple.

> **ADH-YOU:** Cute!

It's true: the kids were cute. And if these ones had quietly played amongst their imaginations, I would not have had any cantankerous objection.

Unfortunately, these particular kids being kids were loud. They rolled toy trucks around and yelled to each other about their strategies in the endeavour, making it difficult for loud-voiced me to talk over them, let alone the groom's soft-spoken grandmother who had travelled from Europe to Canada with plans to tell us all about a favourite memory of her grandchild.

At that point, it seemed to me that it would have been reasonable for the parents of the tiny entertainers to scoop up their collections of pride and joy. Instead, the audience was only able to hear snippets of grandma's speech as it was overpowered by the adorable kids' playing.

> **NOTE:** At the back of the room, a pair of equally young kids watched the proceedings from their chairs and made no disruptive noise during the speeches. These young ones, interestingly, did not seem at all traumatized by their limited play time, and instead played with the same adorable vehemence as their brethren once the speeches were finished.

MOVIES

So you're in a theatre watching a movie and you miss a line of dialogue. Well, you've got to know what they said, of course, so you immediately lean over to your companion:

> **ADH-YOU:** What'd he say?
>
> **YOUR COMPANION:** Um, he lost the gun.
>
> **ADH-YOU:** He lost the rung?
>
> **YOUR COMPANION:** The *gun*.
>
> **ADH-YOU:** Oh, hee, hee, I thought you said rung.

Now, if you look carefully, you might see that the actors' lips were moving throughout your discussion. This means that, in order to retrieve one missed word on your part, you've caused your companion to miss a couple of sentences of subsequent dialogue, which may undermine their enjoyment of the film. So, for future reference, perhaps it would be more efficient to wait for non-dialogue moments to ask your clarifying questions.

Meanwhile, if you're the sort of cat who enjoys talking loudly throughout the movies you watch—to the point that various people nearby swivel their heads in your direction—I have a simple solution for you: don't go out to movies; just watch them at home.

PARTIES

Hosting (Transparency)

My request to party hosts is that, when making invites, you give people an idea of what they're getting into. Personally, I'm one of those dorks who prefers an activity-based event, such as card games or a murder mystery. If it's just going to be people standing around with alcohol in their hands, that sounds like work to me, so I'll probably pass.

> **ADH-YOU:** What a dork!

Yes, well spotted, YOU. So my goal is to help you avoid dorks like me from attending your functions.

> **ADH-YOU:** Hmm . . . all right. I accept your terms.

Thanks, YOU. So, in contrast, I've learned (to my dismay) that some people find activity-based gatherings to be dull.

> **ADH-YOU:** Ah, yeah, activities at parties are lame. I'm not in kindergarten.

Well said, YOU! So, regardless of which type of party you're offering your invitees, if you advise them about what you're planning in advance, then the guests in attendance will mostly be comprised of those who are into what you're supplying.

Attending (To Your Phone)

When you are in a small group interaction—say a dinner party or a book club meeting—if your cell phone vibrates for your attention, and it's truly not feasible to let the call go to voicemail, one good option is to apologize and excuse yourself so that you can have your alternate chat in another room. In contrast, consider this circumstance:

> **HOST:** So I've gathered the seven of you to discuss the protest that's happening tomorrow, and what we should to do about it. My feeling is that we must be prepared for—
>
> **ADH-YOU:** Hello? . . . Yeah, I'm there now . . . Sure, but I'm not at my computer right now. I'll have to

get it to you later ... Well, if you need it that quickly, then *you* call Aaron. You've met him ...

Please notice how the official gathering conversation has stopped while you're on your phone, and how when you eventually end your side chat, the main discussion seems to be in a temporary halting pattern as your friends/colleagues need to restart their conversational engines. Any idea why that might be?

> **ADH-YOU:** Because they were missing my brilliant contribution to the discussion?

Yes, I'm sure that's a big part of it, but I submit that another reason they've suspended their interaction is because your side-chatting was so loud that they felt their conversation couldn't coexist with yours.

Thus, unless your phone call is (A) objectively more important than the conversation it's replacing and (B) so urgent that it could not possibly wait for you to move to a different room, then please assume that you should take your alternate conversation outside the main area.

Attending (To Your Conversational Whims)

If you're at a party and you have something to say, you're one step ahead of many people there, so well done! However, on the occasion that you spot a group with whom you'd like to share your genius, I have a teensy request. When you arrive in their presence, take a peek to see if they are already in the act of conversation. If so, why not smile as you gently join the chat-about and allow them to continue what they've already started instead of taking over the chat with your first conversational impulse?

> **ADH-YOU:** Because I'm really excited about that impulse, obviously.

I know, but eventually, I'm sure, the established topic will run out of talking points, and then you can wow them with your alternative thoughts. Yay! In contrast, when you simply walk into a group and start your soliloquy, you may seem unaware of the fact that you're not the only person in the world.

On a more advanced level, if you see a group that you'd like to join but you don't know exactly what they're discussing, you needn't arrive on the scene and simply demand, "What are you guys talking about?" This is both disruptive and unnecessary.

> **ADH-YOU:** I don't get it. First you tell me not to change the topic, and now you're telling me I shouldn't ask what that topic is!

I know it's confusing, but with practice, the gentle-joining of a chat is not as daunting as it may seem. As we've talked about before, a conversation is not unlike a TV show: the in-progress story will always give you hints as to what brought it to where it is now. So just pay attention. Maybe treat yourself like a detective trying to unravel the mystery of what's being discussed, and I bet you'll figure it out! Yay YOU!

Attending (To Your Food)

Unfortunately, you also have a couple of responsibilities when you're eating food at a party—namely, not talking with your mouth full, or eating with your mouth wide open.

> **ADH-CHEW:** Brt wohy?

I see you have your mouth full right now. So, unfortunately, I'm not able to understand or reply to your question at this time.

Attending (To Others' Nerves)

For many citizens, parties are challenging. A large percentage of us are nervous, awkward, or nervous that something awkward will happen.

> **ADH-YOU:** That's funny. I'm never nervous at parties.

And that's awesome! Nevertheless, whether one is confident or nervous at gatherings, I submit that a party can be strangely more enjoyable if one allows oneself to be an anti-awkwardness crusader.

> **ADH-YOU:** Sorry, mate, I'm not following you.

Well, for instance, let's say you saw someone struggling for the name of a person they were trying to introduce.

> **ADH-YOU:** Yeah, I've seen that. It's pretty funny.

Right, well, if you're interested in being a force for less discomfort at these events, then instead of watching bemusedly, you could try introducing yourself to the unnamed person in order to cause them to publish their name before the suffering introducer has to guess for it.

> **ADH-YOU:** Nah, that would ruin the entertainment.

Fair enough. This option to become an awkwardness destroyer is not a requirement of your ADH-RECOVERY; it's just a suggestion in case you want extra credit.

> **ADH-YOU:** Hmm. I do like extra credit.

Yeah you do!

Chapter 19: *Attending You*

SPORTS

Block You Very Much

When you're watching a game at a stadium or arena, you could greatly improve the quality of life of your fellow patrons by not blocking their views of the proceedings.

> **ADH-YOU:** And, once again, I'm not following you, champ.

Well, you see, a lot of the fun of watching a sport live and in person comes from *seeing* the events at the arena of play. So, if you're late getting to the game, or returning from intermission, maybe you could refrain from walking in front of other spectators during the play.

> **ADH-YOU:** How else am I going to get to my seat? Teleport there?

Hee, hee, yes, *that*, or you could just wait for a break in the play.

> **ADH-YOU:** Fine.

Thanks, YOU. Similarly, if you enjoy holding clever signs for the benefit of television cameras and other fans during games, once again please hold them up *between* the plays, not during them.

Joining The Play

So I must ask: why do you like to run on the field of professional sports competitions when you get drunk?

ADH-YOU: I dunno. It's awesome!

Well put! But, just for fun, I'd like you to consider my mother's explanation for why alleged fans such as yourself enjoy inserting yourselves into sporting events:

> **SETH'S MOM:** People see that the athletes are getting a lot of attention. And they see that they'd like some of it for themselves. But since they're not willing to put in the work to find their own way to legitimately get that attention, they decide to take advantage of the audience already in place for somebody else.

Wow, my mom cuts a little deep, doesn't she? But I kind of see her point. I wonder if you realize that, when you run onto someone else's field, you look like a two-year-old who's upset that someone other than you got a toy.

ADH-YOU: Yeah! How come *they* got the toy? I want it!

Yes, I see your point. But maybe think of it this way: every time you run on the field to borrow an audience gathered for NON-YOUs, you're telling those watching that you need their attention so much that you don't care if you deserve it or not. I don't want to hurt your feelings, but that seems desperate to me. So I say, don't give up! See if you can do something of your own that's worth cheering on. I just hope that someone else doesn't run out into your spotlight while you're in the middle of it.

ADH-YOU: Cute. But no one would dare do that to me.

Good point, YOU.

Chapter 20

Athlete You

Unfortunately, "sportsmanship" means something more than a boat owned by an athlete.

> **ADH-YOU:** Groan!

Hee, hee, thank you. A groan is the highest compliment you can pay a punner.

RECREATIONAL VS. COMPETITIVE

Recreational sports are available in a variety of competition levels, ranging from competitive (*must have certain skill level*) to developmental (*all skill levels welcome*). You might find both styles to be enjoyable, so engage at will.

> **ADH-YOU:** Done and done.

Excellent. My only suggestion is that you pay attention to which one you're attending. If, that is, you've signed up for a sport that is listed as "non-competitive," but you are, in fact, fantastically skilled at it, then you're welcome to join in for practice and socializing, but please avoid destroying the novices.

> **ADH-YOU:** Man, you're a killjoy.

Well observed, YOU! Meanwhile, in the opposite case, if a recreational offering asks for players of a certain minimum skill level, do be careful of overestimating yours such that you slow down the enjoyment of the competitive players.

> **ADH-YOU:** I don't really see a difference in the two levels you're talking about. I always just play my best no matter what.

Good point, YOU. Let me see if I can clarify with an example. I used to play recreational volleyball on both a non-competitive night (for practice and socializing) and a semi-competitive night (for competition and socializing). On the lighter night, the rule was *No hard-spiking the ball.* Several excellent players had no trouble keeping their power spikes in their holsters, and instead focussing their skills on keeping the ball alive to set up their less-skilled brethren. However, occasionally, more advanced egos would guest star in our gatherings, and they apparently did not like the idea of anyone thinking that they couldn't power spike, so they wound up with full swings and proved they were the best. In spite of this impressive result, these ADH-EGOS were not much liked by the people they were trying to impress.

Meanwhile, later in the week, one of the not-so-skilled players arrived at the competitive night, desiring to try a fast-paced game in which spikers were expected to unleash their full strength on the ball. Unfortunately, this meant that, when the ball came into the zone of our not-so-skilled guest, she was rarely able to do anything useful with it, which in turn lessened the experience for everyone.

A more considerate person might have excused themselves from the competition to perhaps return on a later day when their skills were up to standard. Instead, our guest performer stayed for the full event and complained to me afterwards that the players were too competitive. Hmm. What exactly about "competitive players only, please" did she not understand?

> **ADH-YOU:** No, no, I agree with her. If I were ever a lower player, I'd want to improve. And the best way for me to do that would be to play against higher competition. And, think about it: the opposing team should be happy—they'll get to win more.

Eloquently put, as always YOU, but you may be surprised to learn that not everyone takes part in sports just to win; some want challenge and exercise, too. And, while, yes, playing against high-skilled opponents might be great for *your* development, you are simultaneously slowing down everyone else's game and costing them the elite play they were seeking.

So try to keep an eye on the level of play when you join a game. If it slows down significantly after your arrival, or you're the *only* one power spiking, you may have assigned yourself to the wrong group.

PROFESSIONAL

"If You're Not Cheating, You're Not Trying"

European football seems to have amalgamated with the sport of diving. Within the present rules of soccer, there appears to be the following guideline:

A foul occurs when (A) a player is struck by an opponent via kicking or pushing, or (B) a player is almost *struck, and gives a wonderful, acrobatic demonstration of how he or she would have fallen if indeed he or she had been violated.*

I understand that you soccer players are not the only athletes who attempt to convince referees that you've been fouled when you haven't, but you are the most prolific and profound in your efforts. With comprehensive pseudo-agony, your faces writhe as your bodies fly and flail across the pitch after you are nearly tripped.

ADH-YOU: Yeah, it's pretty fun. What's the problem?

Well, in the non-sports world, we call that kind of misrepresentation fraud. And yet, you soccer-divers are rarely sanctioned for your attack on the dignity of the game. You are free to jump up from what appeared to be an amputated leg's worth

Chapter 20: *Athlete You*

of pain and continue sprinting around the field until your next performance.

> **ADH-YOU:** Hey, it's not cheating if you don't get caught!

Brilliant point, but do you not think that such an argument condones well-masked steroids, too?

> **ADH-YOU:** Hey, if you're not cheating, you're not trying.

That is another profound truism, thank you. But why not crown the champion on the basis of whoever has the best skills in the sport, itself? In banking, academics, and card games, cheating is universally considered a big no-no. What's the distinction in fast-paced sports?

> **ADH-YOU:** Hey, if winning a championship for my city is wrong, I don't wanna be right.

That is a noble gesture to your fans, no doubt about it. But if you cheated to acquire your victory, what have you truly achieved?

> **ADH-YOU:** Oh, gee, that's a tough one, maybe that shiny trophy over there.

It *is* shiny, I must admit. But, I wonder, are you really the best at the sport if you won in part because you, as a hockey goaltender, purposely, but surreptitiously knocked your net off its moorings to stop a play that might have yielded the winning goal for the other team? Similarly, if your dream were to be a "best-selling" author, but you fudged the numbers to be ranked as such, have you really accomplished your goal?

> **ADH-YOU:** Hey, it says, "Best-seller," not "Best-truth-teller."

Well put again, poetic YOU! And I should acknowledge that my argument against your lying ways is just a moral one. In reality, as long as simulating injuries is part of the skill set that can help your team win, many ADH-PLAYERS like you will continue to develop their tumbling routines, so it's not really fair for me to ask you stop while so many others continue to profit.

> **ADH-YOU:** Thank you!

Unless, that is, you have started to cure yourself of ADH-ME, in which case your motivation could be maintaining the integrity of the game, as well as your own self-respect. (Oh, and also, you might get more benefit of the doubt from referees.)

You're Number One

Sometimes the rules of your sport won't match your preferences.

> **ADH-YOU:** Well that's not fair!

I know; it's quite cruel.

> **ADH-YOU:** Also, what are you talking about?

Good question, YOU. This concept is sponsored by the 2009 edition of Serena Williams, who was already one of the best female tennis players in the history of her sport, but at the time of the following incident was technically ranked number two in the world.

> **ADH-YOU:** I love Serena. She always says what's on her mind.

Yes, I thought she might be your kind of hero.

> **ADH-YOU:** Hey, wait. Why was she ranked number two in 2009? Wasn't she the best player?

Well, you see, unfortunately for Princess Serena, tennis calculated its rankings using the results from more tournaments than she liked to play. As it was, outcomes from all official tournaments counted towards each player's standing, but Williams preferred to skip a lot of the events so that she could concentrate on the high-glory ones known as the four major "Grand Slam" tournaments.

> **ADH-YOU:** Very clever, Serena! Well done.

Yes, good for her. Indeed, concentrating her training on those big matches, and not burning herself out in the lesser tournaments, may have increased her chances of winning when she did play. She was irked, however, by the fact that she was not officially ranked number one in the world even though she was the then current champion of three grand slams.

> **ADH-YOU:** I'm with Serena. She won more Grand Slams than anyone else. Case closed.

I'm sure you would make a fantastic attorney, but unfortunately, after forensic psychological analysis, we can now see that, like you, Serena was suffering from a bad case of ADH-ME when she made that argument. Similarly, a university student might prefer not to write any essays, and have their grade determined by how they do on the final exam, but sadly it's not up to them to set the rules of the game.

> **ADH-YOU:** Yeah, essays are stupid.

Well put, YOU! But cruelly, in this case, the rules were in place for the good of everyone involved in the sport. You see, if tennis did not count all of their official tournaments in their rankings, then the excluded tournaments would be less valuable to the players, fans, and organizers, and so their revenue and job-creating possibilities would be reduced. For Williams, however, none of that mattered. The people involved in those tournaments were irrelevant to her: she wanted that number one ranking without having to play in tournaments that were beneath her!

> **ADH-YOU:** Not true! You're mischaracterizing my Serena to make her seem self-absorbed.

Fair enough. Perhaps I'm understating Ms. Williams' case: let's ask her to put the argument in her own words. After winning Wimbledon 2009, Serena spoke to reporters and responded to questions about her unjust number 2 ranking. (At the time, Dinara Safina was ranked number one as a result of faring well in a lot of smaller tournaments such as The Italian and Madrid Opens.)

> **WARNING:** Don't be misled by the approval from the reporters of Serena's sarcastic comedy show. As with many of us, reporters can sometimes be star-struck across the head and lose too many brain cells to respond to an ADH-STAR with any critical thinking.

REPORTER: How much of a motivation is it for you to try and regain the world number one ranking?

WILLIAMS: You know, I'm not super motivated. I think if you hold three grand slam titles, then maybe you should be number one, but not in the WTA tour, obviously, so . . .

Enthralled reporters laughed ecstatically.

WILLIAMS (*chuckling*): So, you know, my motivation is maybe just to win another Grand Slam, and stay number two, I guess.

Adoring reporters continued laughing.

REPORTER: Does that disappoint you?

WILLIAMS: No, if it did, I would go crazy thinking about it. I think anyone really could. But, you know, that's just shocking. But, whatever: it is what is. I'd rather definitely be number two and hold three Grand Slams in the past year than be number one and not have any.

REPORTER: Do you see yourself as number one?

WILLIAMS: I see myself as number two. That's where I am. I think Dinara did a great job to be number one. She won Rome and Madrid.

Serena then smirked, and shifted into apparently uncontrollable laughter. In lieu of thinking, the reporters joined in on the chuckles, hoping their heroine would love them.

Safina's supposed crime was to play by the rules established for everyone, and to acquire the most points, only to be mocked for not winning the particular points that Ms. Williams valued. Please don't do that.

You're The Best

I realize that in some sports' circles, in-game boasting is part of the culture. Indeed, some public self-aggrandizers may be perfectly nice people when they're off duty. So, if you're part of a sports culture in which staring down your opponent after you've done something brilliant is expected, then, while I think you're obnoxious, I won't try to stop you.

> **ADH-YOU:** Deal!

> **NOTE:** I'll give you bonus points if you *are* able to step outside your peer pressure and resist such adult bullying.

However, if you are this type of gloating athlete, maybe you could compromise and subdue yourself when you're at the post-game microphone.

Consider, in contrast, the time that your mentor, Richard Sherman—one of the best players in the NFL—won the 2014

Super Bowl because of his exceptional last-minute play, and was asked how he felt about it in a post-game interview with Erin Andrews.

> **ANDREWS:** Richard, let me ask you: the final play, take me through it.
>
> **SHERMAN (*yelling*):** Well, I'm the best corner[back] in the game. When you try me with a sorry receiver like Crabtree, that's the result you're gonna get. Don't you ever talk about me.
>
> **ANDREWS (*with a tone of derision that I will always adore her for*):** Who was talking about you?
>
> **SHERMAN:** Crabtree, don't you open your mouth about the best. Or I'm going to shut it for you real quick.

Some might defend Sherman by pointing out that he screeched this chest-thumping speech right after the greatest battle of his life, and so he was likely intoxicated by the emotion of the moment. But note that rarely have other team sport athletes—who have also dominated profound physical battles—allowed themselves to shout their most arrogant thoughts during their post-game interviews. Richard Sherman is special. The rest of us, though, should avoid this type of unbridled and hostile self-celebration.

"Proving Them Wrong"

When commentators underestimate your athletic prowess, I don't expect you to jump for joy and let such analysis roll off your ego, but I think it's worth remembering that you reside on a pedestal that many covet. Unfortunately (as we'll learn about in Chapter 21), such an exclusive position comes with scrutiny. Your best antidote to this cruelty is to be humble about it.

> **ADH-YOU:** For the one thousandth time, I don't know what you're talking about.

Fair enough, that was a bit vague. Here's an example: I've noticed that whenever you're an underdog in an athletic competition, but you manage to succeed anyway, you tend to deride those who predicted against you. Let's go to the tape:

> **INTERVIEWER:** How does it feel to win after so few thought you had a chance?
>
> **ADH-YOU-UNDERDOG-CHAMPION:** It feels unbelievable! Everyone was counting us out. Nobody believed in us but ourselves, and we proved them all wrong!

By your indignant tone, it seems as though you think the pundits were maliciously targeting you in a manner akin to someone telling a child they would never amount to anything.

> **ADH-YOU:** And why I shouldn't I be indignant? Nobody believed in us, and we proved them all—

Yes, but unlike parents not believing in their kids, I submit that sports prognostications are part of the fun of competitive sports.

> **ADH-YOU:** That's fine. But why did they have to pick *me* to lose?

Great question, YOU. Unfortunately, if predictions are to be made, *someone* has to be estimated to lose. I assure you it's rarely meant as a personal slight against you.

> **ADH-YOU:** Well maybe then they could be nicer about it.

I see your point. I'll ask them to do that. In the meantime, try to remember that the more publicity your sport gets, the more fame and fortune it may help you acquire, regardless of the cruel things the mean pundits say about you.

> **ADH-YOU:** Fine.

If it makes you feel any better, I can report that your notion of protecting athletes from the truth with an always-complimentary spin has been adopted in many children's sports. For instance, when I coached kids' rollerblade hockey, a four-team tournament was divided into "Gold Medal Winner," "Gold Medal Runner-Up," "Silver Medal Winner," and "Silver Medal Runner-Up."

> **ADH-YOU:** Awesome! Looks like everyone did great!

For sure! Although, strangely, one of my ten year-old players said to me afterwards, "Why are we being called 'Silver Medal Runner-Up'? Didn't we come in last?"

> **ADH-YOU:** What a pessimistic kid!

Well put, YOU! I'm sure that's what it was.

Chapter 21

Famous You

It is the best of lives; it is the worst of lives. Being a celebrity comes with notoriety, power of influence, and usually money. At the same time—

> **ADH-YOU:** Sure, but as a celebrity, I also get mean reviews, not much privacy, and a lot of cruel scrutiny when I break up with someone—especially if the person I just broke up with is a celeb, too.

Well said, FAMOUS-YOU. As your agent probably told you when you signed up for celebrity dating, going out with a fellow famous person is the fastest way for you to climb the celebrity alphabet, but if you accidentally fall for your famous partner in dating, it'll hurt like a bad review when you break up and find your sorrow decorating magazine covers.

> **ADH-YOU:** Exactly!

As ever, you have my sympathies. Such mistreatment is undoubtedly related to our society's obsession with celebrity: with great admiration comes great fascination when the object of our appreciation falls. The key to avoiding unnecessary angst, then, is (A) to send the butler to the grocery store when you're down so that you don't have to see what's being written and photographed about you, and (B) to try to remind yourself that being a celebrity has perks, too.

> **ADH-YOU:** Like what?

Well, like the fact that you have more money and influence than the rest of the people you went to high school with have combined. This doesn't justify the abuse you receive, but I hope it softens it.

> **ADH-YOU:** Fine. I'm "lucky" to be in the position I'm in. Tell me something I haven't heard before.

Fair enough. I'm sorry to minimize your pain. My only request is that, when assessing your well-being, try including the perks in your calculations, along with the downsides.

> **YOUR GREATNESS**

Our Language

Society's worship of your celebrity is aided, I believe, by the impressive language we use in your direction. I remember as a kid being startled by *People Magazine*'s annual "Sexiest Man Alive," "Most Beautiful People," and "Most Fascinating People" publications; every year, it seemed to be *celebrities* that adorned the covers. In fact, as far as I could tell, they didn't even do a global search for said most-attractive and fascinating folks, but instead selected only from people featured in Western media.

> **ADH-YOU:** What's your point? It's not my fault the media loves me.

Right, fair enough. I just want you to keep in mind that the media tends to elevate the attributes, achievements, and behaviours of celebrities to superhuman status. That's not your fault, of course, but I think it's worth keeping in mind before you buy into the media's worship of you, and allow yourself to mistreat those around you on the basis of your intrinsic superiority.

> **ADH-YOU:** Holy, convoluted, writer-man.

Fair enough. I just mean to suggest that you take some humility with you when you venture out into the world.

> **ADH-YOU:** Why? Surely, the fans love me for a reason.

Well noted, YOU. Yes, live studio audiences scream for you when you're on talk shows, but how much of that is because of your particular greatness, and how much is because you stumbled into the right role or music producer in the right moment?

I refer you to the humility of David Schwimmer (one of the actor-lottery winners who got a role in the iconic TV show, *Friends*). He's obviously a talented performer, and yet in an interview, I overheard him admitting that getting his career-making part was essentially a stroke of luck. Not that he didn't contribute to the show's success, but Schwimmer seemed aware that there are other actors out there with talent commensurate with his own who could have gotten the part—but he recognized that he was the one who was in the right audition at the right time. Try to bear that in mind when you're about to celebrate yourself in public.

Your Talent

Please understand, dear CELEBRITY-YOU, I don't mean to dismiss your talent. You may have it in abundance. However, are you really so great an author that your children's book would have been published if you weren't already a famous singer?

> **ADH-YOU:** I think it would've done just fine, thanks for asking.

I'm sure you're right in that particular case, but in general I hope you remember that your fame often multiplies for reasons independent of the talent that brought you to the spotlight. Fame, that is, begets more fame.

> **ADH-YOU:** Or maybe my expansive talent begets more fame.

Well I can't argue with that. But another point to consider is that fame is not shared out equally according to talent. Fame is bestowed upon a few people who do the movie acting and studio recording for the rest of us. Meanwhile, other talented people are given exponentially less fame, not because they are exponentially less talented, but because only so many people can be renowned enough to be household names at the same time.

> **ADH-YOU:** All the more impressive that I made it into such an exclusive club.

No doubt, YOU! But try to keep in mind that the means by which you are selected for the job of being a famous entertainer is a combination of talent, luck of opportunity, ambition, intangible fame-begetting activities (such as dating another celebrity), and, of course, looks.

> **NOTE:** I don't want to suggest here that the pretty girl or guy who gets the role isn't also talented, but they may not be any more talented than the less pretty person. I recall that, when the group Milli Vanilli was caught duping the music community by presenting a good-looking duo lip-synching to the music of not-so-good-looking singers, a young Whitney Houston—in the prime of her beauty and musical success—claimed to be baffled by this behaviour.
>
> **HOUSTON:** I made it on my God-given talent!
>
> Hmm, yes, Ms. Houston, you were exceptionally talented, but perhaps you might have acknowledged that it's easier to make it on your divinely-supplied skills when that same deity also imbues you with beauty.

The nature of the entertainment business is that, once you're selected for fame (via the above criteria), your work is viewed by millions or even billions, and so it only takes a tiny fraction of that audience to *like* your work for it to become a hit. Yay, your album sold a million copies, which means that 1/7000th of the world paid to hear you. Not that you shouldn't be proud that so many people wanted to give up their money to listen to you, but you're not necessarily any better at being a musician than Dr. Kidney Transplant and Dr. Without Borders are at being physicians: the leading difference is that they—unlike digital downloads—can't be everywhere at the same time, so they have much less opportunity to gain your popularity.

> **HINT:** Please be careful of claiming that your album or movie was the most popular in history because it sold the most copies (or downloads) ever. Don't forget that our population is getting both bigger and more connected, and so the Beatles and the original Star Wars simply didn't have as many humans available to impress.

THE POWER OF HUMILITY

Another thing I've noticed about CELEBRITY-YOU is that you're willing to be modest about your craft so long as you're receiving compliments for your work. For instance:

> **INTERVIEWER:** So some critics have referred to your latest album as a ground breaking collaboration of poetry and angst.
>
> **ADH-YOU (*smiling*):** Well, that's very humbling. It's certainly my goal to bring my personal angst into my music. I wouldn't necessarily say it's ground breaking, though, as I think Lady Zesto and L. Ron Cool J. pioneered that sound.

Nice! You showed humility by acknowledging your predecessors, without denying the compliment completely by accepting that it matched your aim. But watch what happens to your line of response when the critics aren't so flattering.

> **INTERVIEWER:** However, some critics have found your latest music video to be a poor influence on your young fans because it shows you and other young adults running around a mall terrorizing mall-goers.
>
> **ADH-YOU:** Well, what they are failing to see is that *we* are feeling terrorized by the rules of society. Some people get it when they listen to my music—like those other critics who see the struggle between

my music and my suffering—and some people just don't get it.

Okay, see, I'm a bit confused. A moment ago you were humbled by the critics' love, and now you seem emboldened by their disapproval. Moreover, when you refer to those who dislike your work as "not getting it," you are suggesting that objectively there is a beauty in your ideas that they simply do not have the intelligence or artistic depth to comprehend. Sadly, this illuminates the fact that you measure people's intelligence by their opinion of you, which means, when they praise your work, you are not humbled, after all, but instead are approving of their good judgment.

> **ADH-YOU:** Well I was being modest at first, just to be polite. But, if someone's going to criticize me, then I'm not going to sit back and take it!

Fair enough! I don't have a problem with you faking modesty, but unfortunately, humility works best when it's not disproven a moment later. So, for instance, if you follow it up with a self-congratulating attack on your critics, the disingenuousness of your modesty is tragically highlighted.

> **ADH-YOU:** Well, what am I supposed to do about that?

Here's my suggestion: treat the criticism with the same tentativeness that you did the praise. Just as you pretended that you didn't think the compliments you received were objectively correct, think of each criticism as nothing more than the opinions of another person. This will allow you to be equally intrigued by positive and negative responses to your work. Try this, for instance:

> **INTERVIEWER:** Some of your critics have said that your usage of women in bikinis throughout your music videos is sexist.

ALTERNATE-YOU: Yes, I've heard that, and it concerns me if that's how some people are taking my videos. It certainly wasn't my intent. I was hoping that, by juxtaposing those women with my harsh lyrics, the viewer would get a sense of the harshness of life for women in the bikini model industry. Perhaps that didn't come across as well as I would have liked.

Brilliant! Do you see how ALTERNATE-YOU is now responding to the positive and negative criticism in a consistent manner? In both cases, ALTERNATE-YOU has acknowledged the commentary and contrasted it with what you intended. The audience can now decide for themselves what they think—without the insinuation that if they do not perceive your work in a positive way, they are simply unworthy of it. (Plus, ironically, such humility improves your image more than arrogance does.)

Chapter 22

Getting a Date with You

As you know, you're a great catch.

> **ADH-YOU:** No argument here, pal.

However, sometimes that doesn't come across in your dating efforts—

> **ADH-YOU:** Um, yeah, I really don't need this chapter. I know how to get a date. It's just a matter of showing enough of myself to get them interested before I switch to being aloof and/or hard-to-get. Then they'll have to chase me.

Very clever of you! You are indeed a master of such games. And I'm sure it works much of the time. I have just one wee quibble with it: your method—by virtue of its playing on people's self-doubt—is less likely to appeal to people with self-confidence; and, since you have a good bunch of confidence in yourself, I suspect you may be interested to see if you could attract someone who also possesses self-belief. If I'm right, then get ready to groan because the best technique for luring confident people is to treat them with respect.

> **ADH-YOU:** Is that all? Well, I can fake that!

If only it were so simple. Tragically, the people who are immune to the reverse psychology of playing hard-to-get and aloofness are also adept at recognizing the distinction between performance and sincerity. Your only loophole, then, is to learn to be genuinely decent to your prospective dates.

Chapter 22: *Getting a Date with You*

PICKING UP DATES

The Hunter

The first step in seeking dates is to view individual people as creatures with complex internal workings, as opposed to members of a collective with the identical thoughts and personalities as the rest in their hive.

> **ADH-YOU:** But Chris Rock said—

Yes, I know comedians have told you that generalizations are the key to understanding relationships. But just in case you run into a rare person who doesn't match those factory specifications, I suggest you let the person across from you explain who they are instead of informing them of their personality by virtue of the inferences you've made based on their gender, race, culture, or dietary preferences.

Now let's talk about pick-up lines.

> **ADH-YOU:** Better alert traffic control, because looking at you just made my heart soar.

Hee, hee, thank you. You're very sweet. Sadly, though, the trouble with these prepared "romantic" phrases is that generally they will sound as though they were invented for any person instead of the one with whom you're talking. If you have something in particular to say to *that* person, then go for it; otherwise, it can actually seem impersonal. If you really love your pick-up lines, I suggest using them as a joke once you've started a conversation with your intended friend.

Moreover, when you engage a person, I suggest studying their reactions to you, and lowering your intensity if they seem disconcerted. For instance, if innuendo of a lascivious nature is your preference, but your intended doesn't seem to enjoy your special flavouring, maybe save that style of humour for another audience.

And, finally, even if the object of your attraction is very good looking, they might find it boring if you treat them as though that is their only quality worth considering. As an incredibly attractive person yourself, I'm sure you can appreciate that.

> **ADH-YOU:** Yeah, I guess it's annoying when people don't see beyond this face.

Exactly! While most people with good looks are pleased to have them, you probably want your future spouse to like you for other qualities, too, do you not?

> **ADH-YOU:** Fine. I'll compliment their drink preference, too.

Good enough for now. Thanks, YOU!

The Prey

On the other side of the romance, if you notice that someone is aiming to date you, but you don't feel the same butterflies in your belly for them, then—even if your ego enjoys the warmth of their attraction—try not to lead them on by giving them the impression that you will go for them even though you know you won't.

> **ADH-YOU:** But why should it matter how I treat them if I'm not going to date them anyway?

Right, good point. The official reason is that it would be more kind to your suitor if you didn't give them false hope, but I suppose it's asking a lot of you to take that into consideration when you're enjoying some flattery, which is perhaps your favourite commodity in this world.

> **ADH-YOU:** Hey, if letting people adore me is wrong, I don't wanna be right.

Understood. Would you accept, then, that releasing the fish you don't want back into the sea will help create the impression to other, more compatible suitors who happen to be nearby that (A) you're available, and (B) you're confident enough to forgo a free ego boost for the sake of sparing someone else a futile pursuit?

> **ADH-YOU:** I guess.

Whew, thank you! I didn't have much else to offer you on that one.

Next, then, when it comes to turning down your pursuers, I request that you react with kindness. You see, you never know when the person to whom you direct your understandable disdain may turn out to have feelings of their own. I understand that you are excessively attractive, and it can be presumptuous of certain goblins to even dream of joining you in a waltz. Nevertheless, I am told that there is no chapter in the beautiful person's handbook that says the mere invitation from a lesser being will harm your reputation. To impersonate a kind reply, then, I suggest aiming for a curvature of your lips (this will create the impression of a smile), and then a vocalization of gratitude for the invitation—you might even claim to be flattered—and then, as you decline the invitation, be gentle on the first pass.

> **ADH-YOU:** How could depriving someone of my company possibly be gentle?

Good question, YOU. Maybe pretend that you are explaining to a five year old that you are unable to give them candy at this time (that should create a reasonable facsimile of compassionate attention).

> **ADH-YOU:** Okay, I'll try. But, if I know my stalkers, they're going to keep asking if I go so easy on them.

Fair enough, if they persist in making proposals, then you may precede to a more direct reply ("No really, I'm fine, thank you"). If that doesn't take, you can switch to a smirk as you decline; after that, if they're still insisting, then you are free to unleash your full ADH-ME at them.

ONLINE DATING

Are You A Winner Or A Loser?

I'm not ashamed—although I am a little nervous—to admit that I have tried online dating more than once (and I even married one of the people I met there). As far as my ego is concerned, I believe it's as legitimate as any other means of meeting members of the gender you want to date.

> **ADH-YOU:** Nah, sorry, bud. Online dating is for losers.

I'm sure you're right as always, but before you lock that opinion down, can I ask you to consider where you have met *your* mate(s)? Perhaps you have come across your match(es) at school—

> **ADH-YOU:** Yup, I've dated a lot at school.

And congratulations! That is certainly an ideal way to meet your future spouse, because it allows you to get to know them in casual school situations before going for romance. But, on the off-chance that you aren't attached to a sweetheart when you finish school, what's next? Meet someone at work?

Chapter 22: *Getting a Date with You*

> **ADH-YOU:** Yeah, the new bookkeeper is cute.

Great, but risky. Office romances can be awkward when they're (A) one-sided, and (B) ended.

> **ADH-YOU:** True, it's gonna be very awkward to submit my payroll stubs after we break up.

Good point! So, instead, maybe you go to the bar to meet people?

> **ADH-YOU:** All the time.

You really think that's better than the internet?

> **ADH-YOU:** Yup.

Really? But how deep an intellectual connection can you develop in a noisy bar or club? The internet has its downsides (which we will soon be exploring), but it allows for the unfettered exchange of (written) conversation preceding the first meeting.

> **ADH-YOU:** Whatever. If conversation is so important to you, there are lots of other places you can meet people other than at bars.

Fair enough. So, if not the bar, then perhaps you feel one should just meet someone in their everyday life—at the gym, a cooking class, the library—wherever humans of one's preferred gender are likely to be.

> **ADH-YOU:** You're on fire, deputy.

Thanks, Captain! Certainly, all of these are worthy meeting places, but they require an aptitude for provoking spontaneous romance. To make it work, you must be lucky enough to meet someone you are interested in (and vice versa), and if you want to pursue the chance-romance opportunity, you or they must have the skills to propose a date. This is not easy. And, I submit, it requires a person of particular confidence to initiate.

> **ADH-YOU:** Guilty!

Yes, I know *you* have the necessary self-belief for this pastime; nevertheless, for those of us who are not you, I don't think that a lack of self-assurance in this area implies a lack of fitness to be in a relationship.

Internet dating, then, allows people who are interested in a relationship (and think they're worthy of one) to pursue one without struggling through the turmoil of trying to initiate romance with a stranger or colleague whose return interest they cannot guarantee. Nobody likes making cold calls!

> **ADH-YOU:** If you say so. But why are you telling *me* this? I'm not afraid to flirt with a stranger.

Right, sorry, I defend the legitimacy of online dating because there is still a palpable (although, ever-decreasing) stigma against it in the general community, which is a useful fact to keep in mind if you ever decide to give online dating a try. Thus far, this is how the online version of you has been known to introduce yourself in your profile:

> **ADH-ONLINE-YOU:** Well, I can't believe it. I never thought I'd try this, but, hey, let's give it a shot just to see what all the fuss is about.

Now, I can empathize with your sheepishness to be dipping your toes into these uncool waters, but—

> **ADH-YOU:** Thanks, yeah, it wasn't easy.

I understand. But, by your embarrassed-to-be-there tone, you seem to be implying that the medium is generally for losers, and that you're the *one* person who is cooler than the whole process, but is nevertheless trying it out for a lark. If that's the case, why do you even want to go on a date with one of the rest of us?

> **ADH-YOU:** You said it—for a lark.

Well played. Okay, let me try this from another angle. You may be surprised to discover that we were all instinctively embarrassed the first time we tried online dating so there's really no need to point it out. Instead, if you've decided that the internet is a sufficiently legitimate place to meet people and you're willing to give it a try, then act like it. Simply present yourself and make the case for why you're a good catch; perhaps describe the sort of person you're hoping to be snared by, and then put yourself out there. It can actually be freeing to admit to the whole internet that you, specifically—with all your nuanced traits—would indeed like to meet your match.

Too Good To Be You

Once you make the decision to go for it, please take your time creating your online profile.

> **ADH-YOU:** What's an online profile?

Oh, sorry, most online dating websites set you up with a profile, in which you answer questions about yourself, such as your interests, the traits you're looking for in a partner, your favourite books and movies, and so on.

> **ADH-YOU:** Sounds corny.

I'm sure you're right, and I know your preference—when responding to such questions—will likely be to randomly throw words at the screen. For instance:

> **ADH-YOU**: Hey, this is me. I'm a virgo. And I like... what do I like? I dunno. I like *The Big Bang Theory*. It's on in the background while I'm typing right now. It's the one where Sheldon's mom has an affair. I love that show. Anyway, I also like...

Now, I know that you're simply giving a sincere representation of what you're actually thinking while you're typing, but unfortunately, by treating your online profile as though it's a doodle that you don't need to put any thought into, you are once again accidentally making it seem that you think the process is beneath you.

> **ADH-YOU**: But it *is* beneath me.

Exactly right, but if you're looking for someone who is at least within the vicinity of your greatness, then surely you'll want to give such higher-level candidates the impression that you think that they—unlike the rest of the riffraff—are *close* to being worthy of you?

> **ADH-YOU**: I don't follow.

Right, okay, how about this? In spite of the fact that you're the most amazing catch in the history of the internet, many of the other people online haven't met you, so if you don't give them any information that demonstrates your greatness (other than your attractive picture), then how are those few worthy matches supposed to distinguish you from everyone else?

> **ADH-YOU**: I dunno. I'm me. People can usually tell pretty quick that I'm different from the rest.

I'm sure that's true out in the world, but online—where your future dates can't see your mannerisms and how you're relating to others—it's harder for them to detect your unique flavour of awesomeness. So I suggest adding a dash of panache to your personal presentation. If you're intelligent, talk about something that *you* would find interesting if you had never met you before; if you're a wit, maybe add a funny comment.

> **ADH-YOU:** Done! Here comes the funny!

Great! And don't forget to spell check! When your errors are unchecked, it looks like you don't respect your readers enough to care about how you're coming across, and so once again you may scare off those few people from whom you would like a response.

Finally, I know we talked about this in Chapter 11, but when you write your internet profile, do you go capital free?

> **adh-u:** don't tell me u want me using capitals on my dating profile now, 2! dating's supposed 2 be relaxed. if u could just let me be who i am, that'd be gr8. thanx.

Fair enough: if that's truly who you are in all settings, go for it—why falsely advertise that you're someone different? Just remember that this is not the same as a casual text message with a friend; it's your first correspondence with a stranger. If you would in fact greet a stranger with the honour of capitals, then perhaps in this case, too, it might be worth letting your audience know that you respect them enough to press the occasional shift key.

Cliché Dating

All right, enough lecturing, let's see what you've got so far on your profile:

> **ADH-DATING-YOU:** I like music and long walks on the beach, so contact me if you're interested.

Wow, that's really great. You sound awesome. My only concern is that I'm still not sure you've given your future fans much of a sense of your personality. You may be surprised to learn that, amongst humans, both music and beach-walking are popular pastimes, so you haven't particularly distinguished yourself from the rest of us.

> **ADH-YOU:** Well, I don't think that'll be a problem. Have you seen my picture?

Hee, hee, well put. You are quite the eye candy, aren't you? I'm nervous just typing to you. And the truth is you probably *will* get lots of attention just for your appearance. But again I wonder if you might be interested in meeting someone who likes you for more than just your exquisite appearance?

> **ADH-YOU:** Yeah, I guess.

Well, if you are indeed looking for someone who can spot your inner beauty, I suggest you add some substance to your profile's sparkle. You see, if you use only your looks to garner attention, then it's likely that the only people who seek you out will be those solely interested in your outer beauty. However, if you are looking for someone who is interested in talking to you, then let's see if we can remove some pat phrases from your profile to make sure that no one mistakes your common language for common thought.

> **ADH-YOU:** Well, sometimes the best way to express something is with the simplest phrase.

Yes, fair enough. But the tricky thing is, if you *only* use pat phrases to describe yourself, then—instead of illuminating the content of those clichés favourably in your direction—you may instead be illustrating that you can think of nothing original to say. Which I know isn't true!

For instance, in my time online, I discovered the two most popular phrases that people used to describe themselves were (1) that they "love to laugh," and (2) that they wanted to "live life to the fullest."

> **ADH-YOU:** Hey, that's exactly how I would describe *me*! I love a good laugh: laughter really is the best medicine, after all. And, as for living life to the fullest, I'm totally on board with that plan, too. I'm going to grab life by the "Carpe Diem," and get out there, and be myself, and all that I can be!

Well said, YOU! You sound so great. My only quibble is that, for the person who doesn't know you, there might not be anything in particular that they can learn about *you* from your statements of laugh-loving and full-life-living.

> **ADH-YOU:** No, no, you're *way* off on this one. You can totally tell from that description that I'm really funny and that I love to go out and do cool stuff.

Good point as always, YOU. Let me put this another way: how many people do you know who *don't* love to laugh? How many people, that is, get in a bad mood after a good laugh?

> **ADH-YOU:** I dunno. I don't keep count. What's your point?

Well, in reality, there are few people on earth for whom laughing is not an enjoyable exercise, so, when you say that you "love to laugh," you are really just saying, "I enjoy the same stuff that most humans do." And that's grand, but it doesn't tell your perspective suitor much about you (which is ironic, since you have so much to say about you!).

> **ADH-YOU:** I don't follow.

Okay, consider this. If you put on your profile, "I love to breathe—oxygen in particular," then clearly all you've really told your hoped-for suitors is that you're an Earth-dweller.

> **ADH-YOU:** Of course I'm an Earth-dweller. Where do they think I'm from?

Exactly! The statement was already assumed before you said it, so you didn't really need to say it.

> **ADH-YOU:** Okay, what's your point?

Well, it's the same when you list laughter enjoyment among your chief pleasures. You're stating the obvious.

Instead, then, why not give a little detail about what makes you laugh? Who puts the JC in your comedy taste buds—John Cleese or Jim Carrey? (Or, better yet, both!) Or—and this is getting pretty advanced—instead of announcing that you like humour, why not demonstrate a sprig of whimsy in your profile?

> **FUN FACT:** In my experience, when a person uses the phrase "I love to laugh," the rest of their profile is resoundingly humourless 99% of the time. (I guess such people love to laugh, but are not interested in provoking others to enjoy the same pastime.)

Similarly, when you tell us of your inclination "to live life to the fullest," you are, ironically, giving the emptiest statement imaginable to illustrate your preference. Certainly, there are some people who live more full lives than others, but, once again, I think if you conducted a survey, you would discover that somewhere between 99 and 100% of people hope that their life is filled to the brim with good stuff.

So, as with your love of freedom and a roof over your head, your full-life preference isn't telling us anything that distinguishes you from the other thousands of romance candidates on the dating site. So why not instead list some of the activities that

Chapter 22: *Getting a Date with You*

fill up your life? If you like to seek adventure, fantastic: tell us about some of your adventures.

> **ADH-YOU:** How about this? "I hate sitting at home and watching TV—I'd rather go out to an art gallery or the theatre."

Sure, that's fine. It's maybe a little negative, but at least now other TV-dissenters will be able to find you.

> **ADH-YOU:** Okay, how about, "I love to travel and see the world"?

Once again, that one's a wee bit standard amongst the dating community, but there are a few people who aren't travellers, so it's not a complete waste of profile space. Nevertheless, I would still suggest aiming for a teensy bit more detail. Maybe explain what it is about travel that you like. For instance:

> **ALTERNATE-DATING-YOU:** I love travel because I like being in a place where I'm completely separate from everyone I know. I feel like I can just be a fly in the wall for a while without having to participate in anything if I don't feel like it.

Cool. Very interesting. I'm intrigued, and I'm not even a traveller. Do you see how, with just a couple of specific sentences, ALTERNATE-YOU has said so much more than your all-purpose cliché ever could?

> **ADH-YOU:** I guess. But I really can't be bothered to go into all this detail. I'm a great catch. If people can't see that, screw 'em!

Well put! But remember, even though you are indeed the greatest, there is no way for your potentials to know that unless (A) you're on a psychic dating site, or (B) you tell surfers-by just a little bit about yourself that they couldn't have guessed from the fact that you're human.

Ego-Dating (Self-Congratulations!)

As you know, you're really smart and attractive—a lot more so than most of us.

> **ADH-YOU:** Awe, shucks. That's true.

Yes! And I'm really proud of you for it. However, in human interaction, there is a strange unwritten rule that one ought not claim certain aptitudes—such as intelligence or good looks—for oneself. Instead, it's your observers' job to decide for themselves whether they see those traits in you. As a result, dating profiles that lead with "Smart, sexy single with a great personality" sound more silly than accurate.

> **ADH-YOU:** You're kidding, right? The truth is silly now?

Well queried. How can I explain this? There is nothing wrong with being aware of one's own intelligence or attractiveness, but when you describe yourself using these adjectives, it sounds awkwardly arrogant to the reader. Telling someone that you're sexy is like going on a date and saying, "Don't I smell nice?" You may, indeed, smell swell, but unless you're being playful, it's best to let your date notice and point it out (or not). Below are a few more self-assessments that you may want to avoid.

> **NOTE:** Except when otherwise noted, these self-assessments are paraphrased from actual profiles that I encountered.

(1) ADH-DATING-YOU: I'm really funny.

Yeah, see, humour is in the laugh of the beholder. This doesn't mean that, if your date fails to find you funny, you're not. However, if they don't think that you're funny, why bother telling them that you are? Most people believe themselves to be the best arbiters of funny, so they'll probably trust their own lack of laughing over your insistence to the contrary.

> **HINT:** As suggested in the previous section, if you're looking for someone who will laugh at your jokes, then—instead of announcing that you're hilarious—why not offer a joke or two in your profile? That way, you'll attract people who appreciate your comedy, and weed out those too stupid to get it.

(2) ADH-DATING-YOU: I'm a delight to be around.

Yeah, you are! Tragically, once again, social convention says that it's up to the delighted to point it out.

(3) ADH-DATING-YOU: I'm the life of the party.

This is a tough one. It may, in fact, be interesting to learn that you're a social butterfly who gets the fun going at gatherings. However, the term "life of the party" may again seem awkwardly self-celebrating, so I suggest that—in lieu of diagnosing yourself as the best at parties—you simply describe your friendly intentions. For instance:

> **ALTERNATE-DATING-YOU:** I really like getting to know people, and I enjoy trying to be a catalyst for conversation.

Not bad at all, ALTERNATE-YOU! Even though ALTERNATE-YOU has portrayed you with a positive description, ALTERNATE-YOU is not announcing that you should be commended for it.

(4) ADH-DATING-YOU: I have a great physique.

Once again, there's no doubt about that! But it's an odd thing to say about yourself—especially since your date can probably make their own assessment based on their particular tastes—which may, surprisingly, be different from your own.

(5) ADH-DATING-YOU (on a date with a blind person): I wish you could see what I look like tonight.

Hee, hee, that one's taken from a scene in the movie *Daredevil* in which the love interest of the blind superhero accidentally went a little narcissistic in her seduction attempt.

> **HINT:** If you are dating a blind person, and you're worried that they don't realize how good looking you are, I'll bet their sighted friends will keep them in the loop, so I wouldn't worry about making sure they know.

(6) ADH-DATING-YOU: I've got a great head on my shoulders.

As with humour, instead of declaring your intelligence, why not demonstrate it? (This should both scare off intellect-resisters while enticing smart-people-fans.)

> **ADH-YOU:** How? You want me to write an essay on the theory of relativity?

No, you don't have to go that far. I was just thinking you could say something interesting or unusual that could get your suitors' brains intrigued.

(7) ADH-YOU: Well, I never compliment myself, but my friends tell me I have a great musical ability.

Okay, I stole this one from Mrs. Elton in Jane Austen's *Emma*, because I think her character brilliantly illustrates how ADH-YOU sometimes attempt to get around society's anti-boasting laws (by instead quoting someone else complimenting you). Well done, YOU! It is certainly a less obvious show of ego, but be careful: if you do this too often, your date might start to mentally accuse you of an arrogance loophole.

Ego-Dating (Your Application Process)

When creating your profile, please avoid making it seem too much as though potential matches are applying to work for you. So, for instance, let's look at how you would normally fill out the section in which you are asked to describe your ideal match:

> **ADH-DATING-YOU:** You need to be an animal-lover who is in great shape.

While, of course, there is nothing wrong with noting that you find particular traits essential in a future spouse, do you see how your requirements sound similar to a job posting? This creates the impression that you see yourself as the obvious top prize in any dating scenario, as opposed to simply a person who is putting themselves into the sea to see if they can find another fish with whom to swim.

> **ADH-YOU:** But I *am* the top prize.

Yes, I'm aware, of course, that you are superior to your suitors. But, once again, acting like it may perturb those potentials who just might have been able to live up to your expectations. So, instead of listing qualities that you require in a candidate in order to attain an interview with you, I suggest that you simply describe the type of person you're hoping to meet, perhaps in relation to your own qualities and traits.

> **ALTERNATE-DATING-YOU:** I love animals, so I'm hoping to find someone who loves them, too. And I enjoy staying physically fit and am looking for someone who does the same.

Yay! Well done, ALTERNATE-YOU. Do you see how, instead of displaying yourself as the prize amongst two daters, ALTERNATE-YOU has now made you sound like a human being who is looking for a teammate?

> **ADH-YOU:** I guess. If I must.

Deal!

Online "Hi"

> **NOTE:** This one seems to be most commonly the product of heterosexual men (perhaps because our culture still prefers men to take the lead in suggesting dates with women), so I direct the general rant towards HE-YOU, but, if you're a NON-HE-YOU who takes part in this behaviour, feel free to listen as well.

Allegedly, in the real world, the most successful pick-up line is simply "Hi." I wouldn't be surprised, given that all other pick-up lines may seem contrived by comparison—especially when they are directed at strangers.

However, in the internet world wherein participants set up intricate profiles describing themselves, and then have a mailbox in which to receive messages from interested daters, there is plenty of room and opportunity for a more detailed introduction. Nevertheless, I am told by my female online dating advisors that many men will respond to their profile by sending them a message that simply says, "Hi." Unfortunately, without eye contact and a smile, the result comes across as familiar and yet vacant.

One of my friends has taken to requesting on her profile that men *not* send her a message simply saying "Hi"; instead, she asks them to tell her about themselves and why they wanted to contact her. Alas, she still repeatedly receives the "Hi" message. This either means these gentlemen are ignoring her request or didn't read her profile; in either case, she has no interest in replying, which is sad, since I'm sure "Hi"-YOU are awesome!

> **ADH-YOU:** Hi.

Hello, YOU! Yes, I see you there being delightful. And I know you are a great catch. So, when you send your potential love-interest a message, I suggest you give them something to go on to help them realize your wonderfulness. It's fine to be brief, but try to include a smidge of content, such as a comment about something you liked in your hoped-for new friend's profile; then throw in a quick question and you're done!

> **ADH-YOU:** But, if I have to do that with every profile I pursue, it's going to take hours!

Ahah, I see what's happening. You're dating in bulk. That is, you're simply sending "Hi" to every dater whose picture you like, am I right?

> **ADH-YOU:** You got it. I don't care if most of 'em don't reply. I only need three or four to respond.

I see what you mean. While spamming potential dates may annoy most of them, as long as you hear from a few of them, you're all set.

> **ADH-YOU:** Bingo.

Okay, well, I admit that your "Hi" method certainly is a fast way of starting conversations with the few people who reply. But consider this: in the world of dating, you're a luxury automobile. Am I right?

> **ADH-YOU:** Sounds about right, mate.

So I'm just thinking that, while spam can be an effective way to build a business, it may cost you the high-end customers that you deserve. Do you see what I'm saying?

> **ADH-YOU:** I'm listening.

Well, here's a thought. Instead of spam-dating, try reading the profiles of your candidates and picking out the one(s) you're most interested in, and just replying to those! Then you can tailor your messages to those specific people instead of simply pasting "Hi" into the mailbox of each attractive person on the site. It may seem time-consuming at first, but in the long run, you'll have fewer dates with random "Hi" people who are unworthy of your greatness.

Online Time To Meet

Some online daters prefer to communicate electronically for a long time before they agree to meet. I don't blame you if you find that frustrating.

> **ADH-YOU:** Yeah, what's the hold up? If we don't have chemistry in person, then all this emailing back and forth will have been a waste of time.

I don't want to alarm you, but in principle I agree with you. In fact, my suggestion to all prospective daters is not to spend a lot of time falling into blissful infatuation via online correspondence before meeting. As you suggest, it turns out that online and in-person chemistry don't always overlap, so meeting early can help minimize disappointment.

> **ADH-YOU:** Hmm, now that you agree with me, I think I must have been wrong.

Fair enough, go ahead and take the opposite side of the argument.

> **ADH-YOU:** Well, maybe I *should* be careful. There are a lot of creeps out there. Better to be safe than sorry.

True, but I think the safety issue is actually an easily solved anxiety. Set up that first date at a neutral location, such as a coffee shop or restaurant. Meeting someone at a coffee shop is as safe as going to a coffee shop without date plans and happening to strike up a conversation with a stranger.

> **ADH-YOU:** Fine. No more delays. I'll always set up the meetings right away from now on.

Great, except we should acknowledge that certain people in the dating world (more often women-type people) may not feel comfortable meeting unless they're confident that safety precautions are included in the arrangement. My instruction to ADH-YOU is to *not* take those safety policies personally. She (or he) is not insulting you—they are merely acknowledging that they do not know you yet. While they think that they probably have nothing to worry about, one never knows when a dangerous person might strike, and so they are smartly protecting themselves in advance. You wouldn't want your future spouse to be callous about safety, would you?

> **ADH-YOU:** I guess not.

Yay, YOU! Nevertheless, I have heard several stories from female friends about ADH-DATERS who became annoyed by their safety restrictions. Apparently, ADH-YOU will pout and act wounded by her unwillingness to be picked up in your car for the first date.

> **ADH-YOU:** But I've never hurt a woman in my life.

It's a good point, but I'm afraid it's also your ADH-ME talking. Once again, you are taking knowledge that you happen to have acquired about yourself (that you are a safe and lovely person) and assuming that, because you know it, everyone else should, too.

Expectations

Now before we send you on that first date, let's talk about some of those expectations that you and your date may have for each other.

(1) THEIRS:

One of your habits as an online dater is that you sometimes accidentally claim things about yourself that aren't strictly true.

> **ADH-YOU:** What could you possibly mean by that?

Well, have you ever, I don't know, claimed an occupation that you don't really have, or sent pictures of yourself that are not only flattering, but—through tricks of light and angle—give a definitively false impression of what you look like most of the time?

> **ADH-YOU:** Well that's just good self-promotion. What's wrong with that?

Well, first of all, some of your deceptions—such as a false height claim—will be particularly baffling to your future dates because they are disprovable the moment you meet.

> **ADH-YOU:** Well, how else can I make sure they'll want to go out with me? Most people want someone who looks like that and has a job like that.

Well pondered, YOU. I understand your predicament: *you* know you are a wonderful person, but you're worried that your

Chapter 22: *Getting a Date with You*

looks or job or criminal record are biasing people against you. And so, for their own sake, you feel you must misrepresent certain features about yourself so that your potential love-interests can get to know you first.

> **ADH-YOU:** Bingo. I'm tired of people being prejudiced against ME. So I present a ME.2.0 for them to enjoy.

Well explained, YOU. And I empathize with your frustration. However, I think you're assuming that shallowness, occupation-based-discrimination, and other dating biases are traits that you can cure. People are allowed to be shallow and/or elitist if they want to be. It may mean that they'll miss out on some meaningful moments in life, but, in the end, they can prioritize whatever they like in a match.

> **ADH-YOU:** But, if I tell people I'm an astronaut, I find they're quite intrigued, and that gets me a lot of dates.

I see your point. ASTRONAUT-YOU does sound pretty interesting.

> **ADH-YOU:** Yeah, and you know what: if I tell people online that I speak five languages, I bet I can get them to fall for me before I have to admit the truth.

Right, that does make a lot of sense, but unfortunately, I think most people will second-guess their affectionate disposition towards you when they discover that it was nourished by lies.

> **ADH-YOU:** Wait, so you want me to just list the things about myself that I think people will find *un*attractive.

No, sorry, I'm not suggesting that you turn your profile into a repository of your flaws. I just don't want you to claim facts about yourself that are definitively untrue. Instead, I recommend presenting a positive, but honest portrayal of yourself. In doing so, you may not attract as many suitors, but you will know that the ones you do acquire are interested in the person you actually are.

(2) YOURS:

Now, if you're in the position of feeling misled by a person's online profile, you have my sympathies. But please try not to be too harsh in your response. When you meet a person who you feel doesn't live up to, say, their photo, please consider smiling and having a respectful encounter anyway. (Even if there's no chance for a love connection, there is a chance for learning about a stranger, and not destroying their emotional wellbeing.)

> **ADH-YOU:** But they lied to me. Why do I need to be polite to a fraud?

I see your point (in fact, I wrote about it in the previous section). But the misleaders don't always realize that they've portrayed themselves in a manner that would give you the wrong impression, so maybe you could give them a break and save your anger for someone who isn't in the nervous position of being on a date.

> **ADH-YOU:** Fine, if have to.

Thanks, YOU! You won't regret it.

SPEED-DATING

Seth Goes Speed-Dating

Speed-dating is an all-you-can-meet personality buffet. Several years ago I went inside that strangely sped-up world and lived to blush about it.

It turns out that speed-dating participants range from the obscenely nervous (my insides seemed to think I was about to make a speech, while naked, on a tight rope, being chased by a lion), to the irritatingly confident (imagine my disappointment as I watched Good-Looking Guy warming up by flirting with some attractive women who weren't even staying for the festivities). However, as with most anxiety-provoking activities, once the opening bell rang, the challenge quickly became less daunting.

> **ADH-YOU:** I don't get why you were nervous in the first place. It's just people. You've met people before, haven't you?

Good point, YOU. You're right—it wasn't too bad. In fact, most of us behaved respectfully towards each other even in cases where there wasn't a speedy connection; we seemed to appreciate that we were all taking a leap of nerves to be there. As we progressed through our 23 mini-dates, however, some ADH-CONTESTANTS seemed to become tired and grumpy. I encountered several women who appeared to feel no obligation to assist in running our whirlwind conversations. Their job, apparently, was to sit and wait for my queries, responding to each with one or two glorious words for me to bask in before I asked my next question. Their behaviour was soaked with so much self-certainty that I wondered if I should ask for their autographs.

> **ADH-YOU:** I thought you said I wasn't supposed to lead people on when I'm not interested!

Well caught, YOU. And certainly I was surprised to discover later that several flirtatious woman (including one who treated my wrist as though it was her own personal armrest) left me off their "Let's meet again" list at the end of the evening. But surely there is a middle ground here between (1) hinting that you see romance in a date's future, and (2) rudeness.

> **ADH-YOU:** That's so abstract. Exactly how rude is *too* rude?

Well, consider my mini-date with an ADH-SPEED-DATER (nicknamed "Chicken-wing Girl") who perhaps could have toned down her rudeness a smidge without causing me to fall in love with her.

>**SETH (*arriving, with a smile, at Chicken-Wing Girl's station*):** Hi.
>
>*Chicken-wing Girl took a chomp of her barbecue-flavoured-meal.*
>
>**CHICKEN-WING GIRL:** Hi.
>
>**SETH:** Um, how are you liking the speed-dating so far?
>
>*Chicken-wing Girl shrugged as she considered and then took her next bite.*
>
>**CHICKEN-WING GIRL:** It's fine.
>
>*I waited for her to make a dent in the mouthful.*
>
>**SETH:** So, um, what do you do with your free time?
>
>*Chicken-wing Girl was still clearly much more fascinated with the meal in front of her than the speed-dater opposite her.*
>
>**CHICKEN-WING GIRL:** I'm a nurse.
>
>**SETH:** Oh, cool, do you like the work?
>
>**CHICKEN-WING GIRL (*through a heavy mouthful*):** Yeah, I guess.

SETH (*desperately reaching for a joke to open up the conversation*): So, um, you must have a lot of *patience*?

CHICKEN-WING GIRL: Yup. Lots of patients to look after.

So, as you can see, while I—

> **ADH-YOU:** So you're saying Chicken-wing Girl was . . . impolite?

Great catch, YOU! Yes, while I appreciate that she didn't give a false impression of romantic interest, her unwillingness to pause her meal to show human interest—

> **ADH-YOU:** But maybe she found you to be completely uninteresting, and was really hungry.

Good point, YOU. And it's certainly your right to be unimpressed with your date—and hungry for your food—but expressing your displeasure so transparently is, in polite society, what we call discourteous. So when you're dating (speedily or otherwise), try to remember that for most people going on dates is an anxiety-cultivating endeavour. Please be as gentle on those nerves as you can manage, and I'm sure you'll do brilliantly!

> **ADH-YOU:** I see your point: I *am* brilliant. Okay, I'll try it your way.

Your dates won't regret it! Thanks, YOU.

Seth's Sister Goes Speed-Dating

In the interest of collecting a balanced perspective, I dispatched one of my sisters to try out speed-dating as well. She discovered that most men were polite and respectful, but that many of them were nervous and trying so hard to be perfect that they weren't unique or interesting. Instead, they engaged in what's known as "Empty-Compliment Dating." For instance:

> **FEMALE-DATER:** So what do you do for a living?
>
> **MALE-ADH-DATER:** I work for X company.
>
> **FEMALE-DATER:** Oh, interesting, and what do you—
>
> **MALE-ADH-DATER:** You're pretty.
>
> **FEMALE DATER:** Oh, thanks. So how do you spend your free time?
>
> **MALE-ADH-DATER:** Right now, I'm spending it admiring you. You're beautiful.

No! Perhaps you genuinely like a woman's looks, but, as mentioned earlier, if that's all you can talk to her about, she's going to suspect you have no interest in her character. Please stop that.

> **HINT:** While complimenting someone's eyes may seem sweeter than cheering on their other physical achievements, it is still a looks-based remark and should not be a substitute for content-based reactions to your date. Indeed, if you are a male ADH-DATER, be advised that many women are used to the standard "I love your eyes" loophole to shallowness and so they may not be as impressed as your magazine advice column told you they would be.

Meanwhile, some über-confident guys broke the speed-dating rules and started asking for their mini-dates' phone numbers during their miniature encounters (instead of simply filling out their speed-dating scorecards which would automatically give out contact info to those who indicated mutual interest in each other). This put the ladies in an unnecessarily awkward position. Patience, my friends.

Speed-Dating Gender Breakdown

Comparing heterosexual men and heterosexual women speed-daters yielded interesting results (which I think can provide lessons to all ADH-DATERS). Female ADH-SPEED-DATERS displayed (A) a greater propensity to be unhelpful in the running of the conversation, and (B) an overindulgence in honesty by allowing their grumpiness (i.e. lack of interest) to shine even when their opponent had been perfectly polite. On the other gender, male ADH-SPEED-DATERS demonstrated a greater frequency of (A) banal compliments in lieu of substantive conversation, and (B) asking for full-length dates right away, instead of allowing for the evening to progress as planned.

> **MALE-ADH-YOU-DATER:** Maybe I over-compliment women because they're not participating in the conversation, so I'm grasping for some way of connecting with them.
>
> **FEMALE-ADH-YOU-DATER:** Or maybe I'm "rude" to men because they won't take the hint from my polite lack of interest.

Well put, YOU and YOU! I suppose I can see why the ADH-BEHAVIOURS of the one sex might be contributing to the ADH-BEHAVIOURS of the other. Nevertheless, I request that you treat each date as a new person instead of automatically convicting them of the crimes of your previous date.

Chapter 23

Dating You

Dating often requires a lot of trial and error before you finally land beside a person with whom you feel you could share a relationship, so it may seem silly to waste your best dating behaviour on people you'll most likely never see again. However, if one of those people turns out to be Mr. or Mrs. YOU, there's no way to re-do that first date. As a result, when you tell your friends the story of how you first met, you're stuck with those things you said and did. So, for the sake of those future stories, I recommend aiming for your friendliest you.

ARRIVING AT A DATE

Late

When you're significantly late for a date, you are leaving your date waiting to stew in their own anxieties longer than necessary.

> **ADH-YOU:** I'm not following you, champ.

Well, remember how in the regular, non-dating world, being on time was considered good manners because it demonstrated that you valued your companion's time?

> **ADH-YOU:** But I thought that was just for my meetups with friends. What's it got to do with me being late for someone who barely knows me?

Great question, YOU! It turns out that the above effect is magnified on a date, which, in itself, is a leap of hope that one might be meeting someone with whom one can share a significant connection. To be late for such an encounter may create the impression to your potential betrothed that you are callous towards their enjoyment of life, which in turn may hinder their interest in getting to know you.

Not At All

Another thing to avoid on a date is to—without warning—*not* show up for that date. You see, even though I'm sure you have an excellent reason for not keeping your commitment, the human being who is expecting you doesn't know your eloquent justification and so will be left alone with only their thoughts of why they were unworthy of a simple cancellation call.

You don't really want to provoke such a rotten experience in someone else for no other reason than you didn't feel like letting them know in advance, do you?

> **ADH-YOU:** No, I guess not.

> **ADH-YOU-MALEVOLENT:** Actually, I think it's kinda funny.

Fair enough. I suppose if you're an ADH-MALEVOLENT, you're not going to be deterred by the suffering of another. How about this? The prodding pain of being stood up—while not relevant to you in the moment that you cause it—may suddenly become significant to you a year later when you chance upon one of your discarded candidates. But this time they might happen to be in a position of power over you—say, they're deciding whether you get the coveted job for which you're applying. If they happen to remember you from your profile picture—

> **ADH-MALEVOLENT-YOU:** Of course they'll remember me.

Right! And so, if they also recall that they weren't worthy of a cancellation call, they may think of you with less fondness than they do the other applicants. Thus, for the sake of YOU, please be nicer if you change your mind about going on a date with a NOT-YOU.

THE PAYMENT DEBATE

> **NOTE:** This section is focussed on heterosexual relationships, because the specific problem contained within it tends to be based on a gender diversity in the dating pair.

To my mind, the question of who should pay for the first date is one of the most philosophically intriguing in all of modern Western society.

> **ADH-YOU:** It's actually quite simple.

Well done, and as ever I congratulate you on your superior intellect. But I request that you keep in mind that rest of us aren't as smart as you. So don't be too hard on us if we've got it wrong. Let's consider your two possible positions on this:

(1) It may seem obvious to you that, when men and women go on dates, the gentleman should pay.

> **ADH-YOU:** Yup. Given that's the social convention, if a man doesn't pay, he's being rude.

I see what you're saying. But try not to be too offended if your counterpart on the date sees things differently. Men who don't offer to pay, and women who prefer to share in paying, may not mean to be ungracious, but instead may believe that the notion of men paying for women on dates is antiquated and unnecessarily discriminatory.

> **ADH-YOU:** Fine. But how come when I offer to pay for certain women, they go on a feminist tirade that I'm sexist and presumptuous? I'm just trying to be nice.

Yes, I've heard you mention this one before. But, with all due respect, I'm skeptical that this happens as often as you report it.

> **ADH-YOU:** Oh, it happens.

I believe you, of course—and I'll talk to the feminist ranter in a moment. But I have to admit: it seems far-fetched to think that more than 1% of women would agree to a date with a man only to ridicule him for a gesture that she surely knows most men think they're supposed to offer. If she were truly concerned about any sexist implications of you covering her cost, why wouldn't she simply say the following?

> **EQUAL-PAYER-DATER:** Oh, you know what? I prefer to pay my share. In this day and age, I don't think there's any reason to put the expectation on one gender over the other.

So, let me ask you this: if you did hear such a speech, would you be willing to let her halve her way without taking offence?

> **ADH-YOU:** I guess... if it's that big a deal.

I see, by your tone, that you're not delighted to accept shared payment even when it's requested in a civil way. So, if you were caught in such a situation, and you still really wanted to treat your date, maybe you could say something like this:

> **ALTERNATE-YOU:** Fair enough. If that's your preference, that's fine, but I truly did want to take you out, and I invited you, so I'd like to pay, if you're willing.

Nice! Upon hearing such a respectful offer, she may then decide that she feels comfortable with you paying, but if she doesn't, then there is no reason to fight her on the issue. She is taking a principled position that is important to her, which is not a rejection of you, but a rejection of certain societal notions, and so to hassle her on it would be akin to objecting to your vegetarian date's resistance of steak.

Indeed, if you *are* pushy in your opposition to her resistance, then she may wonder why it's *so* important to you to pay, and she may eventually accuse you of sexist motives.

> **ADH-YOU:** See what I mean? I'm just being nice and she's being rude.

Yes, I'm sorry you got caught in her fire. But please note that she's not necessarily criticizing you because you offered to pay, but perhaps because you wouldn't let her decide for herself whether to accept your generous offer. Does that make any sense?

> **ADH-YOU:** I guess.

Thanks YOU! Meanwhile, if you're the lady of the date, and you're in favour of your fellow dater paying for you, don't forget: it's okay to be gracious about it.

> **ADH-YOU:** What exactly do I have to do?

Well, for instance—if the payment debate hasn't been settled in advance—perhaps you could make a sincere movement towards your wallet when it comes time to pay. And if your date ends up paying, you could try thanking him for the gesture.

> **ADH-YOU:** Fine, how's this, "Thank you *so much* for the meal."

Not bad. And, since I know that was hard for you, I'm not even going to request a redo without the sarcasm.

> **ADH-YOU:** Oh, wow, again, thank *so much*.

(2) Now, on the other side of the ledger, maybe you strongly believe men should *not* be expected to pay for the first date, because you don't like forced gender expectations.

> **ADH-YOU:** Exactly! Can't we just treat each other as equals?

Fair enough. But, given that men paying for the first date has been a convention for a long time, do you think you could go easy on the person who does still think they should follow that expectation?

> **ADH-YOU:** Hey! I'm always nice.

No doubt about it. In fact, as I said to your bizarro self—who believes that men *should* pay for the first date—I suspect that the reported numbers of women yelling at men for simply offering to pay has been inflated by certain confused daters.

> **ADH-YOU:** Exactly! It's a myth.

Nevertheless, in case you have ever accidentally gone directly from receiving a payment-offer to a feminist rant, I must say it sounds like entrapment on your part.

> **ADH-YOU:** But men paying for women is sexist!

You might be right. But would you not say that, even in Western societies where we have freed ourselves of most gender-based requirements, there is still a general carryover of assumption that men will pay for the first few dates?

> **ADH-YOU:** So? I don't care what most people do. I refuse to be disrespected.

Well ranted, YOU! But are you sure your date's individual adherence to convention is always intended with disrespect?

> **ADH-YOU:** Why else would he do it?

Well, most cultures thrive on patterns of behaviour, and generally, on a date, all parties are nervous and want to avoid offending their companion. I'm sure some men pay because they're hoping for traditional gender roles in a relationship (and maybe they're searching for someone who feels the same way), but I suspect that most men pay because they think they're supposed to; in fact, they may have noticed that men who don't financially back their dates are portrayed as cheap in sitcoms. So, if it truly bothers you just to be offered a free meal, then why not warn him in advance? Try this:

> **MALE:** Would you like to go to dinner with me?
>
> **ALTERNATE-YOU:** I'd love to! Although, I should warn you that I prefer to pay for my own meal. Would you be okay with going Dutch?

If he has a problem with that, then tirade at will, but if he doesn't, then are we good?

> **ADH-YOU:** All right, fine.

You're within your rights, of course, to turn down a second date with a wrong-minded first-date payer/non-payer on the grounds that they possess an intellectual position that is untenable with your own, but given that the poor slob has now lost their chance with YOU, the greatest catch of all time, the least you could do is be nice to them for the rest of that first date.

> **ADH-YOU:** I see your point.

ON DATE

Location

On a 2011 episode of *Tyra Banks*, the talk-show host chatted with a researcher who explained to us what "science tells us" we should do on dates. The psychologist-type explained that the best activity to engage in on a date is dinner, because "studies show" if you go to a nice place with someone, they will associate that nice atmosphere with you (particularly, they said, if you're the guy who has selected, and is paying for, the choice). Oh my. This assumes that your goal on a date is to impress the other person.

> **ADH-YOU:** Of course that's my goal! Why else am I wearing these uncomfortable shoes?

Fair enough, I'm sure that sometimes making an impressive impression may be your prime task when you're on a date. Perhaps, for instance, you're not a particularly friendly person, but you enjoy the company of romantic potentials, so you may feel you need to trick them into liking you by having items unrelated to your personality represent you. Understandable. Or maybe your goal is a short-term clothing-optional relationship, and so you don't want to waste the time it takes to divulge your great personality, and instead think it would be more efficient to persuade your date, by a flashy demonstration of wealth, that you're worthy of an out-of-clothing examination. As you wish.

> **ADH-YOU:** Thank you.

However, you may one day find yourself hoping to meet someone who enjoys your personality on its merits, and vice versa, and so your prime goal may shift to finding out who each other are after the music stops. In that case, while it's pleasant to go somewhere nice to demonstrate to the person that the date is important to you, I submit that you may want to avoid inflating the scenery so much that it gets in the way of the interaction between you and your candidate.

On a first date, then, dinner—with all its distractions—may impede your pursuit of getting to know each other. For the purpose of acquiring an initial introduction to each other's personalities, I suggest going for "coffee" where conversation instead of atmosphere can run the show.

> **NOTE:** It is of course not the coffee, itself, that is the essential part of going for coffee; instead, the practice refers to going to a café, which is a comfortable but neutral location at which you and your date can acclimatize yourselves to each others' personalities through conversation over whatever beverage you choose. I point this out for the benefit of Matt Damon's supposedly brilliant character in *Good Will Hunting*, who responded to a "coffee" invitation in the most ADH-CONDESCENDING manner possible, and was not even rebuffed for it:
>
> **SKYLAR:** Here's my number. Maybe we could go out for coffee sometime?
>
> **WILL:** Great, or maybe we could go and just eat a bunch of caramels.
>
> **SKYLAR:** What?
>
> **WILL:** When you think about it, it's just as arbitrary as drinking coffee.
>
> **SKYLAR (*laughing*):** Okay, sounds good.
>
> Yikes, to my ear, the response from Skylar ought to have been:
>
> **ALTERNATE-SKYLAR:** Never mind, I'd rather go for a boring old coffee with someone who doesn't talk down to me.

Your Attention

For all genders and gender-preferences, one neat thing you can do on a date is give your counterpart your full attention. I know you sometimes prefer watching the surrounding people and television screens when you're on a date, but, in the process—

> **ADH-YOU:** But what if my date's boring?

Yes, I realize that sometimes you won't find your date to be as interesting or attractive as the person over there, but sadly the dating rulebook says that, by agreeing to an outing, you have promised your temporary companion an hour or so of your attention. I wish I could change the rules for you, but I can't. If you must look around during the encounter then maybe you could share your observations with your date.

Similarly, it is best if you can avoid interacting with your phone during a date; using it may once again create the impression to the person opposite you that they do not have your attention. If you have something crucial that you must deal with, please apologize to your date in advance and explain that you're going to have to check your phone for calls from X person because of Y important reason, and then restrict yourself only to communication from X.

> **ADH-YOU:** Okay, fine, I'll restrict my phone use to Twitter and Snapchat.

Thanks YOU. Close enough.

Your Questions, Please

I know from experience that some people think they're participating in a job interview while they're on a date. That is, they only answer questions and don't see much point in asking their own questions in return.

> **ADH-YOU:** What's wrong with that? If my date doesn't want to know everything about me, why are they on a date with me?

Good point; very poignant. But how do you think they feel when—

> **ADH-YOU:** Wait a minute, you're not going to tell me once again to "Listen unto others as I would have them listen unto me," are you? It's getting a little tired.

Um, no, I certainly wasn't ... um .... right, yes, here's what I was going to say: dating is like a rehearsal for how your relationship might go. So, if you don't ask any questions of your date, you may give off the impression that you only care about your personality and nothing about theirs.

> **ADH-YOU:** I'm good with that.

But that means that, um, let's see ... um ... if you continue dating, your counterpart may assume that you're not curious about who they are, and in turn how they behave towards you, and so they may feel they have licence to treat you badly.

> **ADH-YOU:** That doesn't sound like much fun!

Exactly, so the best thing to do is to feign some interest just so they know that you're watching them.

However, if that doesn't persuade you, then I'm afraid I'm just going to have to pull rank on this one: annoyingly enough, it's considered good manners to share some of the conversational load during a date, and therefore you're expected to ask the occasional question whether you see a benefit in such queries or not.

> **ADH-YOU:** So, in other words, "Listen unto others, as I would have them listen unto me."

Yeah, I'm afraid so. Sorry about that.

Space Invasion (Touch Barrier)

If you *do* like your date—or at least you like the look of them—please be careful of crossing the invisible but clear boundary into their personal space too quickly. I realize that some people like to move faster into that realm than others, and you don't know if you don't try. However, be advised that, if you try to hold your date's hand before they feel they know you well enough to lock palms, you may seem presumptuous to them—and that's rarely good news for your dating potential. If you're sure it's time to give it a shot, try something less definitive (and thus reversible) to break the touch barrier.

> **ADH-YOU:** Like what?

Well, if I may gender profile for a moment: female daters are more often masters of this skill, as they are able to casually touch their date's arm in such a way that, while the receiver can't be certain if it meant anything, they can be sure that they felt it. So try that out, and watch to see if your date (A) pulls back from you, or (B) reciprocates and/or moves in closer. If they stay where they are, that could still mean that they like you back, so you can continue to find other excuses to contact their arm. But if they pull away, then they're not ready for the touch barrier to be removed, or they're not interested at all, in which case, take a break! The date may be salvageable, but only if you don't rush the matter.

Space Invasion (Romance Barrier)

The same goes for the breaking of the romance barrier. Another of my advisors once went on an internet-provoked date with a gentleman, who—before they were able to get a sense of each other's personality—took her on a romantic boat ride during which he whispered supposedly romantic aphorisms in her ear. He followed this stratagem with an attempt to hold her hand.

Not only was my advisor uncomfortable to receive such gestures from a stranger, she also found them to be disingenuous. He was behaving as though he was in love with her, when, in fact, he had just met her. Therefore, his attempts to woo her felt like just that—a play to manipulate a stranger into feeling something for him because of "moves" that had nothing to do with her, and everything to do with what he perceived all women would swoon over.

It may be that occasionally some lonely people will fall for such games, but do you really want to *trick* someone into temporarily falling for you? Given that you are *you*, I would think no pretence would be required for such a result. Am I wrong?

> **ADH-YOU:** No, I see what you're saying. I am indeed me. What more could anyone ask for?

Nothing at all, YOU!

END DATE

Getting Out

Now, let's say that you're having such a bad time on your date that you would like to end the encounter sooner than might normally be expected. This can be a troubling position to be in for sure, but before you exercise your right to leave the meeting prematurely, I have a question for you to consider. Would it be traumatic to give the date its normal due out of respect for your temporary companion, so that they know that—while you won't be writing wedding vows to each other—you believe they are worthy of an hour of your time?

> **ADH-YOU:** Hmm, sounds crazy. But I'll allow you to make your case.

Thanks, YOU! Okay, so, even if there's no spark warming the air between you, your date may be an interesting person from whom you could learn something. Imagine yourself to be a journalist who has to write a story about this person: *what can you find out?*

> **ADH-YOU:** I guess. But what about those times I find my date to be irritating?

Fair enough. In some cases I don't blame you for being unwilling to proceed with a flailing encounter (perhaps you're caught with someone who isn't contributing to the conversation, is generally rude, and/or is supplying overtly sexual jokes even though you're clearly uncomfortable with that line of witticism). If you really don't feel up to staying any longer—

> **ADH-YOU:** Finally! What's on the menu for ditching this dork?

Well, perhaps you could simply thank your date for meeting you, and then indicate that you should get going.

> **ADH-YOU:** I doubt that'll work. They're going to try to keep me there as long as they can.

I understand your concern. So, if your soon-to-be ex-date questions your plan to shorten the encounter, then I think it's fair to increase your honesty quotient and point out that, while they seem like a very X* person (*choose a compliment that sounds believable without being condescending), you don't feel a romantic connection. They very well may agree with you at that point—if only to protect their own pride—and that will be the end of the matter. But, if they pry further, you can tell them you're sorry, but you've made your decision, and now should get going.

> **HINT:** If you smile, look them in the eye, and state as sincerely as you can that it was great to have had an opportunity to get to know them, then hopefully they'll at least feel respected as they ponder the YOU that got away.

To Rescue Call Or Not To Rescue Call?

Now, in lieu of a straight forward explanation that you're ready to end the date, you may feel it would be easier to go with a rescue call.

> **NOTE:** A rescue call is the clandestine manoeuvre wherein you have a friend call you during your date, so that you can pretend that the call is regarding an emergency that needs your immediate attention. If done well, this allows you to leave the date immediately without much debate.

> **ADH-YOU:** I know what a rescue call is: it's my favourite exit strategy. I'll just do that. We done here?

Not just yet. Before you casually text your friend to activate Operation Rescue Call, it's worth asking yourself if you're sure you can pull it off?

> **ADH-YOU:** Of course I can! Why wouldn't I succeed at this as I do everything else?

Well, you see, most of us aren't professional actors, and so few of us possess the dramatic chops to be persuasive in our attempt to pretend-console our faux-emergency-stricken friend. Indeed, most of us are likely to leave our date recognizing our clumsy falsehood. Now, if they're being a jerk, or if you feel nervous about how they might handle any other reason for you shortening the date, then do what you need to do.

> **ADH-YOU:** Yeah, they are a jerk!

Okay, if you're confident that you're justified in using a rescue call to get out of a date, then do you mind if I give you a couple tips on how to operate it safely?

> **ADH-YOU:** You can try.

Okay, thanks. So, first, let's first look at the origin of the rescue call.

> **ADH-YOU:** Oh, yay, a history lesson! Won't that be exciting?

Well teased, YOU. But it's more interesting than you might expect. The rescue call was invented by the ancient Greek woman, Alexendra Mythophocles, who went on a date with a young philosopher named Socrates and discovered that, while he was certainly smart and articulate, he was a bit condescending, and so she decided that there wouldn't be an encore date. But Socrates wouldn't stop talking, and so she couldn't think of a way to get out of the date gracefully. When she was finally free of him, she vowed that she would never go into a date unprepared again. From then on, whenever she went on a date, she asked a friend to pop by at some point during the encounter. For instance:

> **SOCRATES'S BROTHER:** So, if you believe that you are breathing air, then when you ingest it, are you half-human, half-air?
>
> **ALEXANDRA:** Good question ... you're a lot like your brother, you know?
>
> *Suddenly, Alexandra's friend, Friendoclese, arrived on the scene.*
>
> **FRIENDOCLES (*urgently to Alexandra*):** Hey you! Sorry to interrupt your date, but can I talk to you for a minute?
>
> *A moment later, in private:*

FRIENDOCLES: So how's it going?

ALEXANDRA: Not well. He's just as a much a bore as his brother. We gotta get me outta here.

A moment later:

ALEXANDRA (to Socrates' brother): I'm sorry, Friendocles's chariot has been stolen, so I don't think she should be alone at this time. We'll have to cut this date short.

SOCRATES'S BROTHER: Of course.

As you can see, if you decide you need to activate the emergency protocols of a rescue call, then the key is to invent an imaginary emergency that is severe enough that it needs your immediate assistance, but isn't so upsetting that poor Socrates's brother will worry.

ADH-YOU: Obviously. What else am I going to do?

Well, I have noticed on occasion that when you have been on a bad date, you have been so unconcerned with the feelings of the person you're about to reject that you haven't put much effort into your rescue call performance—i.e. you have been known to fabricate an emergency that is either too extreme to be believable or too insignificant to justify ending the date. Consequently you have made it obvious to your rejected that it was a rescue call. Please avoid that.

For a modern example of a rescue call, see the story, *The Rescue*, below. I'll let you determine for yourself whether it was a well-executed operation or not.

The Rescue

After writing a new (hoping to be humorous) online profile many years ago, I was delighted by an immediate reply from a woman whom I'll refer to as Miss Thing). Miss Thing was apparently so impressed with me that, only moments into our online conversation, she gave me her offline phone number and asked me to call her.

> **MISS THING:** Hello?
>
> **SETH (*attempting to be funny*):** Hi, it's Seth. You may remember me from the internet just now when you gave me your number.
>
> **MISS THING:** Yeah, I remember. It was just a second ago.
>
> **SETH (*embarrassed*):** Right, so . . . How are you?
>
> **MISS THING:** Fine.

Nothing for a moment.

> **SETH (*grasping for a topic*):** So I must ask: what about my profile made you contact me?
>
> **MISS THING:** Your picture.
>
> **SETH:** Oh. You weren't inspired by my tongue-and-cheek public advisory, then?
>
> **MISS THING:** Sorry, didn't read it. But your picture looks good.
>
> **SETH:** Oh. I should warn you, then—I'm no male model.
>
> **MISS THING:** Well, why don't you come by my work so we can get a look at each other? If we like what we see, we can go out.

I pondered doing a strut for her on an imaginary catwalk.

> **SETH:** I don't think that'll work for me. If you wanna meet for coffee, great, but—
>
> **MISS THING:** Fine, we'll go for coffee.

Upon arriving at the café, I quickly recognized my date from her online photo, so I approached with a smile. When she saw me, a frown poured over her. I clearly did not live up to my picture. Oops.

> **SETH:** Hello. Nice to meet you.
>
> **MISS THING (*unhappily*):** Hi.
>
> **SETH:** You still up for coffee?

MISS THING: I guess so.

As we sat down, the disappointed scowl on my date's face had not dissolved.

SETH: So, do you like your job?

MISS THING: It's okay.

I paused, awaiting elaboration, but realizing nothing was coming, I continued.

SETH: Do you find the customers annoying?

MISS THING: Sometimes.

SETH: What do you do when they're rude?

MISS THING: I bring them their food like anyone else.

This suffocating pattern continued for ten minutes. And I wondered how long I had to stay there before it would be appropriate to end it.

SETH: Do you like politics?

MISS THING: Nope.

SETH: Well, I do!

I began desperately babbling about some recent political skirmishes until—bored out of her sulk—my date announced that she had to visit the washroom. While she was away, I fantasized about a date with paint drying. When my actual date returned, I continuing babbling as best I could under the heat of her contempt.

SETH: So nice weather today, eh?

Her phone rang in response. She immediately answered.

MISS THING: Hello? Nope, I'm not busy. Sure, I'll be there in ten minutes.

Oh my! She'd gone to the washroom to provoke a rescue call. I was thus amused as she got off the phone.

MISS THING: Gotta go.

Wait a minute: weren't rescue calls supposed to be emergency-based? I decided to help out.

SETH: Something urgent come up?

MISS THING: No. We're just going for a work out.

I almost laughed as I agreed to this explanation. I was the victim of the first ever non-emergency-based rescue call.

Shall We Meet Again? (Nay! Edition)

Personally, I don't think one needs to be wholly honest at the end of every date. To conclude a self-contained event with a remark such as, "Thanks for coffee—by the way, I don't want to see you again" would be awkward, wouldn't it?

> **ADH-YOU:** I guess, but, if I'm not going to see them again, what do I care if it's awkward?

Good point, but for the sake of contributing to a kinder world, I think it would be fair instead to say, "I had a nice a time, thank you," and then to leave your final assessment for later via email or phone—or not at all, if neither of you shows further interest.

I even think that it's okay, during the end-of-date hug-and-go, for you to avoid awkwardness by casually agreeing with your date's suggestion that "We should do this again." (You can then follow up by email or phone saying that, upon further contemplation, you don't see a romantic future for your pairing, after all, but you wish them the best.) However, try not to be the one to initiate the plans for another date when, in fact, you're not interested. To do so, or to show too much enthusiasm for your date's suggestion, may unnecessarily cause them to tell their friends about the new love of their life who isn't going to be.

Moreover, please don't ask them to call you for a date that you do not want to have! That puts all the pressure on them, only to have you pull the rug out from under their enthusiasm when they find the courage to follow through. For instance:

ADH-YOU: Hello?

PAT: Hi, it's Pat from the other night.

ADH-YOU: Pat? Pat? Were you the one wearing the acid wash jeans?

PAT: Yeah! You remembered!

ADH-YOU (*chortling*): Oh, I remember. Look, no offence, but I'm kind of into fashion, and you're clearly not, so I don't think this is going to work out.

No! That will not do. Please don't request a call just so you can use it to reject them.

> **ADH-YOU:** Man, you're a grinch.

Yes, and I feel guilty about that.

Meanwhile, even in cases where you didn't lead your date on, they might call you for a sequel. If that happens, then feel free to politely respond that you do not see chemistry brewing, and so have to decline. But try not to provide a deluge of explanatory details itemizing why they're not your type. Honesty is nice, but brutal honesty is usually unnecessary.

Shall We Meet Again? (Yay! Edition)

Meanwhile, if you do like your date, why not indicate your preference confidently? Heretofore, you have utilized one of two strategies for expressing your interest:

(1) You display your hopes for an additional date with extreme, your-heart-depends-on-it enthusiasm.

(2) You attempt to cover up your interest by playing a game of hard-to-get.

I'm pleased to report that making a casual but sincere offer to go for an additional date is better than both of these options. You see, on the one hand, if the opposition turns your cheerful invitation down, you've only invested a polite offer and so have nothing to be embarrassed about. On the other hand, if they too are interested, they won't have to acquire translation services to figure out your hard-to-get language.

GHOSTLY BEHAVIOUR

Your prolific creativity in bringing us new ADH-STYLINGS is on impressive display with your modern relationship-distancing strategy known as "Ghosting."

ADH-YOU: I thank you. But could you remind me of the details of my brilliant invention? I lose track of the terms.

Sure thing, YOU. Ghosting refers to cases where you realize that the person you've been dating is no longer adding the flavour to your life that you were seeking, but instead of telling the failed object of your affection about your change of plans, you simply ghost away by discontinuing all communications.

ADH-YOU: Right, yes! Brilliant, isn't it? Saves me the trouble of a break up speech.

Excellent, indeed, YOU! However, I'm afraid there's a problem.

ADH-YOU: Oh my Ghost! What is it this time?

Well, you see, while ghosting may be convenient to you, it's confusing and sometimes cruel to the receiver.

ADH-YOU: Yeah, but this way I don't have to hurt their feelings by telling them why they're not worthy of me. Nice, right?

Nice effort, YOU. But no. In fact, ghosting actually prolongs the pain of the break up as your former heart-warmer tries to figure out if you have indeed broken up or if something else has happened. And then, once they're confident that you *have* broken away, they get to enjoy not only your rejection, but also the fun of wondering why.

> **ADH-YOU:** I don't get it. Why is "wondering why" such a big deal?

Well, you see, when one doesn't have any reason for why one's been rejected, one tends to fill in the blank with every possible explanation.

> **ADH-YOU:** So you want me to tell them exactly why I found them to be so annoying? Geez, sadistic much?

Well queried, YOU. But, no, I'm not asking you to purposely wound your para-no-more; however, a general explanation of where your personalities and/or values don't align might be helpful. Or, if details aren't your forte, simply explaining that you're not spotting a spark is better than vanishing without a text.

> **ADH-YOU:** So I can text the break up! Okay, now we're talking.

Well caught, YOU. Sorry, I was trying to be clever there. No, I would say texting can only be used for a break up announcement if you've been on one or two dates (unless texting is a medium by which you and your soon-to-be-ex often have deep conversations). Beyond that, always add one level of difficulty to what your best guess would be for the most appropriate break up medium.

> **ADH-YOU:** What does that mean?

Sorry, what I mean by that is if it feels to you like a text would be sufficient, please upgrade to a phone call. If a phone call feels right, please upgrade to an in-person conversation.

Chapter 24

Wedding You

At some point in your life, you and your favourite date may choose to get married and have a big wedding to celebrate. Congrat-YOU-lations! Finally, you'll receive some of the recognition and attention you deserve. Nevertheless, if you are a "bridezilla" (or a member of the less-often observed "groomzilla" species) it occurs to me that you might be inadvertently undermining the goodwill of your wedding celebration.

THE WEDDING SCRIPT

> **NOTE:** I enjoy weddings. I've been to many of them as a videographer, an MC, and of course as a guest, and I've found that even the most poorly executed wedding usually provides me with goosebumps. So, despite my criticisms of certain wedding behaviours, please note that this chapter is not provoked by an anti-wedding disposition—quite the opposite is true.

At several of the weddings I've filmed, I've watched baffled as previously grumpy brides and/or grooms have stood up at the podium and broadcasted hearty effusions of love for momentous people in their lives, such as their parents, bridal party, and newly-minted spouse.

> **ADH-YOU:** Why are such positive thoughts baffling? It is a wedding, bud.

Yes, I see your point, but I was startled because, during my filming, I had witnessed the very same purveyors of platitudes snarling at the folks they were now hugging with their words.

At one wedding in particular, I witnessed the bride seeming to care more about her wedding dress than the supposedly significant people in her life. She frequently barked displeasure at both her mother and groom-to-be not only for accidentally stepping on the train of her dress, but also for touching it with their oily hands. Yet, strangely, whenever the professional photographer pointed his camera in the newlywed direction, the growling bride transformed into a sweet butterfly, her face suddenly a beaming expression of affection as she wrapped her arms around the dress-stompers and sighed happily into the lens of the camera. As a result, the pictures do not document a supremely happy day in the wedding couple's life, but instead are merely framing it that way.

> **ADH-YOU:** So you want me to show my grumpiness in the pictures?

No, no, sorry for the confusion. Instead, I was thinking: why not aim for a wedding that includes the merry feelings that the pictures are trying to express? That way, when you look at them later, you will be reminded of moments of genuine happiness instead of pretend happiness.

> **ADH-YOU:** Sounds good. But I can't control my emotions.

I see what you're saying. But, just for the sake of argument, I'd like to suggest in this chapter that—with a slight change in attitude in how you approach your nuptials—you might help yourself to a better time.

> **ADH-YOU:** You've lost me.

Okay, well, I know that at your wedding you have particular stuff that you want to happen, and so it can be stressful if those things aren't occurring in the way or timeline that you would like.

> **ADH-YOU:** Exactly!

Nevertheless, given that your wedding is supposedly an emblem of your affection for someone, what's the point if you're not enjoying each other's company?

> **ADH-YOU:** The point is I had a vision of what I wanted. And it's not happening.

Fair enough, I feel your pain. Nevertheless, every wedding I've ever attended has had some brilliant moments and some not-so-successful ones—indeed, an occasional misstep is almost unavoidable during a one-try event. So, if you're able to react to those few trouble spots as cheerfully as you can muster, both you and your guests will probably have a better time.

> **ADH-YOU:** But Pat was cramming my centrepieces into—

Yes, I'm sure that's annoying. But, before you snap, ask yourself if the items you're protecting are vital enough to justify trampling on a loved one's feelings.

> **ADH-YOU:** In this instance, yes.

I see your point. Nevertheless, one trick I've learned is that saying something politely can be just as effective as barking it.

> **ALTERNATE-YOU:** Hey Pat, it looks like the centrepieces are getting scrunched in there. Do you mind using the bigger box to transport them?

If you're still not persuading 'em with kindness, then by all means let them know that you're stressing and/or explain that you're really worried about the X arrangement, so would they mind checking on it? I suspect you'll get similar results to the ones you got with harshness, and you won't have to worry about any bride/groom voodoo dolls circulating the bridal party.

> **HINT:** You may be shocked to discover that sometimes, when viewing their wedding videos, even the most detail-oriented newlyweds are more excited to see the spontaneous moments of their wedding than whether the flowers were in precisely the right place. Not that you shouldn't aim for the details that matter to you, but if you allow room for your friends to express their appreciation for you in their own (not-scripted-by-you) ways, there's a good chance you'll feel less regret about it later.

YOUR GUEST

Wallets

Being a guest at a wedding is often an expensive endeavour (especially for those who are travelling to your location). Moreover, it would be unusual if you only invited to your wedding people who have the means to purchase expensive wedding gifts. Therefore, to avoid grumblings in the bank accounts of your nearest and dearest, it is polite—if you decide to register for gifts—to make sure that you have a significant number of options that don't require the selling of one's house to purchase.

> **ADH-YOU:** I was just trying to steer people in the direction of gifts that would please me more, which I assumed would please them.

I knew you'd have a good reason! Nevertheless—

> **ADH-YOU:** Fine. I'll put some cheap things on there, too.

Thanks, YOU! I tip my hat to you.

Also, and I know this is probably a controversial matter, but if you have a wedding party and you expect the stars of it to wear an expensive uniform to your event, you might think about covering part of the cost—especially if your friends are not from the wealthy side of the tracks. You see, they are big fans of you and are already willing to put in a lot of time and outfit shopping with you; but going into debt to pay for a single use outfit may leave a sour taste in their wallet when they think back on your beautiful wedding.

Experience

While your wedding is yours, I think you should be careful about taking ownership of the day, itself, and referring to it as *yours*. You see, calling the day yours could give you the ADH-IMPRESSION that you—as the holder of the day—can do anything you like without consideration for the people you've invited to share it with you. Such an option would be a little too tempting for someone of your ADH-HISTORY, so let's avoid that.

> **ADH-YOU:** Well, what else am I supposed to do?

Great question, YOU! Maybe—instead of owning the day—you could think of yourself as *borrowing* it. That way you'll remember it has to be kept in good condition for others.

> **ADH-YOU:** I'm not following you, sweetheart.

Well, I wonder if you could bear in mind that your guests have given up their time to be with you, so it might be worthwhile to treat the quality of their experience at your event as though it matters to you. For example, even though you are the bride or groom, and thus the co-star of the event, you're also the co-host, and so it would be nice if you could avoid keeping your guests waiting too long at the reception before you start the show with your arrival (especially since some of your guests may not know anyone else there).

> **ADH-YOU:** But wait a minute! It's *my* wedding! Why shouldn't I do exactly what I want?

Yes, it is your wedding, but you also chose to invite guests. If you don't want to waste time and fun worrying about hosting, then by all means, have a private ceremony, and then you can do whatever you want. But if you're asking people from all across your continent to "join you in celebrating," then sadly you have an obligation to those who take you up on your offer.

For instance, once the reception starts, I recommend you include something to entertain your guests. In spite of the groans that some people (reflexively?) offer at the thought, I think speeches and/or slide shows are lovely ways to amuse your guests (especially if your productions are well-edited and presented).

> **ADH-YOU:** Groan, speeches are boring!

Fair enough (and thank you for your original response). If you're not into such traditional presentations, that's fine, but please consider some sort of entertainment or activity for your guests who won't have much else to do at your reception.

Meanwhile, if you'd like to increase your personal fun level by taking in lots of alcohol, I suggest that you wait till after the main program to really douse yourself. Drunken speeches are like chilli fries: they may taste good at the time, but they'll leave an unfortunate feeling in your stomach the next day.

I remember, for one of the weddings I filmed, the invitation had said that the hosts would be "honoured" by each guests' attendance. Yet, while the wedding couple had their wedding photos taken, they left their guests waiting for an unusually long period in the reception hall. By the time the wedding elite arrived, it was clear that the wedding *party* had made good use of their transportation's mini-bar, and so were no longer as eloquent as they had been during the ceremony.

> **ADH-YOU:** C'mon, it's a party! Why shouldn't we celebrate?

Yes, I don't think many of your guests would object to you celebrating, alongside them, with some alcohol. But, when you make them wait while you start the celebrations without them in your private, members-only limousine, you may create the impression that your guests' enjoyment of the proceedings is inconsequential compared to your own fun times.

> **ADH-YOU:** I can live with that.

Right, but consider this. When it comes time for your next wedding, your guests may recall feeling mistreated at the last one, and so you may find yourself with a reduced population of fans (and wedding gifts).

> **ADH-YOU:** Hmm, good point. I wouldn't like that.

No, I don't think you would. So plan your wedding as though it won't be your last, and you'll be fine.

YOU'RE GUEST

Meanwhile, when you're a guest at a wedding, it would as always be lovely to hear you step up to the mic to deliver your sweetest and/or funniest wedding message to the headlining couple.

> **ADH-YOU:** Awesome. I'm there!

Excellent. Unfortunately, though, the best way to do that is to prepare something in advance.

> **ADH-YOU:** Awe, man. I have to do homework for a wedding?

I know: it's annoying. But I promise you'll see a difference in appreciation from the attendees.

> **ADH-YOU:** Hmm, I do like appreciation.

Yes you do!

Meanwhile, if you forget to write your poem, song, or anecdote before the event, then be careful of letting your emotions combine with the courage of your alcohol, and seduce you into thinking that you can invent good prose or song lyrics on the spur of a wedding moment. That isn't to say that you shouldn't provide spontaneous speeches or stories, but I would double check with a trusted sober person regarding the content before stumbling towards the open mic.

> **ADH-YOU:** I get it. It's like I need to find a designated speech editor?

Yes, well put, YOU!

Moreover, if at all possible, aim for brevity: it's amazing how what seems in advance to be a short story can go long when you're staring at the faces of smiling people who want the best for your speech (and so can give you the exaggerated impression that every word you say is brilliant). I recall filming a wedding in which one of the groomsmen was so awestruck by how much appreciation the Best Man was getting just for toasting the bride and groom with a few prepared anecdotes that he decided to spontaneously write his own speech to share with the guests. Worry not, he came up with something reasonably sweet, and so the audience was appreciative in reply. Tragically, though, the thrill of the polite applause was too much for our hero, and so he returned to his pen and filled his page with more spur-of-the-moment ponderings. Back to the microphone he went, but this time for much longer, with details that some may have found to be crude and inappropriate; eventually, his friend, the groom, hinted to him that he could share his reminiscences with him later in private.

> **ADH-YOU:** Sounds like the groom was a puritanical prude!

Well, considered, YOU. I'm sure you're right. And I don't ever want you to second guess that everything you say and sing is beautiful. But, if you've got a hankering to share with the rest of the class at the microphone, ask yourself: *is this something that the person or people you're honouring would want publicized for everyone in attendance?*

> **ADH-YOU:** Well, how do *I* know what they want? Do I live in their brain?

Good point, YOU! You don't, do you? Okay, well how about this: imagine it were *your* wedding, and—

> **ADH-YOU:** I'm already married.

Right, okay, but I just want you to imagine back to that day when all of your closest friends and relatives were in attendance. Is the story you're about to tell one that you would have wanted shared at your wedding?

> **ADH-YOU:** Um, why would someone tell a story about my best friend at *my* wedding?

Sorry, I expressed my question badly. Let me rephrase: if the story were about you, is it one which you would want shared in front of *your* wedding audience?

> **ADH-YOU:** Ah, no, I don't really want Great Aunt Betsy to know about that? Obviously.

Okay good, so when you get up to the microphone, I want you to imagine you're telling your story to your *own* friends and family, and that the story is about *you*. If it still seems funny and/

or delightful, then go for it. If not, feel free to excuse yourself from the microphone to get some fresh air. Either way, you go, YOU!

Epilogue

Are You Free of ADH-Me?

ADH-YOU: How would *I* know if I'm cured?

Good point as ever, YOU! If you're not sure if you've cured yourself of ADH-ME, I recommend re-reading the parts of the book that you found to be the most psychologically traumatizing. With increased exposure to these radical concepts, I predict that strange thoughts will eventually infiltrate your mind without warning. For instance, you might suddenly one day think to yourself for no apparent reason:

> **ADH-YOU:** When I board a bus with an open hamburger or container of nail polish remover, I am unduly imposing my vibrant aromas on my fellow passengers.

With that epiphany, bolder ones will likely follow. For instance:

> **ADH-YOU:** When I talk loudly to my neighbour while watching a movie in a theatre, I am the true villain of the production.

When you encounter these realizations, do not scold your former ADH-TENDENCIES. Be thankful (to yourself!) that you have brilliantly escaped your affliction. You now get to join Jane Austen, Jerry Seinfeld, and other commentators on social foibles as they make us chuckle at the etiquette errors of those around us.

Be cautious, though: it's easy to jump off the wagon again as you start to notice how many other ADH-PATIENTS continue to threaten civilized society with their unyielding ME-THINKING. But, in lieu of throwing your newly earned WE-PERSONALITY back, you can feel good that you are not suffering in such painful self-obsession anymore. You no longer need to spend your time hollering out your window at passing cyclists; instead, you can try out previously unimaginable-to-you behaviours such as asking your friends questions, and then listening to the answers, or simply being nice to strangers (I promise it's not as painful as it sounds—some of them will even be friendly back).

Few of us are perfect, but if you behave as though you are not the only sentient creature on Darwin's earth, you may discover that others enjoy being around you more than they did before. Or, better yet, someone else might notice your considerate ways and decide to give up their ADH-ME ways to follow in your WE-EFFORTS. And then you'll be the hero you and I always knew you were.

Your fan, as ever,

Seth McDonough

ACKNOWLEDGMENTS

I would now like to show some appreciation for those who have helped construct this book.

> **ADH-YOU:** Why would you acknowledge someone for work already done? They can't take it back, so there's no need to butter them up anymore.

Hee, hee, good one, funny reader.

> **ADH-YOU:** No, I'm serious.

Oh, okay, well I appreciated people's help, and I want them to feel—

> **ADH-YOU:** Come on. We're not in the middle of the book anymore—I don't want a Pollyanna reason on this one.

Oh, okay, um, would you accept that I might like to work with them again, so—

> **ADH-YOU:** Right, I got you. So you flatter them now so they'll do your work for you again.

Exactly.

> **ADH-YOU:** Okay, go ahead.

Thanks YOU. So, with your generous readerly indulgence, I submit thanks go to the following ADH-ME staff:

EARLY EDITING: Bernice Lever of *The Colour of Words*: thank you for your excellent suggestions and guidance with an early draft of this book. You gave me confidence to try for a second draft.

> **ADH-YOU:** I don't remember a first draft.

Oh, um, this is awkward. You didn't have a speaking role in that draft.

> **ADH-YOU:** Oh.

Yeah, so, um… moving along…

FINAL EDITING: Bethany Root: your editing services were detailed, yet never dogmatic, and thus very persuasive. But, since you didn't write this sentence, I cannot promise good words in it.

> **ADH-YOU:** That last sentence wasn't very good.

I know. That's the joke.

> **ADH-YOU:** If you say so.

Thanks. Anyway, next we have:

FORMATTING: Michelle Argyle at *Melissa Williams Design*: you have been delightful to communicate with, but since I'm submitting this before you could do the actual work, I thank you for your _____ design and your _____ attention to detail. Working with you has been _____.

> **ADH-YOU:** I guess that's clever, but isn't she just going to fill in the blanks with compliments of herself even if she does a bad job?

Fair enough. I guess I'll just have to risk it.

> **ADH-YOU:** Okay, good luck on that.

I'll take it! Next up is:

COVER DESIGN: Calum McDonough: you precisely captured the spirit of the book. And, even though, as my brother, you were obligated to lend me your talents, you nevertheless respected me enough to charge me as much as you would a real client.

> **ADH-YOU:** Seriously, he charged you full price?

Hee, hee, no, he hasn't actually charged me anything yet, but I'm hoping by making a joke about his fee, he'll feel awkward enough about it to forgive my debt.

> **ADH-YOU:** Ahh, okay—respect.

I'm honoured! Next is:

CARTOON DESIGN: Sorrel McDonough and Tarrin McDonough of *The Styrogirls*. Tarrin, even though our sister Sorrel did most of the work on this one, you always shared the credit with her equally. I admire you for that, and I thank you both for your magic rendering of my silly ponderings.

> **ADH-YOU:** So the one sister did nothing, and still wants credit? And you call me self-involved?

No, sorry, I'm just teasing my sister who was busy with other projects while this one was being built. But since the styrogirls are a joint endeavour, she has no choice but to share in the glory.

> **ADH-YOU:** I guess I can get behind that.

I thought you'd like that. And now we have:

STORY CONTRIBUTIONS: Many of the vignettes starring in this book were gently borrowed from my parents (Tom and Marg McDonough), my siblings (Tamsen, Tarrin, Sorrel, and Calum McDonough) my wife (Natalie Anderson), my mother-in-law (Wendy Anderson), one of my favourite friends (Candida Moreira), and myself. I thank us all for our willingness to put our stories on the line for the superior mind of our reader to have their way with.

> **ADH-YOU:** Um, I appreciate the respect, but are you seriously including yourself as one of your muses?

Yeah, I wasn't sure about that either. So you think it's weird to acknowledge that I—

> **ADH-YOU:** Weird, no. I would have taken credit for all the stories. But with your high bragging levels there, you may now want to consider yourself a client of this book, too.

Fair enough. Finally, we're at:

FEEDBACK: During the many years of this book's construction, I have received elite suggestions on these musings from many sources, led by my spouse and honourary editor, Natalie Anderson, whose editorial evangelisms are so passionate that I sometimes accept them even when I'm not convinced—and yet in the long run I'm always glad I did.

> **ADH-YOU:** Come on—is that true? Or are you just sucking up to your spouse because she's had to put up with your pipe dream of a writing career?

Um... no, no, it's, um, no... I totally meant it, but, if you want to talk to me outside of the book, I can give you more detail on that.

> **ADH-YOU:** Hee, hee, I thought so. Looking forward to it.

Meanwhile, I'd also like to send a large bouquet of gratitude to the *Off The Page Writers' Group* (particularly my longtime teammates Robin Spano, Louvain Chalmers, Cheryl Andrichuk, Frank Robinson, Rosemary Carter, Barb Drozdowich, Lily Liu, Malcolm van Delst, David Haines, Sheilagh MacDonald, Deborah White, Katie Ormiston, and the Eric/ks—Mason & D'Souza), as well as loyal commenters on my Sethiquette blog, including Tom Durrie and Vanessa Mackenzie.

> **ADH-YOU:** Sethiquette, really?

Hee, hee, thanks, I thought you'd enjoy that. And, finally, I want to thank YOU, the reader. Without YOU, this book would be museless. YOU stay *YOU.*

> **ADH-YOU:** What? I thought this whole book was about changing me?

Oh, right—stay less *YOU*, YOU.

www.ingramcontent.com/pod-product-compliance
Lightning Source LLC
Chambersburg PA
CBHW072141100526
44589CB00015B/2031